Non-Compliance of National Courts

Remedies in European Community Law and Beyond

Non-Compliance of National Courts

Remedies in European Community Law and Beyond

Bernhard Hofstötter

T·M·C·Asser Press
The Hague

Published by T·M·C·ASSER PRESS
P.O.Box 16163, 2500 BD The Hague, The Netherlands
<www.asserpress.nl>

T·M·C·ASSER PRESS' English language books are distributed exclusively by:

Cambridge University Press, The Edinburgh Building, Shaftesbury Road,
Cambridge CB2 2RU, UK,
or
for customers in the USA, Canada and Mexico:
Cambridge University Press, 100 Brook Hill Drive, West Nyack, NY 10994-2133, USA
<www.cambridge.org>

ISBN 10: 90-6704-205-6
ISBN 13: 978-90-6704-205-5

Si autem [iudex] non negligit, sed iustitiam facit, pronuntiando inique, tunc si civitas habeat iudicem appelationis deputatum ad ipsum, per appellationem adibitur, et si non habeat, indicentur represaliae. Nam est quid imputari civitati quae non deputavit iudicem appelationis.

[But if the judge does not neglect to do justice, but does injustice by pronouncing an unjust judgment, then, if the State has a judge of appeal appointed over him, he will be applied to by way of appeal; and if it has not, reprisals will be declared. For some blame must be imputed to a State which has not appointed a judge of appeal.]

Giovanni da Legnano,
De Bello, De Represaliis et De Duello (Bologna, ca. 1360)
Cap. CL.

The theatre for our study is the international society. The members of the international society are the various States that exist in the world as well as organisations, other entities and individuals. States and organisations cannot be studied without immediate reference to individuals as the abstract entities are nothing but agglomerations of individuals assigning (explicitly or implicitly) various functions to a larger entity.

Ingrid Detter,
The Concept of International Law,
2nd edn. (Stockholm, 1993),
p. 24 et seq.

The judge affects the normative structure of the world in which we live, the structures upon which we rely and with which we contend daily life, the structures that shape us and our actions. In this sense, we all find ourselves ineluctably members of the audience in each great judge´s theatre.

Michael Reisman,
'Judge Shigeru Oda: A Tribute to an International Treasure',
16 *Leiden Journal of International Law* (2003)
p. 57 at p. 58.

PREFACE

Reading the present book reminded me of the sheer quality of the author's work as a student in my European law classes at the K.U. Leuven (Belgium) where he graduated as Master of Laws (LL.M.) magna cum laude.

Bernhard Hofstötter's work contributes substantively to the topic he deals with.

Although the principle of State liability for damage caused to individuals as a result of breaches of Community law has raised enormous interest amongst legal practitioners and theoreticians from the early years of the Community legal order, this principle was only, for the first time, formally recognised by the Court of Justice of the European Communities (ECJ) in its 1991 *Francovich* judgment. Five years later, in its *Brasserie du Pêcheur* judgment the ECJ added, in a case concerning an infringement of Community law by the legislature, that the principle of State liability applied in any case in which a Member State breaches Community law, whatever be the organ of the State whose act or omission was responsible for the breach. In 2003, in its *Köbler* judgment, the ECJ explicitly extended the principle of State liability to cover also judicial acts.

The *Köbler* case is the primary focus of Dr. Hofstötter's book. He explains that the extension of the principle of State liability to the judiciary finds its foundation not only in international law and in the case law of the European Court of Human Rights but also in the general principles common to the legal traditions of the Member States. He examines in great detail the objections raised against the inclusion of national judiciaries for the purpose of State liability for breaches of Community law, such as the independence and impartiality of national judges, and the doctrine of *res judicata*. According to the author, the danger of putting at risk the co-operation between the national courts and the ECJ, which results from the extension of the principle of State liability to the judiciary, was contained in *Köbler* by setting a new and a higher standard of liability.

Dr. Hofstötter also examines the existence of alternative remedies for sanctioning failures of the judiciary to comply with Community law. In this respect he analyses the recent *Commission* v. *Italy* judgment (C-129/00) which seems to indicate that an action for infringement can serve as a means of sanctioning national courts' failures to comply with Community law.

Dr. Hofstötter's book is based on extensive research. Its approach is balanced and constructive. Criticism is either countered or balanced with practical suggestions. Since the extension of State liability to judicial acts has only recently been confirmed in the Community legal order, this book will undoubtedly contribute to the development of the law in this field. It is therefore highly recommended to anyone who is truly involved in contemporary developments in European law.

Luxembourg, June 2005

KOEN LENAERTS

Judge of the Court of Justice of the European Communities

Professor of European Law (K.U. Leuven)

ACKNOWLEDGEMENTS

This book brings together attempts at organising my thoughts in relation to the topic of the 'accountability' of national courts for violations of European Community law. Although, by its very nature, rooted in an analysis of European law, I have made every attempt to put it into a broader public international law framework, which seemed a promising perspective to me. Many of the themes touched upon by this book have occupied me for a number of years. However, they have essentially been put to paper only during my time as a researcher at the Institute of Public International Law, International Trade Law and European Law of the University of St. Gallen (2002–2004).

I would like to express my sincere thanks to Professor Juliane Kokott, currently an Advocate General at the ECJ, and Ulrich Haltern, a Professor at the University of Hannover, both of whom have guided my efforts and allowed me time to work on this book during the period between 2002 and 2004. Both have, in their own ways, contributed to the successful conclusion of this manuscript.

In addition, this book could not have been written without the direct or indirect support of a number of persons. In particular, I would like to thank Professor Erich Schweighofer and Professor August Reinisch, both from the University of Vienna (the former on leave to the European Commission), for their encouragement to pursue research in European law. I am indebted to Judge Professor Koen Lenaerts and Professor Walter van Gerven who have both decisively shaped my views on European law during the time I was a student at K.U. Leuven. Thanks are also due to Dr. Wolf-Dietrich Grussmann and Peter Rodford, who have carefully guided me through a most instructive period of legal in-service training at the European Commission. I benefited tremendously from the experience and expertise of many of my colleagues at the European Institute of Public Administration in Maastricht, where I was employed as a researcher in 2001/2002. For constructive criticism, encouragement and support during my time in St. Gallen, I am grateful to Thorsten Götz, Dr. Julia Raue, Franziska Sprecher, Kerstin Wolny and Dr. Ulrich Zelger. My colleagues at my new academic home – the Institute of European Law of the Universities of Berne, Neuchâtel and Fribourg – have also extended me a warm welcome.

Furthermore, I would like to thank my wife Joanna Weychert for accompanying me on my journey over the last six years, and – *deo volente* – hopefully many more to come. Your patience and support, as well as your insistence on the need to finish what has once been started, have given me strength and courage throughout this project. I am also grateful to Martin Moser for the precious gift of his friendship. Your support and advice – in legal and extra-legal matters – have always been unfailing. Thanks are also due to Alen Močilnikar and my brother Michael Hofstötter.

Finally, I am grateful to T.M.C. Asser Press, and in particular to Philip van Tongeren, for accepting to publish my manuscript with capacious co-operation. I would also like to thank Marjolijn Bastiaans, who has swiftly made the book ready for print. Thanks to Claire E. Stirrup for the proof-reading.

I finished working on the manuscript in September 2004. However, every effort has been made to incorporate essential developments after this date.

This book is dedicated to my parents in gratitude.

Fribourg, June 2005 BERNHARD HOFSTÖTTER

TABLE OF CONTENTS

Preface VII

Acknowledgements IX

Abbreviations XV

Chapter I – Introduction 1

Chapter II – Effectuating Effectiveness in European Community Law 7

1. The 'Transformation of Europe' and a Prior Transformation in Public International Law 9
2. National Courts and 'National Procedural Autonomy' 14
   - 2.1 A strategy of minimum interference 24
   - 2.2 A growing concern over effectiveness 26
   - 2.2.1 Setting aside national 'remedies' 27
   - 2.2.2 Creating new remedies 28
   - 2.2.3 Creating new remedies and spelling out minimum conditions for their exercise 31
   - 2.3 A more balanced approach 33
   - 2.4 *Critique* and conclusion 34
3. State Liability for Judicial Wrongs – Basic Notions 39
   - 3.1 Extension to judicial acts – the problem 39
   - 3.2 *Non-compliant* courts 41
   - 3.3 Primary and secondary proceedings 43

Chapter III – Three Hypotheses on the Necessity of State Liability for Judicial Acts in the Community Legal Order 45

1. International Law Hypothesis I: State Liability As Refined 'State Responsibility' Tailored to the Individualising Nature of the Community Legal Order 49
   - 1.1 Community law refers to public international law 50

1.2 Attribution of courts to the State in public international law 55
1.2.1 From the early days to the twentieth century 55
1.2.2 Contemporary practice 57
1.2.2.1 Separation of attribution from substantive issues 57
1.2.2.2 The ILC's Draft Articles on State Responsibility 58
1.2.2.3 Practice of international courts concerning the attribution of national courts to the State 61
1.2.2.4 Scholarly comment 63
1.2.3 Conclusion 64
1.3 Transferability to Community law? 65
1.4 Conclusion 70
2. International Law-Hypothesis II: The Imperatives of the Protection of Fundamental Rights Are Such As to Require State Liability for Judicial Acts 71
2.1 Procedural guarantees – Articles 6 and 13 of the ECHR 71
2.2 Substantive guarantees – Article 1 of Protocol No. 1 75
2.3 Conclusion 78
3. Comparative Law-Hypothesis: State Liability for Judicial Acts Is a General Principle Common to the Legal Traditions of the Member States 79
3.1 Alleging a general principle 80
3.2 Conclusion 84
4. Conclusion 86

Chapter IV – Reservations for Community Law 89
1. Grounds Causing Hesitation 91
1.1 Judicial independence 91
1.2 The doctrine of *res judicata* 95
1.3 Impartiality of the judiciary 107
1.4 Endangering the spirit of co-operation between the ECJ and national courts? 108
1.5 *Litis finiri opportet* or endless litigation within 'reasonable time' (Article 6 of the ECHR)? 112
1.6 The parallelism between State liability and the community's extra-contractual liability regime 114
1.7 Undesirable power gain for the ECJ? 118
2. Conclusion 120

Chapter V – Which Standard of Liability for Judicial Acts? 123
1. The Additional Standard of 'Manifest Infringement' of Community Law 126
2. Criteria to Be Taken into Account by National Courts 131
   2.1 Breach of the duty to refer pursuant to Article 234(3) of the EC Treaty 132
   2.2 Conclusion 135
3. The Application of the Standard of Manifest Infringement in *Köbler* 136
4. Need to Delimit the Judiciary from the Other State Functions 142
   4.1 What is a court for the purposes of State liability? 144
   4.1.1 Do only courts of last instance trigger State liability? 144
   4.1.2 What is a court of last instance for the purposes of State liability? 146
   4.2 Conclusion 150
5. Conclusion 150

Chapter VI – Necessary Institutional Arrangements in the Member States to Facilitate State Liability for Judicial Acts – A Case Study on Austria 153
1. Community Law Background 155
2. State Liability for Judicial Acts under Austrian law 161
   2.1 State liability pursuant to the law on official liability (*Amtshaftungsgesetz* – AHG) 161
   2.2 State liability pursuant to Article 137 of the Austrian Federal Constitutional Law 170
   2.3 Concluding assessment 171

Chapter VII – Alternative Remedies 177
1. *Kühne & Heitz* and an Approach of 'Try Again'? 179
2. The Action for Infringement 181
   2.1 Deficiencies 182
   2.2 *Commission* v. *Italy* 183
   2.3 Relationship between *Köbler* liability and the action for infringement 188
3. The Residuary Role of the ECrtHR 189
4. Conclusion 191

Chapter VIII – Epilogue 195

Bibliography 207

Table of Cases 217

ABBREVIATIONS

AG	Advocate General
AHG	Amtshaftungsgesetz (Law on Official Liability)
AIIDP	Annuaire de l'Institut international de Droit Public
AJIL	American Journal of International Law
AöR	Archiv des öffentlichen Rechts
BayVBl	Bayrische Verwaltungsblätter
BGBl.	*Bundesgesetzblatt* (Official Gazette of the Republic of Austria)
BVerfGE	*Entscheidungen des Bundesverfassungsgerichts* (Court Reports of the German *Bundesverfassungsgericht*)
Cap.	Capitulum
CFI	Court of First Instance (of the European Communities)
CML Rev.	Common Market Law Review
DVBl.	Deutsche Verwaltungsblätter
EAEC	European Atomic Energy Community
EC	European Community (-ies)
ECHR	European Charter of Human Rights
ECrtHR	European Court of Human Rights
ECJ	European Court of Justice
EComHR	European Commission of Human Rights
ECR	European Court Reports
ECSC	European Coal and Steel Community
ed.	editor, edited
edn.	edition
eds.	editors
EJIL	European Journal of International Law
ELJ	European Law Journal
ELR	European Law Reporter
EL Rev.	European Law Review
EP	European Parliament

EPL	European Public Law
et al.	*et alii*
ETS	European Treaty Series
EU	European Union
EuR	Europarecht
EuZW	Europäische Zeitschrift für Wirtschaftsrecht
EWS	Europäisches Wirtschafts- und Steuerrecht
GA	General Assembly (of the United Nations)
GeoWashIL Rev.	George Washington International Law Review
GJF	Global Jurist Frontiers
Harv. ILJ	Harvard International Law Journal
Ibid.	*Ibidem*
ICLQ	International and Comparative Law Quarterly
ICJ	International Court of Justice
ICSID	International Centre for Settlement of Investment Disputes
i.e.	*id est*
ILC	International Law Commission
ILM	International Legal Materials
ILR	International Law Reports
JGS	*Justizgesetzsammlung* (of the Austrian Empire)
JT	Journal des Tribunaux
JZ	Juristenzeitung
LJIL	Leiden Journal of International Law
mn.	marginal number
n.	note
NJW	Neue Juristische Wochenschrift
nyr	not yet reported
OJ	Official Journal
ÖJZ	Österreichische Juristenzeitung
para.	paragraph
paras.	paragraphs
PCIJ	Permanent Court of International Justice

RDUE	Revue du Droit de l'Union Européenne
RGBl.	*Reichsgesetzblatt* (Official Gazette of the Austrian Empire)
RMCUE	Revue du Marché commun et de l'Union européenne
RTDE	Revue Trimestrielle de Droit Européen
UN	United Nations
UNCIO	United Nations Conference on International Organization Documents
UNTS	United Nations Treaty Series
US	U.S. Supreme Court Reporter
VfSlg.	*Sammlung der Erkenntnisse und Beschlüsse des Verfassungsgerichtshofs* (Court Reports of the Austrian *Verfassungsgerichtshof*)
Vol.	Volume
wbl	Wirtschaftsrechtliche Blätter
WTO	World Trade Organisation
YEL	Yearbook of European Law
YLJ	Yale Law Journal
ZEuS	Zeitschrift für europarechtliche Studien
ZfRV	Zeitschrift für Rechtsvergleichung, internationales Privatrecht und Europarecht

Chapter I
INTRODUCTION

Chapter I
INTRODUCTION

This work deals with the possibilities of remedying the conduct of national courts which is incompliant with European Community law.

Recent months have seen the culmination of a number of judgments handed down by the ECJ which have shed new light on an old problem of Community law. In *Köbler*[1] the principle of State liability as a standard feature of Community law was explicitly extended to judicial acts. The case of *Commission* v. *Italy*[2] provided the first test case for the application of the action for infringement to judicial conduct, and bears witness to a greater willingness than hitherto exhibited on the part of the European Commission to make use of this remedy, also when Member States act in their judicial capacity. More recently, *Kühne & Heitz*[3] saw the Court revisit the principles of legal certainty and *res judicata*, principles crucial to the working of the judiciary. At the same time recent case law of the ECrtHR exhibits a trend towards stressing the responsibility of the State for its judiciary as well as fostering the establishment of legal protection against the judiciary.

In less than a year the judgment in *Köbler* has received considerable attention in scholarly writing, providing for a piecemeal analysis of a number of central issues. By contrast, the interplay with other relevant judicial pronouncements, the case law of the Strasbourg Court, as well as the international law aspects to which the ECJ openly refers, appear to have remained under-researched. It is the investigation of this interplay which justifies a work of this scope, which sets out to put these developments into context and essentially asks which possibilities there are to remedy non-compliant judicial conduct in the Community legal order.

This question seems of prime importance, given the pivotal role played by national courts in the implementation of Community law. At the same

[1] ECJ, Case C-224/01 *Köbler* [2003] ECR I-10239.

[2] ECJ, Case C-129/00 *Commission* v. *Italy* [2003] ECR I-14637.

[3] ECJ, Case C-453/00 *Kühne & Heitz* [2004] ECR I-837.

time it is a problem of the utmost sensitivity; as compared with the other State functions, the judiciary is traditionally perceived as being of a specific nature, and rightly so. The roles of *national courts* within the national constitutional systems as independent and impartial actors, combined with the position they occupy within the Community constitutional structure as interlocutors with the *ECJ,* of the greatest importance for the functioning of the Community judicial system, require a nuanced answer to the question of in how far Member States should be held accountable for the conduct of their courts. The third pole of this tri-polar model is occupied by the *individual*, whose role has been emphasised in the Community legal order since its inception. This focus on individual rights calls for the availability of adequate remedies against judicial wrongs.

In order to be able to fully grasp the complex relationship between individuals, national courts and the Community courts proper, which lies at the heart of the question of remedies against judicial wrongs, a re-reading of the seminal concepts of direct effect and national procedural autonomy will be offered. In the creation of the new remedy of State liability, the Court's huge body of jurisprudence with regard to national remedies, which is not free from inconsistencies, reaches its zenith. If one recognises that the State, in all its capacities could be liable for non-compliant conduct, assuming a remedy of State liability for breaches of Community law has immediate repercussions on the judicial function, as understood as one of the forms of State conduct. This issue will be approached by formulating three hypotheses which will subsequently be checked for their validity. In this exercise international law aspects will play an important role, which is necessitated both by the ECJ's reliance on the law of State responsibility as well as the relevance of the ECrtHR´s case law in the Community legal order. The aim of this analysis, is to see whether an extension of the principle of State liability to judicial acts can build upon a strong dogmatic framework.

In a further step the specific nature of the judiciary will be scrutinised, which may warrant against an inclusion of judicial acts for the purposes of State liability. Only if reservations flowing from the particular role which national judiciaries take in modern States, which, *inter alia*, is characterised by independence and impartiality, can be disposed of satisfactorily, is holding the State liable also when acting in its judicial capacity a viable solution.

Another aspect concerns the substantive conditions giving rise to State liability and, in particular, the standard of liability applicable to judicial wrongs. Is there a need for a specific standard with regard to judicial acts? And if so, at what level should it be anchored? To what degree can the breach of the duty to refer of national courts of last instance trigger State liability? This leads to the related issue of whether only the acts of national courts of last instance can give rise to State liability. Answering in the affirmative will necessitate the development of criteria to define courts of last instance for the purposes of State liability.

The implementation of State liability being, in principle, in the hands of the Member States entails the problem of adequate institutional arrangements in the Member States, which grant individuals the possibility to bring their claims. The two key problems of the shift of powers from national courts of last instance to courts of lower instance, as well as ensuring impartiality of the competent courts will be analysed in detail. Subsequently, possible solutions will be discussed against the background of the relevant provisions of Austrian law.

Finally, the availability of other remedies apart from State liability will be addressed. The Court's judgment in *Commission* v. *Italy* has reignited debate regarding if and to what extent, the action for infringement can serve as a tool for sanctioning failures to comply with Community law by national courts. Despite principled hesitations, there seems to be an emerging trend to deploy this remedy when systematic breaches by national courts – including supreme courts – are at issue. In addition the recent case law of the ECrtHR suggests the existence of another forum for individuals: Addressing the ECrtHR in particular instances of non-compliant judicial conduct with ECHR-implications may serve as an adequate remedy.

Chapter II
EFFECTUATING EFFECTIVENESS IN EUROPEAN COMMUNITY LAW

Chapter II
EFFECTUATING EFFECTIVENESS IN EUROPEAN COMMUNITY LAW

1. THE 'TRANSFORMATION OF EUROPE' AND A PRIOR TRANSFORMATION IN PUBLIC INTERNATIONAL LAW

It has almost become a truism in European legal scholarship that the ECJ, by rendering ground-breaking judgments particularly in the early 1960's, has fostered the transformation and constitutionalisation of Europe. In legal terms, this translates first and foremost into the familiar doctrines of direct effect and supremacy of Community law.[4] As concerns the former, the ECJ made it clear in its 1963 judgment in *van Gend & Loos* that individuals may derive rights directly from Community law which they may invoke before national courts.[5] The Court held that '[t]o ascertain whether the provisions of an international treaty extend so far in their effects it is necessary to consider the spirit, the general scheme and the wording of those provisions'.[6] It is equally well-known that the ECJ eventually stated that 'the Community constitutes a new legal order of international law for the benefit of which the States have limited their sovereign rights, albeit within limited fields, and the subjects of which comprise not only Member States but also their nationals'.[7]

By reason of this judgment, national courts have been transformed into Community law courts, filling the gap left by the remedial system spelled out in the EC Treaty, which by and large omits reference to individuals. The only exception thereto is Article 230(4) of the EC Treaty affording indi-

---

[4] The *locus classicus* of this narrative is J.H.H. Weiler, 'The Transformation of Europe', in J.H.H. Weiler, *The Constitution of Europe – 'Do the New Clothes have an Emperor?' and other Essays on European Integration* (Cambridge, Cambridge University Press 1999) p. 10 at pp. 16 et seq. [reprint of 100 *YLJ* (1991) pp. 2403 et seq.]; see also U. Haltern, 'Integration Through Law', in A. Wiener and Th. Diez, *European Integration Theory* (Oxford, Oxford University Press 2004) p. 177 at pp. 180 et seq.

[5] ECJ, Case 26/62 *van Gend & Loos* [1963] ECR 1 at paras. 10 and 16.

[6] Ibid. at para. 8.

[7] Ibid. at para. 12.

viduals standing in narrowly defined instances in actions for annulment before the ECJ. According to Article 230(4) individuals may challenge decisions addressed to them, decisions addressed to another person or decisions adopted in the form of a regulation. In the two latter cases, an applicant will have to prove that the decision – even if it is in the guise of a regulation – is of direct and individual concern to him. The ECJ's reading of the criterion of individual concern has been predicated on a cautious and fairly restrictive approach, making this remedy available to individuals only in highly exceptional cases.[8] The application of a lowered standard by the CFI[9] as well as – most prominently – AG Jacobs[10] remained episodic and the Court's floodgates seem to be firmly locked for the time being.[11]

The Treaty establishing a Constitution for Europe[12] as adopted by the Heads of States and Governments in June 2004 leaves matters unchanged

---

[8] ECJ, Case 25/62 *Plaumann* [1963] ECR 107, where the Court held that individual concern presupposes that an act not addressed to individuals 'affects them by reason of certain attributes which are peculiar to them or by reason of circumstances in which they are differentiated from all other persons and by virtue of these factors distinguishes them individually just as in the case of the person addressed'. Without detracting from its restrictiveness, the *Plaumann*-formula has been reformulated in more recent cases. See for instance Case T-266/94 *Foreningen af Jernskibs- og Maskinbyggerier i Danmark* [1996] ECR II-1339, where the CFI held in para. 44: 'It is settled case-law that persons other than those to whom a decision is addressed may claim to be individually concerned only if that decision affects them by reason of attributes peculiar to them or by reason of factual circumstances differentiating them from all other persons and, as a result, distinguishing them individually in a like manner to the person addressed'.

[9] CFI, Case T-177/01 *Jégo-Quéré* [2002] ECR II-2365, where the CFI held that in the absence of an otherwise effective remedy the criterion of 'individual concern' should be of no relevance.

[10] Opinion of AG Jacobs in Case C-50/00 P *Unión de Pequeños Agricultores* [2002] ECR I-6677. In this case AG Jacobs forcefully argued for a relaxation of the conventional test of individual concern. No longer should it be necessary for a measure to differentiate an individual from all other persons in order to give him standing (ibid. at paras. 59 et seq.). Quite to the contrary 'it should therefore be accepted that a person is to be regarded as individually concerned by a Community measure where, by reason of his particular circumstances, the measure has, or is liable to have, a substantial adverse effect on his interests' (ibid. at para. 60).

[11] See most recently ECJ, Case C-263/02 P *Jégo-Quéré* [2004] ECR I-3425, and Case C-50/00 P *Unión de Pequeños Agricultores* [2002] ECR I-6677. Both cases marked the way back from the innovative reasoning of the CFI in *Jégo-Quéré* to the classic *Plaumann*-based approach.

[12] [2004] OJ C 310/1.

as far as the requirement of 'direct and individual concern' is at issue. However, as concerns the nature of the contested act, it goes beyond the law as it stands, in omitting the criterion that the challenged act has to be an individual scope act.[13] According to Article III-365 of the Constitution '[a]ny natural or legal person may [...] institute proceedings against an act addressed to that person or which is of direct and individual concern to him or her, and against a regulatory act which is of direct concern to him or her, and does not entail implementing measures'. The notion of regulatory act refers to the newly introduced category of implementing acts known as 'European regulations' (Article I-33(1)(4) of the Constitution), which shall implement 'European laws' (Article I-33(1)(2) of the Constitution) and 'European framework laws' (Article I-33(1)(3) of the Constitution). The definition of a 'European law' given in the Constitution corresponds to that of a regulation pursuant to Article 249(2) of the EC Treaty. *Mutatis mutandis* this holds true of 'European framework laws' and directives in the meaning of Article 249(3) of the EC Treaty. Since European regulations may take the form of either a regulation, or a directive according to conventional terminology, the range of challengeable acts has been significantly widened to cover general scope acts wholesale, which are implementing other general scope acts and which thus far could only be appealed in exceptional cases, characterised by a crying injustice on the merits.[14] This applies regardless of whether the implementing act is a regulation or a directive, with the result that even directives may be challenged.[15] [16] By contrast, pursuant

[13] For the distinction between general scope acts and individual scope acts for the purposes of Art. 230(4) of the EC Treaty see K. Lenaerts and D. Arts, *Procedural Law of the European Union* (London, Sweet & Maxwell 1999) mn. 7-038 et seq.

[14] See for instance ECJ, Case C-309/89 *Codorniu* [1994] ECR I-1853 at paras. 14-33, and CFI, Joined Cases T-480 and T-483/93 *Antillean Rice Mills* [1995] ECR II-2305 at para. 66. For the argument that the hopes triggered by these cases seemingly indicating a trend towards a more flexible approach to *locus standi* of individuals have largely been misplaced cf., A. Arnull, 'Private Applicants and the Action for Annulment since *Codorniu*', 38 *CML Rev.* (2001) pp. 7 et seq. (*passim*).

[15] According to the ECJ's case law relating to Art. 230(4) of the EC Treaty, an application brought by individuals for annulment of a directive is, in principle, inadmissible, the reason being that as a legislative act it cannot be of individual concern to an individual. However, a directive may be of direct and individual concern to an individual, if the latter can show that it has a right which the Community legislature should have taken into account when adopting the directive (CFI, Case T-135/96 *UEAPME* v. *Council* [1998] ECR II-2335 at para. 90). See also CFI, Joined Cases T-172/98 and 175-177/98

to Article III-365(4) *e contrario* of the Constitution legislative measures in the form of 'European (framework) laws' cannot be challenged by individual applicants.

Quite apart from these aspects related to *locus standi* of individuals and its requirements based on the type of the act, the scope *ratione materiae* of the action for annulment is restricted to acts emanating from *Community* organs. So the Community system of legal protection does not provide for a direct right of appeal against national administrative or judicial acts to the European courts proper.

It is hence the national courts which primarily afford legal protection to individuals and form the life-blood of the decentralised enforcement of Community law.

Although the ECJ insisted on going beyond classical international law in finding in favour of direct effect of Community law and, as has been suggested in many quarters, was using activist techniques of legal interpretation previously unheard of in international law[17] at least with regard to direct effect, this submission appears to pay too little deference to a similar transformation in public international law, which was heralded by the case concerning *Jurisdiction of the Courts of Danzig*[18] as early as 1928.[19] Being faced with the issue of a potential direct effect of treaty provisions, which was firmly denied by the Polish government, the PCIJ held as follows:

> 'It may be readily admitted that, according to a well established principle of international law, the *Beamtenabkommen*, being an international agreement, cannot, as such, create direct rights and obligations for private individuals.

Salamander [2000] ECR II-2487, at paras. 27 et seq. On the law as it stands see Lenaerts and Arts, op. cit. n. 13, at mn. 7-044.

[16] See also F. Mayer, 'Individualrechtsschutz im Europäischen Verfassungsrecht', 119 *DVBl.* (2004) p. 606 at p. 610.

[17] K. Alter, *Establishing the Supremacy of European Law* (Oxford, Oxford University Press 2001) p. 17.

[18] PCIJ, Advisory Opinion on the *Jurisdiction of the Courts of Danzig*, 1928, Series B, No. 15.

[19] A similar point is raised by Spiermann, who argues that the ECJ in *van Gend & Loos*, n. 5 above, takes the 'old' international law of coexistence as its point of departure, while neglecting more recent developments towards an international law of co-operation. Cf., O. Spiermann, 'The Other Side of the Story: An Unpopular Essay on the Making of the European Community Legal Order', 10 *EJIL* (1999) p. 763 at pp. 775 et seq.

But it cannot be disputed that *the very object of an international agreement, according to the intention of the contracting Parties, may be the adoption by the parties of some definite rules creating individual rights and obligations and enforceable by the national courts.* That there is such an intention in the present case can be established by reference to the terms of the *Beamtenabkommen*'.[20]

The PCIJ concluded that the 'wording and general tenor of the *Beamtenabkommen* show that its provisions are directly applicable as between the officials and the Administration'.[21]

This judgment has been hailed by Lauterpacht as 'among the most important rendered by the Court'.[22] According to him it 'dealt a decisive blow to the dogma of the impenetrable barrier separating individuals from international law'.[23] In the light of the subsequent development of the European polity, Lauterpacht's assessment predicated on his 'cosmopolitan individualism'[24] almost reads like a prophecy of what was soon to become a common place in European legal thinking:

'The question whether individuals in any given case are subjects of international law and whether that quality extends to the capacity of enforcement must be answered pragmatically by reference to the given situation and to the relevant international instrument'.[25]

The reasoning of the ECJ itself, and in particular its reliance on a purposive Treaty interpretation, is a key example of the legal pragmatism canvassed by Lauterpacht and matches well with the approach taken by the PCIJ. The PCIJ's reference to the very object of an agreement and the intention of the contracting parties, which is inferred from the treaty text itself, roughly corresponds to the ECJ's pragmatic and anti-formalistic Treaty interpreta-

[20] PCIJ, *Jurisdiction of the Courts of Danzig*, n. 18 above, at p. 17 (emphasis added).

[21] Ibid. at p. 18.

[22] H. Lauterpacht, *International Law and Human Rights* (London, Stevens 1950) p. 29.

[23] Ibid. at p. 28.

[24] For this notion see M. Koskenniemi, *The Gentle Civilizer of Nations* (Cambridge, Cambridge University Press 2001) p. 396, who offers a fairly critical appraisal of the writings and teachings of Lauterpacht (ibid. at pp. 353 et seq.).

[25] Lauterpacht, op. cit. n. 22, at p. 27.

tion. The method of treaty interpretation employed by the ECJ has thus not been devised by this very Court, but can, at the very least be traced back to the PCIJ. Direct effect of provisions of Community law is the *consequence* of the application of this method of interpretation. The ECJ may hence be seen as having facilitated the enforcement of Community law by individuals *qua* authoritatively giving the Treaty a certain meaning, employing the said method of treaty interpretation.

In this sense, the notion of direct effect did not necessarily encompass the creation of a new legal order of international law, since it had previously already been conceived in public international law. It is the underlying rationale itself, the idea that an international treaty could by its very nature confer rights on individuals, which is compelling. This idea, which is commonly said to have been developed by the ECJ in 1963, was already present in a judicial pronouncement of 1928. The rhetoric of revolution, which is inherent in the ECJ's invocation of a new legal order of international law, in fact has to give way to a more sober *ex post*-evaluation in terms of an evolutionary process. Subsequently, both Courts' reliance on purposive treaty interpretation has entered Article 31(1) of the 1969 Vienna Convention on the Law of Treaties.[26]

There is no principled difference between the approaches employed by the two courts, although the *scope* and *breadth* of direct participation of individuals, as right holders and law enforcers, in the Community law context is unprecedented.[27] The case involving the *Beamtenabkommen* stands out as a strong ruling, whose relevance for international law has been symbolic and episodic rather than creating a large-scale-involvement of individuals in general international law though.

2. National Courts and 'National Procedural Autonomy'

The consequence of the PCIJ's ruling in the *Jurisdiction of the Courts of Danzig* advisory opinion is readily apparent in that national courts – in

[26] 1155 *UNTS* p. 331.

[27] See S. Weatherill, 'Addressing Problems of Imbalanced Implementation in EC Law: Remedies in an Institutional Perspective', in C. Kilpatrick, et al. (eds.), *The Future of Remedies in Europe* (Oxford, Hart Publishing 2000) p. 87 at pp. 112 et seq.

addition to their role as adjudicators of national law – take the role of international law courts. In more general terms, this phenomenon has been described by Scelle as *dédoublement fonctionnel*, whereby an individual is put in a position of acting for two or more societies.[28] That national courts indeed also have to function as international law courts is confirmed by Article 38 of the Statute of the International Court of Justice, which refers to judicial decisions as a source of international law, whereby a restriction to decisions of international courts or tribunals is absent.[29]

The involvement of national courts is the hallmark of a decentralised, horizontal legal order.[30] This – with additional qualifications – also holds true for the Community legal order. Whereas the framers of the Community Treaties have entrusted the ECJ with the task of authoritatively interpreting 'the law' (Article 220 of the EC Treaty), the prime importance of national courts in the (effective) enforcement of Community law and thereby making the latter a living truth for individuals can hardly be overstated.[31] The lesson from *van Gend & Loos* is that national courts have been transformed into Community law courts with adjudicatory powers encompassing both national and Community law in a like manner. The language employed by AG Léger in *Köbler* clearly echoes the idea of *dédoublement fonctionnel*, hinting at the fact that the designation of national courts as 'Community law courts of ordinary jurisdiction' 'must not be understood literally, but symbolically: where a national court is called upon to apply Community

---

[28] G. Scelle, 'Théorie du gouvernement international', (1935) *AIIDP* pp. 54 et seq.; on the notion of *dédoublement fonctionnel* see also Koskenniemi, op. cit. n. 24, at p. 333.

[29] R. Higgins, *Problems and Process – International law and how we use it* (Oxford, Oxford University Press 1994) p. 208.

[30] On the (exceptional) use of national courts for securing compliance with the decisions of international organisations cf., E. Lauterpacht, 'Implementation of Decisions of International Organizations through National Courts', in S. M. Schwebel (ed.), *The Effectiveness of International Decisions* (Leiden, Sijthoff 1971) pp. 57 et seq.

[31] A. Ward, *Judicial Review and the Rights of Private Parties in EC Law* (Oxford, Oxford University Press 2000) p. 4; T. Tridimas, *The General Principles of EC Law* (Oxford, Oxford University Press 1999) p. 277; K. Alter, op. cit. n. 17, at p. 33; see also the Opinion of AG Léger in *Köbler*, n. 1 above, at para. 53: 'Since the national courts have the function of applying the law, including Community law, they inevitably constitute an essential cog in the Community legal order. At the "crossroads" of a number of legal systems, their role is to make an important contribution to the effective application of Community law and, eventually, to the development of the process of European integration'.

law, it is in its capacity as an organ of a Member State, and not as a Community organ, *as a result of dual functions*'.[32]

Unlike classic public international law, the Community legal order exhibits centralised and decentralised features alike; it is simultaneously horizontal and vertical. The horizontal and decentralised strand is represented by the reliance on national courts in the enforcement of Community law.[33] The vertical and centralised features are linked to the role of the ECJ, which holds a monopoly in the authoritative interpretation of Community law (Article 220 of the EC Treaty). It is the ECJ which takes the role of a neutral adjudicator in the sense that it is a third party, independent of Member States' (political) preferences. In this sense the Member States are no longer the masters of the Treaties.

The focal point of these two aspects is the preliminary reference procedure as envisaged by Article 234 of the EC Treaty.[34] Here national courts and the ECJ enter into a formalised and channelled dialogue,[35] [36] the initiation of which is in principle in the hands of the national courts. It is well known that courts of lower instances *may* refer questions on the interpretation of Community law to the Court (Article 234(1) of the EC Treaty).

---

[32] Opinion of AG Léger *Köbler*, n. 1 above, at para. 66 (emphasis added).

[33] Cf., Tridimas, op. cit. n. 31, at p. 277; C. Keville, 'The principle of effectiveness and the development of a system of remedies at European Community law', in M.C. Lucey and C. Keville (eds.), *Irish Perspectives on EC Law* (Dublin, Round Hall 2003) p. 1 at pp. 2 et seq.

[34] Cf., C. Himsworth, 'Convergence and Divergence in Administrative Law', in P. Beaumont, et al. (eds.), *Convergence and Divergence in European Public Law* (Oxford, Hart Publishing 2002) p. 99 at p. 101, who speaks of the Art. 234-procedure as a 'vital link' between the ECJ and national courts.

[35] It is true that the word dialogue may be a misnomer since it implies the search for a mutually accepted outcome. However, this need not necessarily be the case owing to the centralised features of the Community legal order where ultimately only the ECJ authoritatively interprets the Treaties. A dialogue also connotes the equal rank of the interlocutors, which at least on a formal legal analysis is clearly absent in the relationship between national courts and the ECJ. On the other hand, non-acceptance by the Member States may provoke non-compliance. The spectrum between non-acceptance and non-compliance may be better described by the term negotiation, which presupposes the acceptance of compromises. On this terminological problem see Alter, op. cit. n. 17, at p. 38.

[36] C.W.A. Timmermans, 'The European Union's Judicial System', 41 *CML Rev.* (2004) p. 393 at p. 397 and p. 399; T. Tridimas, 'Enforcing Community Rights in National Courts: Some Recent Developments' in Kilpatrick, op. cit. n. 27, p. 35 at p. 49.

However, they are under an obligation to refer *praeter legem* when they entertain doubts as to the validity of an act of secondary Community law.[37] Finally, national courts whose decisions are no longer subject to (national) review equally have to refer questions concerning the interpretation of Community law to the ECJ. This far-reaching obligation has purportedly been narrowed down by the ECJ and cases of *acte clair* or *acte éclairé* have been excluded from the obligation to refer.[38] And yet the exacting criteria[39] enun-

[37] ECJ, Case 314/85 *Foto Frost* [1987] ECR 4199. On the implications of this judgment see Lenaerts and Arts, op. cit. n. 13, at mn. 2-055 et seq.

[38] ECJ, Case 283/81 *CILFIT* [1982] ECR 3415 at paras. 9 et seq.

[39] Timmermans, loc. cit. n. 36, at p. 401. In *CILFIT*, n. 38 above, the broad concept of *acte clair* as originally advocated by the French *Conseil d'Etat* in the *Cohn-Bendit* case (judgment of 22 December 1978, 15 *RTDE* (1979), p. 157) has been tamed by the ECJ in the following terms: The Court accepted that the correct application of Community law could be 'so obvious as to leave no scope for any reasonable doubt as to the manner in which the question raised is to be solved'. Before reaching this conclusion, however, national courts would have to be convinced that the matter was equally obvious to courts of other Member States and to the Court of Justice (ECJ, *CILFIT*, at para. 16). Thereby 'the characteristic features of Community law and the particular difficulties to which its interpretation gives rise' would have to be observed (ibid. at para. 17). Specifying these idiosyncratic characteristics of Community law the Court insisted on national courts conducting a comparison of *the* different language versions (ibid. at para. 18, emphasis added). More generally, it pointed at the terminology peculiar to Community law; national concepts may differ from homonymous Community law concepts (ibid. at para. 19). In line with the interpretative maxims of Art. 31(1) of the Vienna Convention on the Law of Treaties, the Court finally stressed the need to place every provision of Community law in its context (ibid. at para. 20). Whereas the latter two criteria mentioned barely impact on the original thrust of *acte clair*, it is in particular the requirements to conduct an analysis of all the language versions as well as to arrive at the conviction, that for other courts including the ECJ a given question of Community law would be equally obvious, which remove the subversive potential of *acte clair* for the uniform application and effectiveness of Community law. How, except for cases of *acte éclairé*, – one may ask – could a national court be sure that for the ECJ a point of Community law is equally obvious, unless it asks for a preliminary ruling? The underlying problem seems to be that the question whether something is clear in itself is not a clear question. To a great extent this problem is akin to that of the 'ordinary meaning' clause in Art. 31(1) of the Vienna Convention on the Law of Treaties: 'It assumes what was to be proved; that the expression has a certain meaning instead of another one. The doctrine of "normal" meaning fails to deal with the fact that already the ascertainment of the "normal" requires interpretation and that the very emergence of the dispute conclusively proves this'. See M. Koskenniemi, *From Apology to Utopia: the structure of international legal argument* (Helsinki, Lakimiesliiton Kustannus 1989) pp. 291 et seq. Just as there is no ordinary meaning (in this sense also J.

ciated in *CILFIT*,[40] at least, if taken literally, have a negligible impact on the duty to refer. Just as the Court paid lip-service to the concept of *acte clair* in *CILFIT*, national courts have, unsurprisingly, at best, paid lip-service to the requirement to conduct a complete comparison of the different language versions. A study of German courts shows that largely due to reasons of practicality there is a huge discrepancy between the precepts of *CILFIT* and the practice of national courts.[41] Apart from the language-issue, there are indications that national courts, at times, go beyond the margin of discretion afforded to them by the Court's concept of *acte clair*.[42]

It has been rightly pointed out that the ECJ followed a strategy of 'give and take' in *CILFIT*:[43] It 'gave' approval to the concept of *acte clair* in a

---

Kammerhofer, 'The Binding Nature of Provisional Measures of the International Court of Justice: the "Settlement" of the Issue in the *LaGrand* Case', 16 *LJIL* (2003) p. 81), questions as such are not clear. By way of conclusion, in its quest for ensuring the uniformity of Community law, so far the ECJ has not been willing to significantly narrow down the all-embracing duty to refer in Art. 234(3) of the EC Treaty.

[40] The *CILFIT* approach is now also reflected in Art. 104(3) of the Rules of Procedure of the Court which provides for a fast-track procedure in case of preliminary references (a) being identical to questions already decided by the Court; (b) whose answer can be clearly deduced from the Court's case law; and (c) which leave no reasonable doubt about the answer.

[41] I. Schübel-Pfister, *Sprache und Gemeinschaftsrecht – Die Auslegung der mehrsprachig verbindlichen Rechtstexte durch den Europäischen Gerichtshof* (Berlin, Duncker & Humblot 2004) pp. 328 et seq., who at the same time opines that *CILFIT* concerned a *Sonderfall* motivated by the need to stop the abuse of *acte clair* by a national court of last instance, which should not be generalised without hesitation (ibid. at pp. 331 et seq.). On a more abstract level, Tomuschat – taking the ECJ's ruling in *Francovich* and the 'isolationist' thrust of German comment thereupon as an example – laments the state of the science of European law characterised by a discursive fragmentation alongside language borders, with the inherent potential of making legal cultures in Europe drift apart. See C. Tomuschat, 'Das Francovich-Urteil des EuGH – Ein Lehrstück zum Europarecht', in O. Due, et al. (eds.), *Festschrift für Ulrich Everling*, Vol. 2 (Baden-Baden, Nomos 1995) p. 1585 at pp. 1608 et seq.

[42] A recent example is the case of *Katsarou* v. *Greece*, judgment of 25 September 1998, in which the Greek Conseil d'Etat read Art. 126 of the EC Treaty as a derogation from the free movement of workers. The recognition of a Belgian diploma in Greece was therefore denied. The Conseil d'Etat arrived at this doubtful conclusion without asking the Court for a preliminary ruling. For a more detailed analysis of this case see T. Tridimas, 'Knocking on Heaven's Door: Fragmentation, Efficiency and Defiance in the Preliminary Reference Procedure', 40 *CML Rev.* (2003) p. 9 at p. 43.

[43] H, Rasmussen, 'The European Court's Acte Clair Strategy in CILFIT', 9 *EL Rev.* (1984) p. 242.

Community law setting, thereby accepting it in principle. At the same time, it made *acte clair* a Community law-concept whose exercise is linked to an extremely exacting clarity-threshold, and in this way 'took' away much of its practicality.[44] The Court's underlying objective is clear: The creation of divergent views on Community law *qua* judgments of national courts, against whose decisions there is no judicial remedy under national law needs to be ruled out as far as possible.[45]

In a number of Member States the Article 234(3) procedure has been internalised by relating the duty to refer with specific guarantees connected to the administration of justice, as enshrined in national constitutions. In this way, the violation of the duty to refer and hence of Community law is perceived as a violation of national law.[46] This attitude is apparent from the jurisprudence of the German *Bundesverfassungsgericht*: In light of the German *Bundesverwaltungsgericht* – a national court of last instance – failing to refer preliminary questions related to the interpretation of a number of directives, the *Bundesverfassungsgericht* found a breach of the duty to refer pursuant to Article 234(3) of the EC Treaty, which at the same time amounts to a breach of the right to the *gesetzlicher Richter* as guaranteed in Article 101 of the German Basic Law.[47] Along the same lines the Austrian *Verfassungsgerichtshof* assumes a violation of Article 83(2) of the Austrian Federal Constitutional Law – the right to the *gesetzlicher Richter* – whenever an administrative authority under obligation to refer fails to do so.[48]

---

[44] It is to be noted that the pending case in C-495/03 *Intermodal Transports* [2004] OJ C 21/23 may afford another opportunity to the Court to alter or refine its *CILFIT* formula. The questions put by the Dutch *Hoge Raad* basically seek to clarify, whether a national court should refer questions on the Combined Nomenclature (cf., Art. 1 of Regulation 2658/87/EEC on the tariff and statistical nomenclature and on the Common Customs Tariff [1987] OJ L 256) to the ECJ, when a party to a dispute concerning classification in the Combined Nomenclature of a certain product invokes a decision by a customs authority laid down in binding tariff information issued to a third party in respect of a similar product and the national court takes the view that that binding tariff information is at variance with the Combined Nomenclature. In essence, this question dwells on the *CILFIT*-requirement of the matter being equally obvious to courts of other Member States, before a national court may assume *acte clair*.

[45] F. Mancini and D. Keeling, 'From *CILFIT* to *ERT*: The Constitutional Challenge Facing the European Court', 11 *YEL* (1991) p. 1 at p. 4.

[46] K. Lenaerts, 'Interlocking Legal Orders in the European Union and Comparative Law', 52 *ICLQ* (2003) p. 873 at pp. 881 et seq.

[47] German *Bundesverfassungsgericht*, judgment of 9 January 2001, 1 BvR 1036/99.

[48] Austrian *Verfassungsgerichtshof*, judgment of 10 June 1999, B 1809/97.

The dialectical and formalised relationship between national courts and the ECJ is crucial for ensuring the uniform application of Community law. Recently, and in line with the liberal agenda, including the idea of 'transgovernmental networks' of American interdisciplinary legal thinking,[49] it has been identified as an important (vertical) dimension of a further-reaching global community of courts,[50] which is characterised by 'constitutional cross-fertilisation' as well as 'both active cooperation and vigorous conflict among national courts involved in transnational litigation between private parties across borders'.[51]

The preliminary reference procedure supplements the domestic systems of legal remedies which are embodiments of what is commonly referred to as 'national procedural autonomy'.

In the absence of a general Community competence for the harmonisation of national procedural rules, attempts at harmonisation by means of Community legislative activity necessarily had to remain selective and piecemeal.[52] Thus, substantive rights derived from Community law in most instances will have to be enforced in the context of national procedural laws. The maxim of *ubi ius, ibi remedium* holds true for the Community

---

[49] Cf., Koskenniemi, op. cit. n. 24, pp. 480 et seq., and in particular p. 488.

[50] A.-M. Slaughter, 'A Global Community of Courts', 44 *Harv. ILJ* (2003) p. 191 at pp. 215 et seq.

[51] Ibid. at p. 193.

[52] For an overview of the Community's legislative achievements in this field see T. Heukels and J. Tib, 'Towards Homogeneity in the Field of Legal Remedies: Convergence and Divergence', in Beaumont, op. cit. n. 34, p. 111 at pp. 122 et seq. Notable examples relate to the fields of public procurement, electronic communications including telecommunications, and information on the environment. In the law of public procurement Directives 89/665/EEC and 92/13/EEC contain detailed rules, both as to institutional aspects as well as to applicable procedures, including the suspensive effect of certain procedures and interlocutory proceedings (ibid. at p. 123). The new Framework Directive (2002/21/EC) in the electronic communications sector, building on its predecessors, stipulates detailed conditions as to the organisation of national regulatory authorities (Art. 3) as well as rights of appeal against their decisions (Art. 4); see W.-D. Grussmann, 'Europäische Regulierungsschwerpunkte für den Bereich der elektronischen Kommunikation im Jahr 2003', 17 *wbl* (2003) p. 306 at pp. 308 et seq. Finally, Art. 4 of Directive 90/313/EEC on the freedom of access to information on the environment requires the availability of a judicial or administrative review of decisions refusing information; on this issue cf., A. Epiney and K. Sollberger, *Verwaltungsgerichtlicher Rechtsschutz in Umweltangelegenheiten* (Berne, Stämpfli 2003) p. 147.

order as well,[53] even if combined with an element of rigorous decentralisation. This entails a complex interplay of supra-national law and national procedural laws, the latter often being ill-suited to fostering effective enforcement of Community law.[54] This situation has also been characterised as one of 'relentless conflicts'.[55]

The underlying tension results from the fact that rights derived from Community law must have a uniform content and be uniformly applied, whereas the remedies to which they give rise, only in an idealist vision can be entirely uniform.[56] The ECJ has stressed the requirement of the uniform application of Community law on a number of instances.[57] Nevertheless it is clear that in the light of the Member States' procedural autonomy the maxim of uniformity has to be of a relative and fluid nature.[58] It cannot take the force of an absolute principle such as direct effect, supremacy and access to courts can,[59] without putting into doubt its fundamental importance.

Not least for this reason, the exercise of Member States' autonomy has not remained unfettered. In fact, the case law of the ECJ has encroached in various ways on this concept or rather what its designation augurs, thereby

---

[53] Cf., the programmatic statement in ECJ, Case C-188/95 *Fantask* [1997] ECR I-6783 at para. 38, whereas – with regard to the remedy of restitution – the existence of a remedy 'is a consequence of, and an adjunct to, the rights conferred on individuals by the Community provisions as interpreted by the Court'.

[54] Lenaerts and Arts, op. cit. n. 13, at mn. 3-002.

[55] Lenaerts, loc. cit. n. 46, p. 880.

[56] W. van Gerven, 'Of Rights, Remedies and Procedures', 37 *CML Rev.* (2000) p. 501 at p. 521.

[57] Already in Case 6/64 *Costa/ENEL* [1964] ECR 585, the Court held that 'the executive force of Community law cannot vary from one State to another in deference to subsequent domestic laws, without jeopardizing the attainment of the objectives of the Treaty'. In *Foto Frost*, n. 37 above, the requirement of uniform application was held to be 'particularly imperative when the validity of a Community act is in question' (at para. 15). Furthermore, in Joined Cases C-143/88 and 92/89 *Zuckerfabrik Süderdithmarschen* [1991] ECR I-415, the ECJ referred to uniform application as a 'fundamental requirement of the Community legal order' (at para. 26). Finally, the Court in Joined Cases C-46/93 and C-48/93 *Brasserie du Pêcheur* [1996] ECR I-1029, pointed to the 'fundamental requirement of the Community legal order that Community law be uniformly applied' (at para. 32).

[58] van Gerven, loc. cit. n. 56, at p. 505.

[59] Ibid. at p. 522.

taking away much of its substance.[60] It has thus been suggested as more appropriate to refer to national procedural *competence* instead of national procedural autonomy.[61] In the light of increasingly intrusive action by the ECJ from the point of view of national law, in recent years even the concept as such has not remained unchallenged, and it has been proposed to do away with the misleading expression of procedural autonomy, which does not correspond to reality.[62] In this view the role of national procedural law is merely ancillary: Its purpose from a Community law perspective is to serve Community law. Thus, as soon as a national rule endangers the effective application of Community law it would have to be set aside.[63] Since national procedural laws would fill in a gap in Community law, these laws would be subordinate to Community law and hence potentially have to be set aside in a given case. It would therefore be ill-suited to refer to an 'autonomy' of the Member States.[64]

Quite apart from the question whether the notion of national procedural autonomy is an adequate shorthand for the relationship between Community law and national procedural laws, the idea of the merely ancillary nature of national procedural laws has to be rejected since it is based on a misconception of the separation of competences between the Communities and the Member States. Central to Kakouris' argument is the (valid) assumption of a gap in Community law when it comes to remedies. However, it is hard to argue that for this very reason, the Member States in filling the gap would in fact exercise a prerogative of the Community, when applying their national procedural laws. This view could only be upheld when presuming the existence of an (exclusive) general Community competence to harmonise national procedural laws. Although it may be desirable from a

[60] A. Barav, 'Omnipotent Courts', in D. Curtin and T. Heukels (eds.), *Institutional Dynamics of European Integration* (Dordrecht, M. Nijhoff 1994) p. 265 at p. 269, who even refers to the principle as 'defunct'. See also the fairly outspoken comment by Keville, who notes in the light of effectiveness-oriented threads in the Court's case law that it would be 'somewhat disingenious' of the ECJ to still insist that it is through national remedies and national rules of procedure that Community law is enforced; Keville, loc. cit. n. 33, at p. 4; see also Weatherill, loc. cit. n. 27, at p. 99 and pp. 107 et seq.

[61] van Gerven, loc. cit. n. 56, at p. 502.

[62] C. Kakouris, 'Do the Member States possess judicial procedural "autonomy"?', 34 *CML Rev.* (1997) p. 1389 at p. 1395 and p. 1411.

[63] Ibid. at p. 1408.

[64] Ibid. at p. 1396.

political point of view, such a general Community competence is however absent from the Treaties.[65] That the phrasing of, 'in the absence of Community rules in the matter'[66] as a precondition of the applicability of national procedural laws should imply, 'that the Community is competent to establish its own harmonised system of procedural laws by means of secondary law'[67] remains opaque and difficult to reconcile with the canon of juristic methods of interpretation. In fact the *Rewe* judgment makes it clear that, '[w]here necessary, Articles 100 to 102 [now Articles 95 to 97] and 235 [now 308] of the Treaty enable appropriate measures to be taken to remedy differences between the provisions laid down by law, regulation or administrative action in member States if they are likely to distort or harm the functioning of the common market'.[68] This is a far cry from the comprehensive Community competence alleged by Kakouris. In the light of the principle of conferred powers as enshrined in Article 5 of the EC Treaty, the Member States' competence in the fields of procedural law which are not covered by partial Community harmonisation, thus has to be the starting point.[69] The need for a uniform and effective application of Community law of itself, cannot justify a reversal of competences.

In a number of cases, though, the ECJ did not refrain from judge-made harmonisation of national procedural laws. Three different approaches – with a number of sub-strands – may be traced in the large body of case law of the ECJ concerning procedural rules and remedies of the Member States, all of them highlighting different values on a continuum with the uniform and effective application of Community law and the preservation of national procedural laws at opposite ends.

---

[65] van Gerven, loc. cit. n. 56, at p. 502.

[66] See for instance ECJ, Case 33/76 *Rewe* [1976] ECR 1989, at para. 5; Case 45/76 *Comet* [1976] ECR 2043, at para. 13, and Joined Cases C-6/90 and C-9/90 *Francovich* [1991] ECR I-5357, at para. 42.

[67] Kakouris, loc. cit. n. 62, at p. 1395.

[68] ECJ, *Rewe*, n. 66 above, at para. 5.

[69] S. Prechal, 'EC Requirements for an effective remedy', in J. Lonbay and A. Biondi (eds.), *Remedies for Breach of EC Law* (Chichester, J. Wiley & Sons 1997) p. 3.

2.1 A strategy of minimum interference

The *Rewe*[70]-formula, applying 'in the absence of Community rules in the matter',[71] emphasises national procedural autonomy and pays maximum deference to national laws. At the same time it encompasses a minimum harmonisation of national procedural laws on the basis of the constraining principles of equivalence and effectiveness: Only national rules meeting the double standard of (1) not being less favourable when applied in a Community law context than in cases involving similar domestic claims[72] and, (2) not rendering the exercise of rights conferred by Community law virtually impossible or excessively difficult[73] will be found to be in conformity with Community law. Instances in which the ECJ has found violations of one or the other of these cumulative principles have remained relatively few.[74] However, as will be seen, the negative criterion of effectiveness (i.e., not rendering the exercise of rights conferred by Community law virtually impossible or excessively difficult) has been converted into a positive and more exacting criterion of effectiveness, which has served as justification for the 'creation' of novel remedies by the Court. In the case of State liability the ECJ went as far as to spell out uniform (minimum) conditions. By way of contrast, the classic *Rewe*-approach has been applied in cases concerning time-limits and limitation periods, national rules governing the reimbursement of national charges levied contrary to Community law, as well as rules on evidence and sanctions.[75]

[70] ECJ, *Rewe*, n. 66 above.

[71] Ibid. at para. 5.

[72] Ibid. at para. 6. The comparison between national and Community law claims has to be conducted by reference to the nature of the rights which they seek to protect: ECJ, Case C-261/95 *Palmisani* 1997 ECR I-4025 and Joined Cases C-65 and C-111/95 *Shingara and Radiom* [1997] ECR I-3343.

[73] ECJ, *Rewe*, n. 66 above, at para. 5.

[74] A well-known example in which the Court found a violation of the principle of effectiveness is Case C-208/90 *Emmott* [1991] ECR I-4269. However, the ambit of this case was persistently narrowed down in subsequent rulings. On the *Emmott*-saga cf., Chapter II. 2.4 below. For further examples cf., Heukels and Tib, loc. cit. n. 52, at p. 116.

[75] K. Lenaerts and D. Arts, *Europees Procesrecht*, 3rd edn. (Antwerp, Maklu 2003) mn. 94 et seq.; *idem*, op. cit. n. 13, at mn. 3-006 et seq.; Heukels and Tib, loc. cit. n. 52, at p. 115; see also Prechal, loc. cit. n. 69, at p. 4.

Paying maximum deference to national procedural laws also had another limb in the case law of the ECJ: In *Rewe* v. *Hauptzollamt Kiel*[76] the Court made it clear that the Treaty 'was not intended to create new remedies in the national courts to ensure the observance of Community law other than those already laid down by national law'.[77] This blunt and unambiguous statement in favour of national procedural autonomy was – as will be seen – subsequently hollowed out and in fact reversed, so that it can be no longer considered to be good law.

The minimum-interference strategy employed by the Court best reflects executive federalism, and finds its correspondence in the separation of power-model provided for in Article 249(3) of the EC Treaty with regard to directives. It is the Member States which, bound only as to the result to be achieved, apply means of their own choice in implementing a directive. By way of analogy, it is the Member States' procedural laws, bound only to the requirements of equivalence and effectiveness, which govern the enforcement of Community law rules before national courts. At the same time the *Rewe*-approach pays maximum deference to the principle of subsidiarity. The Protocol on the Application of the Principles of Subsidiarity and Proportionality[78] annexed to the Treaty of Amsterdam is fairly outspoken on the relationship between Community law and national laws:

> 'Regarding the nature and the extent of Community action, Community measures should leave as much scope for national decisions as possible, consistent with securing the aim of the measure and observing the requirements of the Treaty. *While respecting Community law, care should be taken to respect well established national arrangements and the organisation and working of Member States' legal systems*. Where appropriate and subject to the need for proper enforcement, Community measures should provide Member States with alternative ways to achieve the objectives of the measures.'[79]

Understood as a substantive device, the principle of subsidiarity lifts restrictions on the Member States in shaping their policies,[80] which would

---

[76] ECJ, Case 158/80 *Rewe* v. *Hauptzollamt Kiel* [1981] ECR 1805.

[77] Ibid. at para. 44.

[78] [1997] OJ C 340/105.

[79] Ibid. at para. 7 (emphasis added).

[80] K. Lenaerts and P. van Nuffel, *Constitutional Law of the European Union*, 2nd edn. (London, Sweet & Maxwell 2005), mn. 5-028.

loom large in its absence. Acting as a filter between Community competence and the possibility to exercise it,[81] it is inherent in the principle that it may enter into conflict with the uniformity of Community law as well as its effective application. A subsidiarity-based approach may hence prove insufficient in the light of far-reaching differences in European legal cultures and national procedural laws. The idea of the uniform application of Community law called for more.

2.2 A growing concern over effectiveness

In particularly acute instances and, under favourable legal and political climates,[82] the ECJ has responded to the danger of a fragmented Community legal order with interventionism, relying extensively on the notion of effectiveness,[83] this time – in contrast to the negative effectiveness-limb of the *Rewe*-formula – understood as a positively formulated obligation on the Member States. Plaintiffs should be afforded an *effective remedy* before national courts to assert their rights or to claim breaches of their rights.[84] This line in the case law exhibits a particular affinity between the principle of effectiveness and the right of judicial protection as a fundamental right.[85] [86]

The potential tensions between the Court's minimum-approach and the more assertive purpose-oriented effectiveness-strategy are readily apparent, since national procedural laws may lack exactly that which the principle of effectiveness requires: an *effective* remedy. In a number of instances, the Court has thus abandoned the earlier no-new-remedies rule, filling the gap at the price of heavy inroads into national procedural autonomy.

---

[81] Ibid.

[82] Tridimas argues that the creation of the remedy of State liability by the Court is largely owed to the favourable political background set by the Commission's internal market strategy, as programmatically sketched out in the 1985 White Paper (COM(85) 310 final), the Court's own previous case law setting the tone towards effectiveness, and the particularly wanting facts of the *Francovich* case, n. 66 above. See Tridimas, op. cit. n. 31, at p. 324.

[83] See also Keville, loc. cit. n. 33, at p. 4.

[84] Ibid. at p. 1 (n. 1).

[85] Cf., in particular Arts. 6 and 13 of the European Convention on Human Rights 1950, 213 *UNTS* p. 111, as well as Art. 47 of the Charta of Human Rights of the European Union [2000] OJ C 364/1.

[86] Tridimas, op. cit. n. 31, at pp. 291 et seq.

2.2.1 *Setting aside national 'remedies'*

The judgment in *Simmenthal II*,[87] the sequel to *Simmenthal I*,[88] is instrumental in this respect. In *Simmenthal I* the Court was confronted with a clear-cut question of substantive Community law. On the occasion of the importation of meat to Italy, Italian law required the imposition of certain inspection fees on the importers. Finding these fees to be incompatible with the customs union established by Community law, the ECJ ordered the national tax authorities to repay the taxes unduly claimed. In contrast, the tax authorities submitted that the case law of the Italian Constitutional Court was such as to hold a measure in conflict with Community law also unconstitutional. Therefore the Constitutional Court would have to decide whenever there was a conflict between Community law and a subsequent provision of Italian law. The upshot would be that a national court could not set aside an Italian law in force which had been found to violate Community law. On the contrary, it would be required to await the decision of the Constitutional Court in this matter.

Italian law thus contained a procedural device, which would have to be employed in the particular circumstances of the case.[89]

The ECJ was firm in discarding the line of reasoning suggested by the Italian tax authorities and held that a provision of national law to the effect that a national court could not set aside of its own motion any national rules incompatible with Community law had to be set aside. It linked the national provision at issue with the concept of effectiveness and ruled that the impairment of effectiveness, by requiring the competent court to stay passive would be 'incompatible with those requirements which are the very essence of Community law'.[90] The underlying rationale of effectiveness, understood as making Community law a living truth without undue delay, induced the Court to finally hold that

> 'a national court which is called upon, within the limits of its jurisdiction, to apply provisions of Community law is under a duty to *give full effect to those provisions*, if necessary refusing of its own motion to apply any conflicting

[87] ECJ, Case 106/77 *Simmenthal II* [1978] ECR 629.
[88] ECJ, Case 35/76 *Simmenthal I* [1976] ECR 1871.
[89] ECJ, *Simmenthal II*, n. 87 above, at para. 24.
[90] Ibid. at para. 22.

provision of national legislation, even if adopted subsequently, and it is not necessary for the Court to request or await the prior setting aside of such provision by legislative of other constitutional means.'[91]

The positive requirement of effectiveness going beyond a mere minimum guarantee as envisaged in *Rewe*, thus was interpreted as requiring a national rule – and even one of constitutional rank – to be set aside. With the judgment in *Simmenthal II* the ECJ marked the negative potential of a reliance on the requirement of effectiveness. The positive and arguably law-making potential became apparent in subsequent cases.

2.2.2 *Creating new remedies*

Whereas the judgment in *Simmenthal II* can be read as the first step in the direction of requiring national courts to provide full and effective protection of Community rights,[92] the apex of this development was yet to come. Two decisions paved the way for the necessary creation of new remedies on the Member States level and deserve brief discussion in this context. In the case of *Johnston*,[93] which involved issues of sex discrimination in the admission to core police functions, the Court recognised the general principle of effective judicial protection. Inspired by 'a general principle of law which underlies the constitutional tradition of the Member States', which also finds expression in Article 6 and 13 of the ECHR,[94] the ECJ held that – within the framework of the dispute set by Article 6 of the Sex Discrimination Directive[95] – all persons would have the right to obtain an effective remedy in a competent court against measures, which they consider to be contrary to the principle of equal treatment for men and women laid down in the directive.[96] Mrs Johnston's contract with the Police had not been extended in the

[91] Ibid. at para. 24 (emphasis added).

[92] Tridimas, op. cit. n. 31, at p. 278.

[93] ECJ, Case 222/84 *Johnston* [1986] ECR 1651.

[94] Ibid. at para. 18.

[95] Art. 6 of Directive 76/207/EEC [1976] OJ L 39/40, reads as follows: 'Member States shall introduce into their national legal systems such measures as are necessary to enable all persons who consider themselves wronged by failure to apply to them the principle of equal treatment [...] to pursue their claims by judicial process possibly after recourse to other competent authorities'.

[96] ECJ, *Johnston*, n. 93 above, at para. 19.

light of an act taken by the competent authority in conformity with British law, which foresaw that women should not be assigned to operations involving the carrying of firearms. It is important to note that according to British law, sex discrimination was immaterial, if a particular act was in the interest of safeguarding national security, public safety or public order. A certificate to this extent if provided by the competent Secretary of State, was to be regarded as conclusive evidence.

In the face of the issue of public security, which from a national perspective was particularly sensitive given that the province of Ulster was involved, the Court unequivocally required there to be a remedy for aggrieved parties to challenge the certificate approving of sex discrimination. Here the Court clearly exemplified that the two-pronged *Rewe*-test in fact could be more exacting than to require only the non-discriminatory nature and application of national rules or rendering not impossible in practise the exercise of rights conferred by Community law. Instead the Court expanded the effectiveness-limb of the *Rewe*-formula to require adequate and effective protection.[97]

Particularly in cases where a fundamental right rooted in the constitutional traditions of the Member States is at issue, the Court will be prepared to reign in a rule of national procedural law.[98] In *Johnston,* Britain was in effect required to provide for a remedy in a situation where there was none according to national procedural law, even though this remedy would not be new in the sense that it was created by Community law. Rather national law was required to provide for a *national* remedy and therefore for some kind of judicial review.[99]

The principle of effective judicial review as extrapolated in *Johnston* was applied in *Heylens*[100] in similar legal circumstances. Again the national legal situation was characterised by the absence of a remedy at the disposal of a party to legal proceedings. His Belgian football trainer's diploma being refused recognition by the competent French authorities, and therefore his free movement being curtailed, Mr. Heylens was faced with a decision,

[97] P. Craig and G. de Búrca, *EU Law - Text, Cases and Materials*, 3rd edn. (Oxford, Oxford University Press 2003) p. 237; Prechal, loc. cit. n. 69, at p. 6.
[98] Lenaerts, loc. cit. n. 46, at p. 887.
[99] See also ECJ, Case C-97/91 *Borelli* [1992] ECR I-6330.
[100] ECJ, Case 222/84 *UNECTEF* v. *Heylens* [1987] ECR 4097.

which had been handed down without any reasons given and could not be appealed under national law. Again the Court underscored the importance of securing effective protection of the rights granted by Community law to individuals. The existence of a remedy of a judicial nature was necessitated by the effective protection of the 'fundamental right' of free access to employment.[101] Again *national* law was thus required to provide for some kind of judicial review.

On the basis of this strand of case law, it was only a small step for the Court to require a particular type of remedy in given circumstances.[102] This step was taken in *Factortame I*,[103] where the Court required a national court to disapply a common law rule according to which courts did not have the power to grant an interim injunction against the Crown. Having regard to the effectiveness of Community law, the Court held that where a national court considers it necessary to grant interim relief for the protection of alleged Community rights, it is obliged to make such relief available, despite national law to the contrary.[104] In effect, the ECJ created a remedy of interim relief which otherwise would not have been available. Whereas in *Johnston* and *Heylens* the Court was concerned with some kind of judicial review, that would have to be available on the Member State level, *Factortame I* goes further in mandating a particular kind of remedy.

The effectiveness-oriented approach to remedies has been said to be 'characterised by a resolute if not unwavering will on the Court of Justice to ensure that private parties are afforded with tangible means of securing rights derived from the EC Treaty and secondary legislation'.[105] All the more, this holds true for the creation of new remedies coupled with the stipulation of uniform conditions as apparent from the case law with regard to interim relief subsequent to *Factortame* as well as from the remedy of *Francovich* liability.

---

[101] Ibid. at para. 14.

[102] Prechal, loc. cit. n. 69, at p. 7; *eadem*, 'Community Law in National Courts: The Lessons from van Schijndel', 35 *CML Rev.* (1998) p. 681 at pp. 688 et seq.

[103] ECJ, Case C-213/89 *Factortame* [1990] ECR I-2433.

[104] Ibid. at paras. 20 et seq.

[105] A. Ward, 'The Limits of the Uniform Application of Community Law and Effective Judicial Review: A Look Post-Amsterdam', in Kilpatrick, op. cit. n. 27, p. 213 at p. 215 et seq.

2.2.3 *Creating new remedies and spelling out minimum conditions for their exercise*

While in *Factortame I* the Court had not answered the question according to which criteria national courts were to grant interim relief,[106] the answer was given in *Zuckerfabrik Süderdithmarschen*[107] – albeit with respect to Community legislative acts – along the following harmonising lines: The grant of interim relief must be necessary 'to avoid serious and irreparable damage' and due account must be taken of the Community interest. If there is a financial risk for the Community in granting interim relief, adequate financial guarantees must be required from the applicant.[108]

The apex of the Court's interventionist line of case law was reached with the development of the principle of State liability as a remedy rooted in Community law.[109] At the same time the case law in this field illustrates the creative role which the Court has played.[110]

Against the then conventional wisdom, that the liability of States for breaches of Community law was governed by national law,[111] and against the absence of any textual reference to State liability in the Treaties, the Court opted for a judge-made harmonisation of the field, which initially was exclusively motivated by the principle of effectiveness[112] and Article 10 of the EC Treaty.[113] The Court explicitly referred to its case law on direct effect[114] and thereby, managed to present the principle of State liability as the logical consequence of the empowerment of individuals to invoke Community law before national courts. Individuals should not be left with a potentially unsatisfactory domestic legal situation, once a provision of Community law did not qualify as directly effective. Furthermore, even in the light of a directly effective provision, damages sustained *qua* State action,

[106] Cf., Barav, loc. cit. n. 60, at p. 272, who argues that the ECJ essentially ignored this question put by the House of Lords.

[107] ECJ, *Zuckerfabrik Süderdithmarschen*, n. 57 above.

[108] Ibid. at paras. 28-32.

[109] Craig and de Búrca, op. cit. n. 97, at p. 257.

[110] Tridimas, op. cit. n. 31, at p. 313.

[111] In this sense for instance ECJ, Case 39/72 *Commission* v. *Italy* [1973] ECR 101, at para. 11.

[112] ECJ, *Francovich*, n. 66 above, at paras. 33-34.

[113] Ibid. at para. 36.

[114] Ibid. at para. 30.

and or omission, should ultimately not be borne by individuals. Only on account of linking substantive *rights* with a *remedy*, individuals could live up to their role of enforcement agents of Community law, which they had been given in *van Gend & Loos*. In this sense, the principle of State liability could indeed be read as inherent in the Treaty[115] and would contribute to the attainment of full effectiveness of Community law.

Not least with regard to winning Member State support, the Court supplemented its reasoning in *Brasserie du Pêcheur*[116] by referring to the non-contractual liability of the Community as set out in Article 288(2) of the EC Treaty, as but an expression of a more fundamental principle common to the Member States legal orders, whereas an unlawful act or omission gives rise to an obligation to make good the damage caused.[117] Already here the idea of the Community and the Member States belonging to the same constitutional order was apparent: The Court declared that the conditions under which a Member State may incur liability cannot, without particular justification, differ from those governing the liability of the Community law.[118] Originally presented as a one-way street (the conditions of State liability should be determined by reference to the conditions for extra-contractual liability of the Community), the door for a veritable cross-fertilisation was opened in *Bergaderm*.[119] Here, the Court for the first time relied on its case law on State liability in order to determine the conditions of the Community's extra-contractual liability.[120]

Whereas the procedural details of State liability have been left to the discretion of the Member States, subject to the provisos of equivalence and effectiveness,[121] the basic conditions have been harmonised in the follow-

---

[115] Ibid. at para. 35.

[116] ECJ, *Brasserie du Pêcheur*, n. 57 above.

[117] Ibid. at para. 29.

[118] Ibid. at para. 42. It is noteworthy that this point already raised by AG Mischo in *Francovich* had not been taken up by the Court then.

[119] ECJ, Case C-352/98 P *Bergaderm* [2000] ECR I-5291.

[120] See also W. van Gerven, 'Bridging the Gap between Community and National Laws: Towards a Principle of Homogeneity in the Field of Legal Remedies?', 32 *CML Rev.* (1995) p. 679, who already in 1995 declared that the relationship between Community law and national law was no longer a one-way street, if it ever had been one, but gave rise to a continuous interplay between both, in particular in the field of legal protection.

[121] ECJ, *Brasserie du Pêcheur*, n. 57 above, at para. 67. An example of the application of the principles of effectiveness and equivalence to a national time limit in connection with damages actions is the case in *Palmisani*, n. 72 above.

ing familiar terms: (1) The rule of law infringed must be intended to confer rights on individuals; (2) the breach of the rule must be sufficiently serious, meaning that the Member State concerned has manifestly and gravely disregarded the limits on its discretions; and (3) there must be a direct causal link between the breach and the damage suffered.[122]

2.3 A more balanced approach

Recent years have seen the emergence of a more balanced approach with regard to the tension, between uniformity and effectiveness on the one hand, and national procedural autonomy on the other. The cases in *van Schijndel*[123] and *Peterbroeck*,[124] both of which, concerned the capacity/obligation of national courts to raise points of Community law of their own motion, afforded the ECJ with the possibility to first develop this new concept. The latter is based on a sort of remedial rule of reason which rests on the following assumption:

> 'In its case-law, the Court accepted that all procedural rules restrict to some extent the right of affected parties to rely on Community law and that the principle of effectiveness was not infringed by e.g. "the laying down of reasonable periods of limitation of actions", as well as of time-limits for complaints and legal actions, as there are normal procedural rules that exist in all legal systems and which are justified by the mandatory requirement of legal certainty.'[125]

In both cases, the Court opted for a context-specific analysis of national procedural laws whereby, the interest in preserving key characteristics of the national legal systems, such as the principle of legal certainty, needs to be balanced with the Community interest of uniformity and effectiveness.[126] Therefore, finding a rule of national law in breach of the requirements of effectiveness and equivalence will not automatically make it objectionable

---

[122] ECJ, *Brasserie du Pêcheur*, n. 57 above, at para. 51 in conjunction with para. 55.

[123] ECJ, Cases C-430-431/93 *van Schijndel* [1995] ECR I-4705.

[124] ECJ, Case C-312/93 *Peterbroeck* [1995] ECR I-4599.

[125] H. Schermers and D. Waelbrock, *Judicial Protection in the European Union*, 6th edn. (The Hague, Kluwer 2002) § 395.

[126] ECJ, *van Schijndel*, n. 123 above, at paras. 19 et seq.; ECJ, *Peterbroeck*, n. 124 above, at para. 14.

from the point of view of Community law, since it may still be justified under the procedural rule of reason. On the other hand, as the post-*van Schijndel* case law evidences, the old *Rewe* approach has not ceased to exist. Only in cases, which are not about clear-cut and manifest violations of the double requirements of effectiveness and equivalence, the rule of reason test will apply.[127]

2.4 *Critique* and conclusion

Taking a look at the case law with respect to the relationship between national procedural law and Community law, one cannot but, get the impression of an 'unsystematic body of rules',[128] which is predicated on varying levels of scrutiny of national procedural laws. As has been seen, the Court will at times be prepared to overrule national procedural laws, whereas on other occasions it will satisfy itself with minimum interference or will bring to bear a more balanced approach. However, it is far from clear, which approach the Court will apply to a given case. Instead the art of casuistry is the prevailing judicial model, with serious setbacks in terms of legal certainty.[129] Attempts at categorising the case law and, putting single cases into suitable pigeon-holes are not lacking. Indeed, by and large, the case law seems amenable to such systemising attempts. Nonetheless, this should not overshadow the fact that although, it may be possible to logically structure and explain the body of case law in an *ex post* analysis, this exercise is of only limited relevance for the predictability of future legal decisions.[130] Arguably, here the European Union, as a union based on the rule of law (Article 6 of the EU Treaty), scores badly and reveals weaknesses that are such as to negatively affect the position of the individual in the Community legal order. Individuals seeking justice must be stunned by the sheer casuistry and, the many instances of subtly distinguishing cases from earlier case law exhibited by the Court's practice, and thus may be left utterly confused. In the end their sole consolation may be that *iura novit curia*.

[127] See ECJ, Case C-212/94 *FMC plc* [1996] ECR I-389, at paras. 71 et seq.
[128] Tridimas, op. cit. n. 31, at p. 278.
[129] Cf., Keville, loc. cit. n. 33, at p. 15.
[130] C. Kilpatrick, 'The Future of Remedies in Europe', in Kilpatrick, op. cit. n. 27, p. 1 at p. 10.

A great degree of legal uncertainty is in particular apparent in approaches 2.1 and 2.3 discussed above. In particular, the criterion of effectiveness being open to different perceptions about the level of effectiveness to be achieved is only an imprecise yardstick when it comes to the application of the *Rewe*-formula. A perfect illustration of the uncertainties and ambiguities surrounding the Court's case law in this regard is offered by *Emmott,*[131] and the subsequent case law steadily narrowing down the ambit of what seemed to be a clear-cut rule.[132] In *Emmott,* the Court held that so long as a directive has not been properly transposed into national law, Member States must not rely on national time limits restricting the exercise of rights conferred by the directive. A defaulting Member State can therefore, not rely on an individual's delay in claiming rights derived from the directive subject to non-transposition. Initial doubts about the general applicability of the rule declared in *Emmott* arose with the arrival of the judgment in *Steenhorst-Neerings.*[133] In this case, which concerned a national rule restricting the retroactive effect of claims for benefits, which would have been due, had the directive been transposed in time, the Court did not find a violation of the requirement of effectiveness, since the rule in *Steenhorst-Neerings* by way of contrast to that in *Emmott* did not make the exercise of the rights flowing from the directive impossible; it only restricted their retroactive effect. On the face of the different rules at issue in the two cases, this ruling could still be reconciled with *Emmott*, even though the effect of both national rules could be exactly the same.[134] In *Johnson,*[135] the judgment in *Steenhorst-Neerings* was confirmed as to its outcome. However, this time the need to distinguish this case from *Emmott* was explained by reference to the fact that the rule found in *Emmott* had been justified by the particular circumstances of the case, in which a time limit had the result of depriving the applicant of any opportunity whatsoever to rely on her right

[131] ECJ, *Emmott*, n. 74 above.

[132] For detailed accounts of this saga see L. Flynn, 'Whatever Happened to Emmott? The Perfecting of Community Rules on National Time-Limits', in Kilpatrick, op. cit. n. 27, pp. 51 et seq.; T. Tridimas, 'Enforcing Community Rights in National Courts: Some Recent Developments', in Kilpatrick, op. cit. n. 27, p. 35 at pp. 41 et seq.; *idem*, op. cit. n. 31, at pp. 282 et seq.; Craig and de Búrca, op. cit. n. 97, at pp. 241 et seq.

[133] ECJ, Case C-338/91 *Steenhorst-Neerings* [1993] ECR I-5475.

[134] Flynn, loc. cit. n. 132, at p. 57.

[135] ECJ, Case C-410/92 *Johnson* [1994] ECR I-5483.

to equal treatment under the directive.[136] Finally in *Fantask*[137] which concerned national limitation periods applicable to claims based on a directive not fully implemented, the finding in *Emmott* was reversed altogether. Even though this case concerned a national time limit fairly similar to the one at issue in *Emmott*, the Court had no hesitation to recognise it as living up to the requirement of effectiveness. The reasoning of *Emmott,* was confined to the particular facts of the case, which had been such as to deprive the applicant of the possibility to rely on her right to equal treatment.[138] What had started as a general rule in *Emmott* was, in the end, confined to a ruling tailored to the particular needs of the case. In spite of this shift, the Court was at pains to demonstrate an organic and incremental development of its case law by *ex post* offering an explanation of how *Emmott* should have been read from the start. However, in *Emmott* itself, those considerations were not at all present. What in fact had happened, was a change from a more assertive to a more sovereignty-friendly approach, which may have been motivated by the creation of an alternative remedy shortly after *Emmott*: the remedy of State liability.[139] Due to the possibility of a damage action against the defaulting Member State, the *Emmott*-rule no longer seemed to be required for the protection of individuals. Nevertheless, confusion writ large must have been the prevailing state of mind of individuals concerned during the period from *Emmott* to *Fantask.*

The approach heralded by *van Schijndel* and *Peterbroeck* in turn is fraught with interpretative uncertainties. National courts are left with the obscure task of balancing rules of national procedural laws with the effectiveness of Community law. The guidance offered by the Court so far has been limited to ascertaining a possible impingement on effectiveness by 'reference to the role of that provision in the procedure, its progress and its special features, viewed as a whole, before the various national instances'.[140] Hereby the basic legal principles of the national judicial system, such as the protection of the rights of the defence, the principle of legal certainty and the proper conduct of the procedure must be taken into consideration.[141] In

[136] Ibid. at para. 26.
[137] ECJ, *Fantask,* n. 53 above.
[138] Ibid. at para. 51.
[139] Flynn, loc. cit. n. 132, at p. 63.
[140] ECJ, *van Schijndel*, n. 123 above, at para. 19.
[141] Ibid.

order to give more specific guidance the Court would have to delve into the murky waters that are national laws, which *ex definitione* is not its task.[142] On the other hand, the discretion afforded by this formula is seemingly endless, and the result of its application to a given case seems uncertain. This is exemplified by the *van Schijndel* and *Peterbroeck* cases themselves where the Court, in apparently comparable legal circumstances, arrived at directly opposite conclusions. In *van Schijndel,* the Court held that Community law did not require national courts to raise, of their own motion, a breach of Community law.[143] However, this did not prevent the Court from finding in *Peterbroeck*, that a rule of Belgian law, according to which, a breach of Community law could not be raised by a court of its own motion had to be disqualified in the light of effectiveness.[144] True, it depends on the precise circumstances of the case,[145] but how the facts in *van Schijndel* could be distinguished from those in *Peterbroeck* itself, was not directly apparent from the cases and was left for *ex post* justifications in the legal literature.[146] Also the subsequent case law, with regard to the capacity of national courts to raise Community law of their own motion, leaves the impression of a highly casuistic body where the peculiarities of the case at hand seem to be everything, and the rule itself, nothing.[147] This strand in the case law, can thus be welcomed as it provides a conceptual framework which helps in the resolution of difficult cases.[148] However, the considerable degree of uncertainty overshadowing this approach makes the prediction of future legal decisions difficult.[149]

---

[142] Prechal, loc. cit. n. 69, at p. 691.

[143] ECJ, *van Schijndel*, n. 123 above, at para. 22.

[144] ECJ, *Peterbroeck*, n. 124 above, at paras. 15 et seq.

[145] Craig and de Búrca, op. cit. n. 97, at p. 251.

[146] For an *ex post*-explanation see van Gerven, loc. cit. n. 56, at p. 532; see also Prechal, loc. cit. n. 69, at p. 691 and pp. 693 et seq.

[147] The Court's case-specific analysis and its different results, *inter alia*, can be gleaned from Cases C-72/95 *Kraaijeveld* [1996] ECR I-5403, C-446/98 *Fazenda Pública* [2000] ECR I-11435, Joined Cases C-240 to 244/98 *Océano Grupo* [2000] ECR I-4491, and Case C-126/97 *Eco Swiss* [1999] ECR I-3055.

[148] Prechal, loc. cit. n. 69, at p. 693.

[149] Craig and de Búrca, op. cit. n. 97, at p. 252; Prechal, loc. cit. n. 69, at pp. 692 et seq.; but see also Tridimas, op. cit. n. 31, at p. 302, who reads this line of the case law as an expression of the Court's preference to follow a case-by-case approach rather than to take into account major changes in the national legal systems.

The body of case law with regard to approaches 2.1 and 2.3 could also be explained in terms of rule and exception. The spectrum of the Court's case law reaches from concern over equity in concrete cases such as in *Emmott*, to the enunciation of rules of more general application. Nevertheless, an answer to the question of what then is the rule, and the 'tailored' application to the particular merits of a case, at least from an *ex ante*-perspective, has to remain open-ended.

By contrast the approach discussed under 2.2. above is more tenable in terms of legal certainty and effectiveness, but, at the expense of maximum intrusion into national legal orders. The judge-made harmonisation of the conditions of interim relief and State liability brings about a transparent legal regime, which by and large, takes away the dependence of the individual on prior interpretative activities of national courts and the ECJ.

The approach advocated by van Gerven[150] takes up this point and at the same time confines its crushing force for national procedural autonomy: The fact that Community law requires that individuals have access to an independent Community, or national court, in order to enforce their rights derived from Community law does not mean that those rights must be fully secured in a uniform manner throughout the Community. By way of contrast, van Gerven distinguishes between the 'constitutive' and the 'executive' elements of a remedy. National remedies should be identical as to principle (or as regards their 'constitutive' elements), but, need not be identical as regards their content and extent (their 'executive' elements). Due to the close link between right and remedy the 'constitutive' conditions of the remedy should be the same as the substantive law conditions for the underlying right to arise.[151] In short, whereas the 'constitutive' conditions should be left to the Community legislature or judiciary the 'executive' elements should fall under the heading of national procedural autonomy.

This approach has the benefit of fixing uniformity at a high level, without, losing sight of national procedural autonomy. It keeps divergences within limits and, at the same time, provides for limited uniformity. Only the 'executive' elements would have to be assessed in the light of the procedural rule of reason. At the same time, legal certainty would be fostered by a more systematic and transparent harmonisation.

---

150 van Gerven, loc. cit. n. 56, at pp. 521 et seq.

151 Ibid. at p. 525.

A cure for the deficiencies and inconsistencies would also be dependent on the will of the Member States to equip the Community with a general harmonising competence in the field, as well as to work towards their result-oriented exercise. On the other hand, a harmonisation of national procedural laws may well prove to be a mission impossible in the light of different legal cultures within Europe. Therefore, exactly for these reasons a cure does not seem to be attainable for the time being.

3. State Liability for Judicial Wrongs – Basic Notions

3.1 Extension to judicial acts – the problem

Putting courts and tribunals instead of diplomatic conferences in the driving seat of applying, and thus shaping international law, the issue of the accountability of courts becomes apparent. Courts may err in the application of international law. The question arises as to which means should therefore be put in place to remedy potentially wrongful interpretations and applications of international law. Admittedly, from a legal point of view, this seems of little relevance for international tribunals proper: They normally decide disputes definitively, without there being a possible means of appeal.[152] They are the supreme courts of the international legal order, and wrong applications of international law will – in the absence of any alternative fora – have to be accepted.[153] Nevertheless, misinterpretation of international law will lead to a weakening of the authority of judicial pronouncements and eventually, to non-compliance.

However, the situation is different for national courts applying Community law. Pursuant to Article 220 of the EC Treaty the ECJ holds a monopoly in authoritatively interpreting the Treaties. At the same time, national courts are called upon to apply Community law, relying on the system of precedent established by the ECJ's case law.[154] The decentralisation of law

[152] Cf., Art. 60 of the ICJ Statute, 15 *UNCIO* p. 335.

[153] In the absence of an appeal one can detect a *Fehlerkalkül* on the international plane. On this notion see A.J. Merkl, *Die Lehre von der Rechtskraft entwickelt aus dem Rechtsbegriff: eine rechtstheoretische Untersuchung* (Leipzig, Deuticke 1923) p. 293.

[154] Cf., ECJ, Joined Cases 28 to 30/62 *Da Costa & Schaake* [1963] ECR 31, and ECJ, *CILFIT*, n. 38 above, at paras. 8 et seq; see also Craig and de Búrca, op. cit. n. 97, at p. 442.

enforcement in the European Union will lead to a situation where the rulings of national courts may not be in line, with what has been held by the Union's Supreme Court. More generally, national courts may go astray in applying the Treaties. This problem is exacerbated by the fact, that by means of the concept of direct effect, national courts have been entrusted with a pivotal role in the implementation of Community law. Even though the principle of supremacy has been a success writ large, and is by and large recognised by the Member States,[155] instances of uneasiness remain. Is it State liability for judicial acts that can fill the gap? And what about the procedure as per Article 226? Can it operate as an adequate redress in case of national courts not complying with Community law?

For a number of reasons, the recognition of State liability for judicial acts appears problematic at first sight. Frequently voiced concerns relating to the independence of the judiciary should prevent the possibility arising of suing a State for damages when an act of the judiciary is at issue. Furthermore, the argument of *res judicata* would make it impossible to review acts of a court of last instance in the course of legal actions dealing with a State's liability in damages. Permitting this course of action could provoke a conflict with legal certainty, and would therefore, weaken instead of strengthen the legal position of individuals in the administration of justice. Other concerns relate to the specific role of the judiciary, as attributed by modern constitutions. This argument, in essence, translates into a fear of jeopardising the separation of powers, should judicial acts ever form the basis of State liability.

None of these concerns have prevented the ECJ from holding that the principle of State liability also pertains to judicial acts of national supreme courts, albeit under stricter ramifications than applied hitherto.[156] It is therefore appropriate to analyse and review the Court's reasoning in detail and to see how legitimate concerns have been accommodated.

It will become apparent that the inclusion of judicial acts as capable of resulting to State liability has developed incrementally and could already be inferred from prior judicial pronouncements of the ECJ, albeit in the form of *obiter dictum*. It will further be shown that none of the objections raised against this development are entirely convincing. Legitimate con-

[155] Alter, op. cit. n. 17, at pp. 1 et seq.
[156] ECJ, *Köbler*, n. 1 above, at paras. 30 et seq.

cerns can be accommodated by certain safeguards, without there being the need to rule out the extension of State liability to judicial wrongs in principle. Furthermore, it will be demonstrated that the legal protection of individuals would be incomplete if one were to restrict the doctrine of State liability to legislative and administrative acts. As in public international law, State liability potentially needs to cover all the State functions without privileging the judiciary. As will be demonstrated, the reasoning in support of the principle of State liability put forward by the ECJ, applies with equal strength to acts of the judiciary and warrants their inclusion in the State liability regime of the European Communities.

3.2 *Non-compliant* courts

Whereas in international law this problem is fraught with uncertainties connected to the decentralised enforcement of international law and the absence of an ultimate judge with mandatory jurisdiction, the notion of non-compliance can be formulated in a fairly straightforward manner in the Community law context.

In most instances, an international law-analysis would have to face the question of '*Who* will ultimately decide?' ('*Quis iudicabit*') in case of dispute. In the absence of conventional dispute-settlement-mechanisms[157] or – more specifically – instances in which States, in one form or another, have consented to the jurisdiction of the ICJ,[158] it will be for the States, party to a particular convention, to decide on issues of non-compliance. In other words, the actors, themselves, will interpret the rules of the game. Such a decentralised interpretation of international law in the end, leaves issues of non-compliance to the prerogative of the States involved and permits for a self-interested and instrumentalised use of the law.[159] Ultimately, State ob-

[157] An example of the creation of a quasi-judicial treaty-based dispute-settlement-mechanism is the *Understanding on Rules and Procedures Governing the Settlement of Disputes*, 33 *ILM* (1994) p. 112, within the framework of the WTO. For further (regional) examples cf., I. Streho, 'Regional Organizations' Judicial System Compared: Is the European Model Transposable and Should It Be?', 27 *Review of Asian and Pacific Studies* (2004) p. 57 at pp. 59 et seq.

[158] On the possible ways to establish the jurisdiction of the ICJ cf., Art. 38 of the ICJ Statute.

[159] Alter, op. cit. n. 17, at p. 211.

jectives are the highest values of the system, albeit glossed over by individual-centric tendencies such as humanitarian law and the recognition of human rights.[160]

Differences relating to interpretation can then, only be smoothed out by having recourse to *diplomatic* means; *legal* means are absent. The Vienna Convention on Diplomatic Relations,[161] whose provisions are illuminated exclusively by national practice, may serve as a case in point. Apart from academic discourse, the question of non-compliance will have to remain unanswered in the absence of States finding a common language.

By contrast, Article 220 of the EC Treaty answers the question of '*Who* will ultimately decide?' in a standardised and uniform manner. It is for the ECJ to ensure that in the interpretation and application of Community law, the law is observed. In this way the Court is entrusted with the role of a final arbitrator. Its judicial pronouncements authoritatively interpret Community law and non-compliance, therefore becomes an issue to be addressed by the ECJ. This does not necessarily require the ECJ to decide on a case-by-case basis as to compliance or non-compliance. Quite to the contrary, the Community legal order is based on a system of precedent in the sense, that national courts are bound by earlier rulings of the ECJ, as they authoritatively declare what the law is. National courts can rely on these findings, regardless of whether the proceedings are similar or whether the questions answered are strictly identical.[162]

Consequently, in the Community law context, non-compliance can be defined as taking or having taken decisions which are not in conformity with Community law *as interpreted by the ECJ*. For the present purposes, the notion of non-compliant courts will thus refer to national courts taking or having taken decisions which are not in conformity with Community law *as interpreted by the ECJ*.

---

[160] Cf., in particular ICJ, Advisory Opinion on the *Legality of the Threat or Use of Nuclear Weapons* [1996] ICJ Reports, at para. 96; see also M. Koskenniemi, 'What is international law for?', in M. Evans (ed.), *International Law* (Oxford, Oxford University Press 2003) p. 89 at p. 95.

[161] 500 *UNTS* p. 95.

[162] ECJ, *CILFIT*, n. 38 above, at paras. 13-15, and ECJ, *Da Costa & Schaake*, n. 154 above.

3.3 Primary and secondary proceedings

Applying the doctrine of State liability to judicial acts gives rise to a distinction between primary and secondary proceedings, which in turn follows from the common differentiation between primary and secondary remedies (*Primär- und Sekundäransprüche*).[163] Both types of proceedings concern different matters in dispute: Secondary proceedings are directed towards *compensation* for the damages resulting from a non-compliant judgment, leaving the source of the damage untouched.[164] In contrast, primary proceedings concern claims relating to the framework of the dispute of the original judgment, which due to non-compliance, subsequently becomes the source of the damage suffered. For the sake of argumentative clarity this distinction will be applied throughout the present work.

[163] For this distinction in national and Community law cf., F. Ossenbühl, *Staatshaftungsrecht*, 5th edn. (Munich, C.H. Beck 1998) pp. 564 et seq. and pp. 611 et seq. For the analogous distinction between primary and secondary obligations in public international law – this time viewed from the perspective of the State – see J. Crawford, *The International Law Commission's Articles on State Responsibility – Introduction, Text and Commentaries* (Cambridge, Cambridge University Press 2002) pp. 14 et seq.

[164] Ossenbühl, op. cit. n. 163, at p. 564.

Chapter III
THREE HYPOTHESES ON THE NECESSITY OF STATE LIABILITY FOR JUDICIAL ACTS IN THE COMMUNITY LEGAL ORDER

Chapter III
THREE HYPOTHESES ON THE NECESSITY OF STATE LIABILITY FOR JUDICIAL ACTS IN THE COMMUNITY LEGAL ORDER

As has been set out above, the ECJ was at pains to provide a dogmatic foundation for its finding of the principle of State liability in *Francovich*,[165] which subsequently was supplemented and refined in *Brasserie du Pêcheur*.[166] The contours of the Court's reasoning are marked by its invocation of the expansive concept of the full effectiveness of Community law along with the need to acknowledge State liability as the logical corollary and complementary tool to the then, already long-standing, concept of direct effect. Furthermore, Article 10 of the EC Treaty as well as an international law analysis confirmed the Court's reasoning, the latter aiming at establishing an analogy between Community law and international law. Finally, in *Brasserie du Pêcheur* the Court hinted at Article 288(2) of the EC Treaty as an expression of a more general principle inherent in the legal orders of the Member States as well as of the Community, according to which damages have to be made good.

From a dogmatic perspective the full effectiveness-argument remains vague and unsatisfactory: Its virtually all-embracing nature and the extensive reliance on it by the Court make it both problematic and unreliable as a yardstick for the preview of future *legal* decisions. Rather than a dogmatic tool, it can be better understood as a kind of *Vorverständnis* or an 'offener, mehrschichtiger, und konkretisierungsbedürftiger normativer Ausgangspunkt'[167] which the Court may have recourse to, in particular when confronted with issues of prime constitutional importance for the Community; a tool which cannot necessarily be freed from its purport as a political vision.[168]

---

[165] n. 66 above.

[166] n. 57 above.

[167] W. Kahl in C. Calliess and M. Ruffert (eds.), *Kommentar zu EU-Vertrag und EG-Vertrag*, 2nd edn. (Neuwied, Luchterhand 2002) commentary on Art. 10 of the EC Treaty, mn. 6.

[168] Tomuschat, loc. cit. n. 41, at pp. 1593 et seq.

Despite the obvious significance of the full-effectiveness argument for the question of State liability for judicial acts, in this context an attempt shall be made to root this problem in a more systematic and dogmatically reliable context. To be sure, there can be few doubts that a reasoning merely based on the full effectiveness of Community law would be instrumental in extending the principle of State liability to judicial acts. Consequently, there seems to be no need for a more in-depth analysis of this line of reasoning, which in any event could be a smoke-screen for holding 'accountable' national judiciaries via the trigger of State liability.

Instead of reopening the discussion of the interpretative maxim of full effectiveness with a view to State liability for judicial acts, which can certainly justify an extension to judicial acts[169] but is only in parts amenable to precise deductions,[170] a more dogmatic approach will be chosen here, with the aim of revealing a firm foundation on which to base State liability for judicial acts. However, this will admittedly be influenced by effectiveness-related considerations.

For this purpose three hypotheses on the necessity of State liability in the Community legal order will be formulated, which subsequently will be tested for their validity. Two of the hypotheses are rooted in the Court's well-established case law on State liability, one brings in more general aspects, which so far have not been taken up by the ECJ. These two hypotheses concern the relationship between Community law and international law: *International law hypothesis I* will bring together the concept of State responsibility as one of the benchmarks of the international legal order with the more recent concept of State liability in the Community law context. *International law hypothesis II* is concerned with the protection of fundamental rights – both procedural and substantive – in the Community law context. It rests on the unequivocal recognition by the ECJ of fundamental rights as general principles of Community law, which are inspired by con-

---

[169] Cf., ECJ, *Köbler*, n. 1 above, at para. 33: 'In the light of the essential role played by the judiciary in the protection of the rights derived by individuals from Community rules, *the full effectiveness of those rules would be called in question* and the protection of those rights would be weakened if individuals were precluded from being able, under certain conditions, to obtain reparation when their rights are affected by an infringement of Community law attributable to a decision of a court of a Member State adjudicating at last instance.' (emphasis added).

[170] Tomuschat, loc. cit. n. 41, at p. 1594.

stitutional principles common to the Member States as well as, international commitments for the protection of human rights entered into by the Member States, most prominently the ECHR.[171] The third hypothesis (= *comparative law hypothesis*) takes up this comparative attitude and is taken from the Court's judgment in *Brasserie du Pêcheur*. It extends the Court's reasoning to judicial acts, whereas the principle of non-contractual liability of the Community as enshrined in Article 288(2) of the EC Treaty is but an expression of the general principle familiar to the Member States' legal orders that an unlawful act or omission gives rise to an obligation to make good the damages caused.[172]

The insights expected from this approach will concern both, the dogmatic foundation of State liability for judicial acts, as well as a better understanding of the system of State liability as a whole. The ECJ's move towards the inclusion of judicial acts for the purpose of State liability will be put in an international and national context, which may also shed light on its motivation.

1. International Law Hypothesis I: State Liability As Refined 'State Responsibility' Tailored to the Individualising Nature of the Community Legal Order

In this section the particular role of the national judiciaries will be considered. This State function is characterised by a number of traits that distinguish it substantially from the legislature and in particular, the administrative branch and which may be such as to plead in favor of a more balanced approach when it comes to the attribution of its acts to the State. Indeed, not least for these reasons, it has been suggested within the realm of Community law that State liability for judicial acts should be 'surely unthinkable'.[173]

However, it will be shown that it is not appropriate to exclude the judiciary from triggering a Member State's liability. This result will be strongly supported by an analysis of the rules on State responsibility of States for

---

[171] ECJ, Case 11/70 *Internationale Handelsgesellschaft* [1970] ECR 1125, at para. 4, and Case 4/73 *Nold* [1974] ECR 491, at para. 13.

[172] ECJ, *Brasserie du Pêcheur*, n. 57 above, at para. 29.

[173] J. Steiner, 'From direct effects to *Francovich*: shifting means of enforcement of Community Law', 18 *EL Rev.* (1993) p. 11.

internationally wrongful acts which are widely recognised as customary international law in the international community. There are no indications that the acts of courts should be treated more benevolently in the Community legal order than is the case in public international law. By contrast, the peculiarities of Community law require a comprehensive and inclusive theory of the State organs committing the State for the purposes of State liability.

1.1 Community law refers to public international law

In *Brasserie du Pêcheur*[174] the ECJ, having held in favour of the principle of State liability of the Member States in *Francovich*,[175] was given the opportunity to refine and further explain its reasoning, as well as the conditions leading to liability. Even though *Brasserie du Pêcheur* concerned a clear case of a breach of Community law by the German legislature, the Court did not satisfy itself with finding this breach. In an *obiter dictum* the ECJ explained that the principle of State liability would hold good for any breach of Community law, regardless of the organ of the State whose act or omission was responsible for the breach.[176] It further explained that 'in view of the fundamental requirement of the Community legal order that Community law be uniformly applied [...], the obligation to make good damage caused to individuals by breaches of Community law cannot depend on domestic rules as to the division of powers between constitutional authorities'.[177] What the Court essentially said here was that, in the absence of any Community rules on the attribution of powers within the States, the States were by and large free to attribute powers to the various State functions. In this task States were only in part limited by international commitments, such as the ECHR and in particular, its Article 6. In the light of this constitutional freedom of the Member States, there should not be any recourse to a back door escape route, thus allowing States to evade State liability *qua* attributing State powers in a particular manner. In addition, the ambit of State liability should not vary between the Member States, a result that could only be achieved by equivalising all the State functions. In spite of

[174] ECJ, *Brasserie du Pêcheur*, n. 57 above.
[175] ECJ, *Francovich*, n. 66 above.
[176] ECJ, *Brasserie du Pêcheur*, n. 57 above, at paras. 31 et seq.
[177] Ibid. at para. 33.

the Court's *obiter dictum* in *Brasserie du Pêcheur*, legal scholarship was divided on the question as to whether or not the principle of State liability should extend to judicial acts.[178]

Even more so than in *Brasserie du Pêcheur*,[179] the Court's reasoning in *Köbler* was further corroborated by a reference to public international law. The Court explained that 'in international law a State whose liability for breach of an international commitment is in issue will be viewed as a single entity, irrespective of whether the breach that gave rise to the damages is attributable to the legislature, the judiciary or the executive'.[180]

The ECJ, therefore partly aligned the law of State liability with that of State responsibility. It is submitted that State liability can thus be conceptualised as a form of State responsibility, albeit not in the classical sense. The crucial point here, is that individuals themselves can bring an action for damages in the Community legal order once a right which has been intended to be conferred on them has been breached in a particularly qualified manner. In the words of AG Léger, '[i]n Community law, State liability can be – directly – put in issue by individuals'.[181] This very feature is absent from the law of State responsibility, which is still State-centric, insofar as requiring the customary rules of diplomatic protection to form the missing link between the individual and the incriminated State. 'State liability is thus only indirectly put in issue by individuals'.[182] Exactly for this reason it has been argued that looking at State liability as mandated by Community law from the viewpoint of State responsibility would not succeed in describing Member State liability, acknowledging at the same time

---

[178] M. Ruffert in Calliess and Ruffert, op. cit. n. 167, commentary on Art. 288 of the EC Treaty, mn. 35 with further references.

[179] Cf., ECJ, *Brasserie du Pêcheur*, n. 57 above, at para. 34.

[180] ECJ, *Köbler*, n. 1 above, at para. 34.

[181] Opinion of AG Léger in *Köbler*, n. 1 above, at para. 46 (n. 37).

[182] Ibid.; AG Léger does not distinguish between the related and yet distinct concepts of State liability and State responsibility in public international law. Arguably these concepts are bound to become ever more mingled: Cf., W. van Gerven (ed.), *Cases, Materials and Text on National, Supranational and International Tort Law* (Oxford, Hart Publishing 2000) p. 595 and A. Rosas, 'State Responsibility under Civil Liability Regimes', in O. Bring and S. Mahmoudi, *Current International Law Issues – Nordic Perspectives, Essays in Honour of Jerzy Sztucki* (Dordrecht, M. Nijhoff 1994) p. 161 at pp. 180 et seq.

that State responsibility could be useful as a 'source of theoretical inspiration'.[183]

It has already been stated that the ECJ refers to public international law for the purpose of attributing the actions or omissions of State organs to the State. The significance of this reference will require to be analysed in greater detail. However, if this analogy holds true, there is a clear parallel between State liability as devised in the Community legal order and the law of State responsibility. As concerns the aspect of individualism versus State centrism which could stand in the way of looking at State liability through the looking glass of State responsibility, it is necessary to consider the subjects of public international law and Community law respectively. It is in line with conventional wisdom that States are the traditional and primary subjects of public international law.[184] By contrast, the recognition of the individual in public international law has only been gradual and piecemeal: The door was opened in *Jurisdiction of the Courts of Danzig,* which emphasised the role of the individual in public international law,[185] and yet the instances of States intending to confer rights on individuals have been limited in subject-matter and hence also in number. Most notably in human rights treaties, individuals have been recognised as subjects of international law and have been afforded standing on the international plane.[186] However, this trend is fairly recent[187] and could as of yet, not affect the old body of customary rules on State responsibility, which still takes the State as the point of departure. Thus individuals take a 'lopsided position' in public interna-

---

[183] I. Lee, 'In Search of a Theory of State Liability in the European Union', 9 *Harvard Jean Monnet Working Paper* (1999) p. 1 at pp. 18 et seq.

[184] A. Cassese, *International Law* (Oxford, Oxford University Press 2001) p. 46.

[185] See Chapter II.1 above.

[186] Cf., for instance Art. 34 of the ECHR which provides that '[t]he Court may receive applications from any person, non-governmental organisation or group of individuals claiming to be the victim of a violation by one of the High Contracting Parties of the rights set forth in the Convention or the protocols thereto. The High Contracting Parties undertake not to hinder in any way the effective exercise of this right'.

[187] It should be noted, however, that in a book published as early as 1927, which was based on a series of lectures delivered at Columbia University in 1926, Politis discerned the growing acknowledgement of the individual in public international law going hand in hand with the emergence of an international criminal law. See N. Politis, *Les nouvelles tendences du droit international* (Paris, Hachette 1927) pp. 185 et seq.

tional law, characterised by a lack of correspondence between duties imposed and rights or remedies granted.[188]

In contrast, the 'new legal order of international law' created by the Community treaties has almost from its inception fully recognised the individual as a subject of Community law. As was emphatically stated in *van Gend & Loos*, the subjects of the Community legal order not only comprise Member States but also their nationals.[189] Thus, the nature of the Community legal order is such as to lead to the transfer of the State responsibility claim from the State to the individual.[190]

There is a further argument in support of an alignment of State responsibility and State liability in the Community law context: Apart from cessation and non-repetition of an internationally wrongful act (Article 30 of the ILC Draft Articles on State Responsibility), State responsibility aims at achieving full reparation for the injury caused by an internationally wrongful act (Article 31 of the ILC Draft Articles). According to Article 34 of the ILC Draft Articles full reparation for the injury caused by an internationally wrongful act shall take the form of restitution, compensation and satisfaction, either singly or in combination. Finally, compensation shall be granted, insofar as restitution – i.e., to re-establish the *status quo ante* (Article 35 of the ILC Draft Articles) – does not make good the damage; the compensation shall cover any financially assessable damage including loss of profits insofar as established (Article 36 of the ILC Draft Articles). In the realm of Community law Member States are obliged to pay compensation for harm caused to individuals by breaches of Community law for which they can be held responsible.

It follows then, that Community law accommodates the full involvement of individuals in the Community legal order by putting into their hands the remedy of an action for damages. The aim of this action is to obtain compensation for harm caused by the State. In this respect a difference between the law of State responsibility and the Community State liability regime cannot be detected. What is different is the subjects involved, and this difference is due to the merely partial recognition of individuals in international law, which is still characterised by mediatisation.

---

188 Cassese, op. cit. n. 184, at p. 85.

189 ECJ, *van Gend & Loos*, n. 5 above, at paras. 10 and 16.

190 Ruffert, loc. cit. n. 178, at mn. 31.

It therefore grants weight to the parallels between the two concepts, to view State liability as a modified and developed form of State responsibility, which takes into account the specific characteristics of Community law, in particular its individualistic tendency. This finding is not in contradiction with Weiler, who explains that there is no room for State responsibility, *at least not in the classical sense*, in the Community legal order.[191] As has been already indicated it is not about re-introducing State responsibility in its classical form into the Community legal order, for which in the light of the Articles 226 et seq. of the EC Treaty there is no place, but rather extrapolating State liability as a form of State responsibility designed to account for the unprecedented involvement of individuals in the Community legal order.

This view is further supported by the case law of the European Court of Human Rights. As is well known, individuals of the States party to the ECHR may file complaints with the European Court of Human Rights (Article 34 of the ECHR as amended by Protocol No. 11).[192] If the Court finds a complete or partial failure of a State party to comply with the Convention's obligations, it shall – under certain conditions – afford 'just satisfaction' to the injured party,[193] the latter being an individual benefiting from the Convention's guarantees. Again, there is no State acting as an intermediary between an individual and the Court. Yet, according to its settled case law, the Court 'does not have to specify which national authority is responsible for any breach of the Convention: *the sole issue is the State's international responsibility*'.[194] Hence, the system of the ECHR aligns State responsibility with the possibility of obtaining redress for individuals.

---

[191] Weiler, loc. cit. n. 4, at p. 29.

[192] Protocol No. 11 to the Convention for the Protection of Human Rights and Fundamental Freedoms, restructuring the control machinery established thereby, ETS No. 155, entering into force on 1 November 1998 and providing for a permanent court which took over the competences of the former Commission of Human Rights.

[193] Art. 50 of the ECHR reads as follows: 'If the Court finds that a decision or a measure taken by a legal authority or any other authority of a High Contracting Party is completely or partially in conflict with the obligations arising from the [...] Convention, and if the internal law of the said Party allows only a partial reparation to be made for the consequences of this decision or measure, the decision of the Court shall, if necessary, afford just satisfaction to the injured party'.

[194] ECrtHR, *Lingens* v. *Austria*, judgment of 8 July 1986, A.103, at para. 46 (emphasis added), and *Zimmermann and Steiner* v. *Switzerland*, judgment of 13 July 1983, A.66, at para. 32 (with slightly different wording).

The consequence of the far-reaching parallels between State responsibility and the Community regime of State liability is that rules of attribution should not be different in the two areas, unless required by the particular features of Community law. At this stage it is therefore necessary to consider the attribution of courts to the State in public international law in greater detail.

1.2 Attribution of courts to the State in public international law

1.2.1 *From the early days to the twentieth century*

It is surprising and noteworthy that one can travel back in the history of public international law and still find an abundance of State practice evidencing the idea of attribution of acts or omissions of courts to States. The multi-facetted concept of denial of justice[195] used to lie at the heart of this attribution and to act as a trigger for the entitlement to reprisals.[196] Instances of this early form of State responsibility date back to the early Middle Ages, whereby the first examples can be found in 9th century bilateral treaties between Italian sovereign territories.[197] In fact the notion of denial of justice was inseparably linked with the concept of reprisals until the 19th century.[198] This link occasioned a blurring of its meaning: Whereas Grotius – in line with earlier authors[199] – associated denial of justice with instances where '*in fontem aut debitorem iudicium intra tempus idoneum obtineri nequeat*',[200] and thereby clearly focused on the conduct of the *judge*, for de

[195] For a meticulous study of the origin and evolution of this concept see H. Spiegel, 'Origin and development of denial of justice', 32 *AJIL* (1938) p. 62 at pp. 63 et seq.; for its purport in modern international law see I. Brownlie, *Principles of Public International Law*, 6th edn. (Oxford, Oxford University Press 2003) p. 434 and pp. 506 et seq.; M. Shaw, *International Law*, 5th edn. (Cambridge, Cambridge University Press 2003) p. 735; I. Seidl-Hohenveldern and T. Stein, *Völkerrecht*, 10th edn. (Cologne, Heymanns 2000) mn. 1638 and mn. 1666; and O. Lissitzyn, 'The meaning of the term denial of justice in international law', 30 *AJIL* (1936) pp. 632 et seq.

[196] Spiegel, loc. cit. n. 195, at pp. 64 et seq.

[197] Ibid. at p. 64.

[198] Ibid. at p. 76.

[199] See for instance G. da Legnano, *Tractatus de bello, de represaliis et de duello*, modern edn. by T.E. Holland (Oxford, Oxford University Press 1917) Cap. CL.

[200] H. Grotius, *De iure belli ac pacis: libri tres* (Paris 1625) Book III, Chapter II, § V (my translation: 'where a judgment cannot be obtained against a criminal or a debtor within a reasonable time').

Vattel the concept appeared much more comprehensive, namely as the failure to redress prior wrong, being the sole condition to start reprisals.[201] The original meaning of denial of justice as a failure to grant protective justice to aliens was therefore superseded by, or at least superimposed on a much broader concept.

The decoupling of denial of justice and reprisals has again led to a focus on the concept's original thrust.[202] However, both strands of thinking have been identified for roughly the first quarter of the 20th century.[203] The award of an ICSID Arbitration Tribunal in *AMCO* v. *Indonesia*[204] dating from 1989 is still resonant of the doctrinal uncertainties surrounding the concept of denial of justice. Here the tribunal stated that

> '[i]ndeed it is common ground in international law that the international responsibility of a State is not committed by the acts of its municipal Courts, except where such acts amount to *denial of justice*. Now, *however broadly the concept of denial of justice may be construed and applied*, the Tribunal is of the view that the proceedings in the Jakarta Courts do not lead us to consider that there was one in the instant case'.[205]

Apparently, the concept of denial of justice has meant different things at different times. Nevertheless it is undisputed and hence safe to assume that at all times it has at least, included *acts or omissions of the judiciary*; an important line of reasoning has even equated it with *judicial* acts or omissions. From the point of view of attribution we can therefore conclude that

---

[201] Spiegel, loc. cit. n. 195, at p. 75.

[202] Ibid. at p. 77.

[203] Lissitzyn, loc. cit. n. 195, at p. 633, who distinguishes between a group of writers applying the term to all forms of internationally illegal treatment of aliens, and another group applying it only to some of the internationally illegal acts of a State. The latter group is divided into the following subgroups along the following criteria: (a) refusal to grant access to or hearing in a court; (b) all or most acts of the judiciary; (c) failure of a foreigner to obtain through local legal means reparation for injuries caused to him, and (d) internationally illegal acts of whatsoever branch of government. According to Lissitzyn, also State practice and international judicial practice are far from attaching a uniform meaning to the concept; ibid. at pp. 635 et seq.

[204] *AMCO* v. *Indonesia* (Merits) 89 *ILR* 451.

[205] Ibid. (emphasis added).

the acts of courts have been imputed to States over a long period of time spanning periods even before the beginning of modern public international law. The trigger for this attribution was the substantive concept of denial of justice.

1.2.2 *Contemporary practice*

1.2.2.1 Separation of attribution from substantive issues

The notion of denial of justice couples substantive aspects with issues of attribution. In a narrow understanding, it means (1) that the judiciary has failed to grant protective justice to aliens and (2) that – implicitly – these judicial acts or omissions can be imputed to a State. However, the question of the attribution of courts to a State can be separated from the substantive aspects conditioning State responsibility. Indeed it is warranted to distinguish between the attribution of conduct to a State and the characterisation of this conduct as internationally wrongful. As stated by the ILC, '[t]o show that conduct is attributable to the State says nothing, as such, about the legality or otherwise of that conduct'.[206]

A State is liable for a denial of justice committed by its courts.[207] Thus, denial of justice appears as a sufficient but not a necessary condition of attribution, and in a number of instances, State responsibility triggered by judicial acts will involve the notion of denial of justice.[208] However, the attribution of courts to the State potentially goes beyond this category. One may for instance think of the application and interpretation of treaties being delegated to the judiciary. As McNair explains '[i]f, however, the courts commit errors in that task or decline to give effect to the treaty or are unable to do so because the necessary change in, or addition to, the national law has not been made, their judgments involve the State in a breach of treaty'.[209]

---

[206] ILC, *Commentaries on the Responsibility of States for internationally wrongful acts*, Chapter II, printed in Crawford, op. cit. n. 163, at pp. 91 et seq.

[207] Seidl-Hohenveldern and Stein, op. cit. n. 195, at mn. 1666.

[208] Cf., Brownlie, op. cit. n. 195, at p. 434, who explains that the activity of the judiciary relates *substantially* to the rubric of 'Denial of Justice'.

[209] A. McNair, *Law of Treaties*, reprint of the 1st edn. of 1961 (Oxford, Clarendon 1998) p. 346.

Only the law concerning attribution of State organs to a State shall be sketched out in the following. By contrast, the myriad forms of substantive criteria upon which a State can be held accountable for judicial acts are beyond the scope of this work.

1.2.2.2 The ILC's Draft Articles on State Responsibility

In public international law, the rules governing the attribution of acts of State organs and other entities, to States belong to the domain of the 'secondary' rules[210] of State responsibility. By and large they form part of customary international law. The ILC's attempt at codifying them has been fruitful and resulted in the Draft Articles on State Responsibility of States for internationally wrongful acts,[211] whose second reading was concluded in 2001. The ILC decided to recommend the UN General Assembly to take note of the draft articles in a resolution and to annexe them to that resolution; the General Assembly should consider at a later stage, in the light of the importance of the topic, the possibility of convening an international conference of plenipotentiaries to examine the draft articles with a view to concluding a convention on the topic.[212]

General Assembly Resolution 56/83[213] welcomed the conclusion of the work of the ILC on the issue of State responsibility as well as the adoption of the draft articles[214] which are annexed to the resolution and commended them to the attention of governments.[215] Equally, the General Assembly decided to include in the provisional agenda of its 59th session an item entitled 'Responsibility of States for internationally wrongful acts'.[216] On 17 September 2004, the General Assembly decided to include the item on the

---

[210] For this notion and its origins see J. Crawford, op. cit. n. 163, at p. 14.

[211] According to the ILC's commentaries on the Draft articles they 'seek to formulate, by way of codification and progressive development, the basic rules of international law concerning the responsibility of States for their internationally wrongful acts'; cf., ILC, *Commentaries*, n. 206 above, general introduction, at para. 1. For an overview of the drafting process lasting for more than 40 years cf., Crawford, op. cit. n. 163, at pp. 1 et seq.

[212] Official Records of the General Assembly, 56th Session, Supplement No. 10 and corrigendum (A/56/10 and Corr. 1), at paras. 72 and 73.

[213] Res. 56/83 of the General Assembly (12 December 2001), A/RES/56/83.

[214] Ibid. at para. 1.

[215] Ibid. at para. 3.

[216] Ibid. at para. 4.

responsibility of States for internationally wrongful acts in its agenda and allocated it to the Sixth Committee. The latter recommended to the General Assembly the adoption of a resolution (1) commending once again the articles on State responsibility to the attention of governments; (2) requesting the Secretary-General to invite governments to submit comments on any future action; (3) requesting the Secretary-General to prepare a compilation of decisions of international (judicial) bodies, which refer to the articles, and to invite governments to submit information on their practice in this regard; and (4) deciding to include in the provisional agenda of its sixty-second session the item 'Responsibility of States for internationally wrongful acts'.[217]

Even before the formal conclusion of the ILC's work on the topic, frequent reference had been made to them in international practice and the jurisprudence of international courts and tribunals.[218]

The point of departure is that the subject of international law answerable in thc context of State responsibility is always a State[219] which – as a juridical abstraction – can only act through its organs.

Article 4(1) of the ILC Draft Articles deals with the core cases of attribution, before addressing in subsequent articles, instances of more remote links of conduct to States. Article 4(1) reads as follows:

> 'Conduct of organs of a State
>
> The conduct of any State organ shall be considered an act of that State under international law, whether the organ exercises legislative, executive, judicial or any other functions, whatever position it holds in the organization of the State, and whatever its character as an organ of the central government or of a territorial unit of the State.'

The notion of State organs that can be attributed to the State is all-embracing. In fact, Article 4 stresses the principle of the unity of the State. Regard-

[217] Report of the Sixth Committee (22 November 2004), A/59/505.

[218] See for instance ICJ, Advisory Opinion on *Difference relating to Immunity from Legal Process of a Special Rapporteur of the Commission of Human Rights* [1999] ICJ Reports, at para. 62.

[219] K. Zemanck, et al., 'Die völkerrechtliche Verantwortlichkeit und die Sanktionen des Völkerrechts', in H. Neuhold, et al. (eds.), *Österreichisches Handbuch des Völkerrechts*, 4th edn. (Vienna, Manz 2004) mn. 2711 et seq.

less of the State function from which an act emanates, it can be attributed to the State. As will be seen this principle is well-recognised in the practice of international courts as well as scholarly writing.

In addition, this concept of State organs extends to decentralised organs. Acts of organs of the central government are but one instance of attribution.

The rationale behind this wide definition of the organs of a State is most illuminating for the present purposes, and is touched upon in the ILC's commentary. Firstly, it is common ground that no category of organs is specifically designated for the commission of internationally wrongful acts. Indeed the contrary is true, for virtually any State organ may be the source of such an act.[220] This plurality of potential authors needs to find reflection in an all-inclusive definition of State organs, excluding none of the State functions *prima facie* from attribution.

The second reason is closely linked to this first one: There is no international customary rule on the separation of powers, and even if such were to exist in principle, its purport would be far from uniform.[221] The explanation that many organs exercise some combination of public powers of a legislative, executive or judicial character[222] is certainly indicative of the current state of the separation of powers viewed from a global perspective. However, it is submitted that the latter argument may be of lesser relevance for the European polity, which *cum grano salis* lives up to stricter standards of separation of powers.

One can add a third reason, warranting the attribution of the judiciary to the State, which follows from a systematic interpretation of the rules on attribution of actors to the State. Article 4 of the Draft Articles on State responsibility is only concerned with the core cases of attribution, namely instances where State organs are acting. Nevertheless, customary international law recognises a number of instances of attribution going beyond these core cases. Such cases have been addressed in Articles 5 to 11 of the Draft Articles, which arguably do not reflect customary international law on all points. Be that as it may, it would appear illogical to view for instance private conduct subsequently adopted by a State as its own, as was the case

220 ILC, *Commentaries*, n. 206 above, Commentary on Art. 4 of the Draft articles on State Responsibility, at mn. (5).

221 Ibid. at mn. (6).

222 Ibid.

in *Diplomatic and Consular Staff*[223] as conduct of the State,[224] while excluding the conduct of a particular category of State organs from attribution. This proposition receives further support from the recognition of *de facto* State organs whose acts are also imputable to States.[225] In other words, if public international law recognises conduct much more remote from the State as State conduct and hence relaxes the required degree of State involvement, it is all the more imperative that the attribution of State organs is complete, and inclusive of the judiciary.

1.2.2.3 Practice of international courts concerning the attribution of national courts to the State

The principle of the unity of the State is supported by a number of cases decided by international courts and tribunals. Various pronouncements of the PCIJ have taken a view on this issue, vigorously supporting the unitary conception of the State. An example taken from the case law of this Court is the judgment in *Certain German Interests in Polish Upper Silesia (Merits)*, where the PCIJ equated the acts of the legislative branch with those of the administration and 'legal decisions'.[226] More specifically, with regard to the attribution of the judiciary the advisory opinion in *Jurisdiction of the Courts of Danzig*[227] as well as the judgment in *Lotus*[228] are cases in point.

More recently the ICJ has relied on the principle of attribution of courts to the State in two cases which deserve mentioning: In *Difference Relating to Immunity from Legal Process of a Special Rapporteur of the Commission on Human Rights*[229] the Court was asked by the UN Economic and Social Council for an advisory opinion. The legal issues concerned the application in Malaysian courts, of the Convention on the Privileges and Immunities of the United Nations[230] to a Special Rapporteur of the Commission

223 ICJ, *Diplomatic and Consular Staff* [1980] ICJ Reports, at para. 74.

224 On this issue see also Art. 11 of the Draft Articles.

225 Cf., Art. 5 of the Draft Articles; see also Cassese, op. cit. n. 184, at p. 189 with further references.

226 PCIJ, *Certain German Interests in Polish Upper Silesia (Merits),* 1926, Series A, No. 7, p. 19.

227 PCIJ, *Jurisdiction of the Courts of Danzig*, n. 18 above, at p. 24.

228 PCIJ, *Lotus*, 1927, Series A, No. 10, p. 24.

229 ICJ, *Difference relating to Immunity*, n. 218 above, at para. 62.

230 1 *UNTS* p. 15.

on Human Rights on the independence of judges and lawyers. The Court held that '[a]ccording to a well-established rule of international law, the conduct of any organ must be regarded as an act of that State'.[231] It found confirmation of this customary rule in Article 6, of the then provisionally adopted, Draft Articles on State Responsibility, which corresponds to Article 4 of the Draft Articles adopted in 2001. The Court further stated that 'the conduct of an organ of a State – even an organ independent of the executive power – must be regarded as an act of that State'.[232]

It is noteworthy that in effect the judiciary is treated along the same lines as the executive. Both had failed to comply with international obligations and in both instances, their acts were imputed to Malaysia. It would have been possible to impute a failure to provide clear instructions on how to dispose of issues of immunity to the judiciary exclusively to the legislature or administration. Therefore the Court could have reasoned that the legislature or government should have provided adequate safeguards for the judiciary to comply with the international law duty of deciding immunity-issues expeditiously *in limine litis*. It is conspicuous that this is the position which had been adopted by the UN Secretary-General in the course of the proceedings before the ICJ: According to his reasoning, the government should have intervened in the proceedings in order to uphold and ensure respect for the Special Rapporteur's immunity, which – in this instance – would not have had to be regarded as an interference with the independence of the judiciary.[233] Instead, the Court acknowledged a duty incumbent on the courts themselves, which lead it to the issue of attribution of courts to the State.

Again the principle of the unity of the State for the purposes of State responsibility was restated by the ICJ in the order indicating provisional measures in the *LaGrand* case,[234] this time in connection with decentralised authorities. Here the Court held as follows:

---

231 ICJ, *Difference relating to Immunity*, n. 218 above, at para. 62.

232 Ibid. at para. 63.

233 Written Statement submitted to the International Court of Justice on behalf of the Secretary-General of the United Nations (*Difference relating to Immunity*), at paras. 58 et seq.

234 ICJ, *LaGrand* (Provisional Measures) [1999] ICJ Reports.

> 'Whereas the international responsibility of a State is engaged by the action of the competent organs and authorities acting in that State, *whatever they may be* [...];'[235]

In conclusion, there remains no doubt about the all-embracing nature of the attribution of State organs to the State. As can be seen, this principle as laid down in the Draft Articles on State Responsibility is borne out by the practice of the ICJ which – particularly in recent years – has put express reliance on it.

1.2.2.4 Scholarly comment

In *Difference Relating to Immunity* the ICJ has been at ease in dispelling the reservation of the independence of the judiciary against the inclusion of courts.[236] Although not expressly articulated thus far, it can be presumed that the ICJ would equally dispose of the reservation of the doctrine of *res judicata* as irrelevant for the purposes of international law. Again this would follow from the rationale of attribution to the State as made clear in the ILC's commentary on the Draft Articles on State Responsibility.[237]

That the judiciary indeed has to be equated to the legislature and the executive for the purposes of international law is, by now, uncontested in dogmatic literature.[238] When Henkin, et al., expressly raised the question of whether the attribution of judicial conduct to the State would run counter to the independence of the judiciary and the principle of *res judicata*, they answered it in the negative.[239] Writing in 1993, they contend that indeed in the past these tenets had been invoked against the attribution of judicial

---

[235] Ibid. at para. 28 (emphasis added).

[236] ICJ, *Difference relating to immunity*, n. 218 above, at para. 63.

[237] See Chapter III.1.2.2.2 above.

[238] Brownlie, op. cit. n. 195, at p. 452 and pp. 531 et seq.; Cassese, op. cit. n. 184, at pp. 187 et seq.; J. Crawford and S. Olleson, 'The Nature and Forms of International Responsibility', in Evans, op. cit. n. 160, at p. 455; K. Doehring, *Völkerrecht*, 2nd edn. (Heidelberg, C.F. Müller 2004) mn. 831; L. Henkin, et al., *International Law*, 3rd edn. (St. Paul, West Publishing 1993) p. 550; Shaw, op. cit. n. 195, at pp. 701 et seq.; M. Schröder, 'Verantwortlichkeit, Völkerstrafrecht, Streitbeilegung und Sanktionen', in Graf Vitzthum (ed.), *Völkerrecht*, 3rd edn. (Berlin, De Gruyter 2004) p. 545 at p. 547; only with regard to denial of justice Seidl-Hohenveldern and Stein, op. cit. n. 195, at mn. 1666.

[239] Henkin, op. cit. n. 238, at p. 550.

acts to the State; yet, in recent years the responsibility of States for acts of the judiciary had been generally recognised.[240] This result is in accordance with the ILC's Draft Articles as well as the jurisprudence of the ICJ. Furthermore, Seidl-Hohenveldern and Stein, in passing, make reference to the specificities of the judiciary, albeit only in connection with the more restrained concept of denial of justice: According to them a State is liable, 'haftet' in German, also for denial of justice and cannot claim the constitutionally guaranteed independence of the judiciary.[241] Again, the argumentation is based on an all-embracing concept of the State and its organs. Despite the particular role attributed to the judiciary within the State, this could not be such as to exclude the responsibility of a State for the conduct of its courts on the international level. It remains unclear whether or not according to these commentators, the attribution of courts to the State, goes beyond the concept of denial of justice.

1.2.3 *Conclusion*

Summing up, it has become apparent that the unitary concept of the State and its organs is firmly entrenched in public international law. The ILC's Draft Articles on State responsibility are a reflection of international practice on this point, and hence codify customary international law. Both judicial pronouncements and legal literature show awareness of the specific characteristics of the judiciary, predicated on its independence and the doctrine of *res judicata*. However, none of these characteristics is such as to justify an exclusion of acts of the judiciary from the imputation to the State.

The international legal situation with regard to the particular guarantees attached to judicial acts by national law – in particular *res judicata* – thus appears best to be reflected by Article 27 of the Vienna Convention on the Law of Treaties[242] according to which States must not invoke provisions of their internal laws as a justification for their failure to perform a treaty. By way of analogy, States are barred from invoking the specific nature of the judiciary, which results from national enactments, possibly of constitutional rank, in order to prevent the imputation of judicial acts to them. In the light

---

[240] Ibid.
[241] Seidl-Hohenveldern and Stein, op. cit. n. 195, at mn. 1666.
[242] n. 26 above.

of the lack of a permissive norm of customary international law to the contrary, such 'positive discrimination' in favour of courts has to be left aside for the purposes of international law. According to a well-known *dictum* of the PCIJ '[f]rom the standpoint of International Law and of the Court which is its organ, *municipal laws are merely facts which express the will and constitute the activities of States*, in the same manner as do legal decisions or administrative measures'.[243] Consequently, national rules shielding the State from international responsibility for the conduct of its courts are of no legal relevance in the realm of international law.

1.3 **Transferability to Community law?**

Having examined the imputability of judicial acts to the State in public international law, the next step will be to examine whether, and if so to what extent, those findings can be transferred to the realm of Community law.

By way of preliminary remark it is pertinent to keep in mind that the European Union as it stands today has developed into an autonomous system that overlays and supersedes the general framework of international law.[244] Whereas the former system rests upon the progressive creation of an ever closer union,[245] logically entailing an ever more limited sovereignty of the Member States,[246] classic international law is characterised by State objectives and State survival being the highest objectives of the system.[247] More specifically, the Community legal order operates as a *sub-system* of public international law, which, though not a *self-contained regime*,[248] derogates from the law of State responsibility of general public international law as traditionally understood, which is based on the ideas of reciprocity and of counter-measures.[249] This, *inter alia*, is apparent from the procedure

---

[243] PCIJ, *Certain German Interests*, n. 226 above, at p. 19 (emphasis added).

[244] Koskenniemi, loc. cit. n. 160, at p. 94.

[245] Cf., Art. 1(2) of the EU Treaty.

[246] On the limitation of sovereignty of the Member States of the then EEC see already ECJ, *van Gend & Loos*, n. 5 above, at para. 9.

[247] Koskenniemi, loc. cit. n. 160, at p. 95.

[248] For a detailed discussion of the European Union as an open sub-system of public international law see A. Marschik, *Subsysteme im Völkerrecht – Ist die Europäische Union ein 'Self-Contained Regime'?* (Berlin, Duncker & Humblot 1997) pp. 221 et seq.

[249] Weiler, loc. cit. n. 4, at p. 29.

spelled out in Article 226 of the EC Treaty, as well as from the role of enforcement agents entrusted to individuals, effectuated by Article 234 of the EC Treaty. Only in exceptional circumstances will there be a retreat to the more general *system* of public international law.[250]

Nevertheless, the Court in *Köbler*, more so than hitherto, emphasised the analogy between Community and international law as concerns the attribution of the judiciary to the State. The Court reasoned as follows:

> 'In international law a State which incurs liability for breach of an international commitment is viewed as a single entity, irrespective of whether the breach which gave rise to the damage is attributable to the legislature, the judiciary or the executive. That principle must apply *a fortiori* in the Community legal order since all State authorities, including the legislature, are bound in performing their tasks to comply with the rules laid down by Community law which directly govern the situation of individuals.'[251]

The Court's starting point is thus the unlimited attribution of judicial conduct to the State in public international law, a proposition which, in the light of the foregoing analysis, can clearly be said to reflect the current state of public international law. In a second step, the ECJ sees no reason against implanting this rule of customary international law into the Community legal order. In this manner it elevates this principle to a rule of Community law. The Court finds justification for this argument in the idiosyncratic features of Community law, which all the more so, would require the inclusion of courts for the purposes of State liability.

On account of a purely international legal analysis, the transposition of the rule, codified in Article 4 of the ILC Draft Articles on State Responsibility, to the Community legal order is a well reasoned move. As has already been indicated, the principle of the unity of the State rests on the assumption that no category of State organs, as such, is specifically designated for the commission of internationally wrongful acts, as well as on the lack of uniformity in the separation of powers in a comparative perspective.[252] Both rationales are of equal relevance in the Community legal or-

[250] Marschik, op. cit. n. 248, at pp. 274 et seq.

[251] ECJ, *Köbler*, n. 1 above, at para. 32.

[252] ILC, *Commentaries*, n. 206 above, Commentary on Art. 4 of the Draft Articles on State Responsibility, at mn. (5) and (6).

der. Clearly, all State functions are involved in the application and implementation of Community law, and here courts even take a predominant role. Equally, Community law is in principle free of particular rules on how and by which kind of State function it is to be implemented on the national level. In connection with infringement proceedings, the Court has made it clear that the separation of powers in a federal State cannot shield the State from responsibility.[253]

This analysis is borne out by the particular features of Community law which reinforce the Court's *a fortori* reasoning. Here the Court highlights the importance of ensuring the effectiveness of Community law which is particularly imperative '[i]n the light of the essential role played by the judiciary in the protection of the rights derived by individuals from Community rules'.[254] The doctrine of effectiveness would thus require that individuals can obtain reparation for an infringement of Community law *qua* a decision of a national court of last instance.[255] The particular rank in the national judicial hierarchy as a court whose decisions are no longer subject to appeal under national (and Community) law is additionally adduced, receiving further support from the rationale of the duty to refer under Article 234(3) of the EC Treaty.[256]

> 'Consequently, it follows from the requirements inherent in the protection of the rights of individuals relying on Community law that they must have the possibility of obtaining redress in the national courts for the damage caused by the infringement of those rights owing to a decision of a court adjudicating at last instance'.[257]

Having acknowledged the principle of Member State liability in *Francovich* as being inherent in the Treaties,[258] combined with the particular role played by national courts, almost of itself gives rise to the necessity of including the acts of national courts for the purposes of State liability. The reliance on

---

[253] ECJ, Case 239/85 *Commission* v. *Belgium* [1986] ECR 3645, at paras. 13 et seq.; see also ECJ, *Brasserie du Pêcheur*, n. 57 above, at para. 33.

[254] ECJ, *Köbler*, n. 1 above, at para. 33.

[255] Ibid.

[256] Ibid. at paras. 34 et seq.

[257] Ibid. at para. 36.

[258] ECJ, *Francovich*, n. 66 above, at para. 35.

the effectiveness of Community law thus stresses the incremental character of the Court's finding in *Köbler*. Indeed, from the perspective of effectiveness it would be an untenable result to exclude courts specifically for the purposes of State liability, given their pivotal importance in the protection of individual rights. The penetration by Community law into the fabric of national legal orders has entailed a dramatic alteration in the constitutional status of the national judicial authorities.[259] A consequence of the importance attributed to them, must be that their conduct is able to give rise to a claim of State liability.

It is evident that the *Köbler* judgment can also be read as protective of another feature of the Community legal order, namely supremacy. Despite supremacy being firmly established in the judicial realities of the European polity, instances of national supreme courts refusing deference to this principle are not lacking.[260] The Court's acceptance of State liability for judicial acts brings about a further incentive for compliance by national courts of last instance, not least with regard to the duty to refer under Article 234(3) of the EC Treaty.

It is conspicuous that the Court does not refer to Article 10 of the EC Treaty in *Köbler*, which had served as additional justification for holding a principle of State liability in *Francovich*.[261] The Member States' obligation to take all appropriate measures, whether general or particular, to ensure fulfilment of their obligations under Community law flowing from this Article could also be sustainable with regard to State liability for judicial acts.

The Court's reliance on an analogy with international law has been criticised on two counts: Classen has referred to it as unconvincing, since national courts could not solely refer to international law as the guiding criterion for their decisions, at least not without entailing problems of supremacy over national law.[262] The concern of this author is directed against the absence of supremacy of international law with the consequence of national courts not necessarily being able to directly rely on a provision of

---

[259] Barav, loc. cit. n. 60, at p. 301.

[260] Cf., Chapter IV.1.4 below; for detailed discussions of a number of examples see also N. Solar, *Vorlagepflichtverletzung mitgliedstaatlicher Gerichte und ihre Sanierung* (Vienna, Neuer Wissenschaftlicher Verlag 2004) pp. 83 et seq.

[261] ECJ, *Francovich*, n. 66 above, at para. 36.

[262] C.D. Classen, 41 *CML Rev.* (2004) p. 813 at pp. 817 et seq.

international law. This criticism seems to be misconceived: In fact the Court does not invite or require national courts to directly rely on a principle of international law. Instead the ECJ formulates an analogy between the international and the Community legal order with the result of implanting the international law rule on the attribution of State organs to the State into the Community legal order. Like in the former, States should also be liable for the conduct of their courts in Community law. As the Court explains, this result is necessitated in particular by the effectiveness of Community law. Since Community law enjoys supremacy, there is no problem for national courts to rely on such a rule of *Community* law. In contrast, the Court does not suggest that the legal situation should be governed directly by a rule of *international* law, which only would give rise to the supremacy-problem described by Classen.

A second criticism against the reference to public international law in *Köbler* has been levelled by Wegener who argues that the Community legal order has ripened into a legal order closer to national law than to international law. A reference to international law would therefore be misplaced.[263] It is true that the degree of integration in the Community legal order is unprecedented and thus exhibits features familiar from national law. On the other hand, the international law basis of Community law cannot be denied[264] nor has it ceased to exist simply by the fact of reaching a high degree of integration.[265] The international law character of European Union law including Community law is highlighted by correctly referring to the Constitution as 'Treaty establishing a Constitution for Europe'.[266] Even if one accepts Wegener's submission, there is no reason not to draw inspira-

---

[263] B. Wegener, '(Fehl-)Urteilsverantwortung und Richterspruchprivileg in der Haftung der Mitgliedstaaten für die Verletzung von Gemeinschaftsrecht', 39 *EuR* (2004) p. 84 at p. 86.

[264] Cf., ECJ, *van Gend & Loos*, n. 5 above, at para. 25, according to which the 'Community constitutes a new legal order *of international law*' (emphasis added); see also ECJ, Case 294/83 *Les Verts* [1986] ECR 1339, at para. 23: 'It must be emphasised in this regard that the European Economic Community is a community based on the rule of law, inasmuch as neither its Member States nor its institutions can avoid a review of the question whether the measures adopted by them are in conformity with *the basic constitutional charter, the Treaty*'. (emphasis added).

[265] Marschik, op. cit. n. 248, at p. 221 with further references.

[266] [2004] OJ C 310/1.

tion from a rule of public international law for the purposes of fostering the effectiveness of the Community legal order.

1.4 **Conclusion**

The attribution of the conduct of courts to the State reflects a long-standing principle of public international law, which has recently been confirmed, most notably, by the ILC Draft Articles on State responsibility as well as a number of judicial pronouncements of the ICJ. Within the open sub-system of the Community legal order the classic law of State responsibility is dormant, and it is only in exceptional cases, which are beyond the scope of the present work, that it may be activated. Nevertheless in the Community legal order, the law of State responsibility finds reflection in the doctrine of State liability, which places individuals in the driving seat and hands them a powerful remedy. State liability combines the virtues of State responsibility with the individualising nature of Community law, and thus overcomes the State-centric nature of the classic law of State responsibility. This difference as to the nature of the applicant corresponds to the fully-fledged legal subjectivity of individuals in the Community legal order and their purely piecemeal involvement in classic international law, and is consequently not such as to mandate different rules of attribution of judicial conduct to the State. In contrast, the individualising nature of Community law, which, *inter alia*, finds expression in the requirement of the full effectiveness of Community law, all the more so suggests a comprehensive notion of the State for the purposes of liability, which must be inclusive of the judiciary. The primordial role played by national courts in the application of Community law, together with their importance in making Community law a tangible reality for individuals, fully supports this finding.

The transfer of the international law rules on the attribution of courts to the State to the Community legal order is therefore sound, and offers a solid basis for finding in favor of a principle of State liability in the Community legal order.

2. International Law-Hypothesis II: The Imperatives of the Protection of Fundamental Rights Are Such As to Require State Liability for Judicial Acts

It is a well-known fact that the European Union, although not formally a party to the ECHR,[267] is bound to respect fundamental rights, as guaranteed by the ECHR, and as they result from the constitutional traditions common to the Member States, as general principles of Community law (Article 6(2) of the EU Treaty). In this way the jurisprudence of the ECrtHR serves as an important source of reference, whenever the ECJ applies and interprets Community law in the light of the ECHR.[268] Recent years have seen important developments in the case law of the ECrtHR with respect to States' responsibility for the judicial function, predating the *Köbler* judgment. It is thus important to review this case law and to examine whether it can be read as actually imposing an obligation on the Community to provide for a principle of State liability for judicial wrongs *qua* the general principles of Community law as a source of primary Community law. For this purpose a distinction can be drawn between consequences derived from procedural and from substantive guarantees, as interpreted by the ECrtHR.

2.1 Procedural guarantees – Articles 6 and 13 of the ECHR

In the case of *Kudła*[269] the ECrtHR redefined the relationship between Articles 6 and 13 of the ECHR, the former providing, *inter alia*, for a hearing to be conducted within reasonable time, the latter stipulating the right to an effective remedy before a national authority in case of the violation of a right under the Convention. According to conventional jurisprudence of the

---

[267] But cf., Art. I-9(2) of the Constitution, according to which the Union shall accede to the European Convention for the Protection of Human Rights and Fundamental Freedoms. At the same time such accession shall not affect the Union's competences as defined in the Constitution.

[268] Lenaerts and van Nuffel, op. cit. n. 80, at mn. 17-075; Craig and de Búrca, op. cit. n. 97, at p. 337; for an overview of the ECJ's fundamental rights jurisprudence see J. Kokott, 'Der Grundrechtsschutz im europäischen Gemeinschaftsrecht', 121 *AöR* (1996) pp. 599 et seq. and Craig and de Búrca, *ibid*, at pp. 319 et seq.

[269] ECrtHR, *Kudła* v. *Poland*, judgment of 26 October 2000, Reports of Judgments and Decisions 2000-XI.

ECrtHR, Article 13 of the ECHR is attributed a subsidiary character only.[270] Having found a violation of Article 6 of the ECHR, the Court would not go on to examine a violation of Article 13 separately, since it considered Article 6 as *lex specialis* superseding Article 13. At the same time it appeared that Article 6 of the ECHR would not be interpreted by the ECrtHR such as to require a system of State liability for judicial acts.[271]

However, in *Kudła*, the Court departed from its previous standing case law, since according to its reasoning the question whether the applicant in a given case did benefit from fair trial within a reasonable time was 'a separate legal issue' from that of whether national law provided for an effective remedy to air a complaint on this ground.[272] Thus, the Court came to interpret Article 13 as a guarantee in its own right, which would not be consumed by the applicability of Article 6. The reasoning in support of this finding is dictated by blatant pragmatism. So, the Court explains, that the time has come to review its case law in the light of the accumulation of applications before it, concerning the reasonable time-requirement.[273] In addition it draws attention to the existence of a serious possibility of undermining the rule of law within national legal orders, when excessive delays in the administration of justice occur in respect of which litigants have no domestic remedy.[274] In the long run this might result in the undesirable result of a weakening of the protection of human rights.[275] Apparently, the Court sees itself compelled to mitigate the consequences of the direct access to it, which had been realised by means of Protocol No. 11.[276] The previous filtering function of the European Commission of Human Rights

---

[270] See for instance *Brualla Gómez de la Torre* v. *Spain*, judgment of 19 December 1997, Reports 1997-VIII, at para. 41; *BAT* v. *The Netherlands*, judgment of 20 November 1995, A.331, at para. 89; *de Geouffre de la Pradelle* v. *France*, judgment of 16 December 1992, A.253-B, at paras. 36 et seq.; *Sporrong and Lönnroth* v. *Sweden*, judgment of 23 September 1982, A.52, at para. 88.

[271] J. Pfander, 'Government Accountability in Europe: A Comparative Assessment', 35 *GeoWashIL Rev.* (2003) p. 611 at p. 642 with further references.

[272] ECrtHR, *Kudła* v. *Poland*, n. 269 above, at para. 147.

[273] Ibid. at para. 148.

[274] Ibid.

[275] Ibid. at para. 155.

[276] n. 192 above.

having ceased to exist,[277] confronted the Court with a significant amount of additional litigation, primarily with regard to the notion of reasonable time in the sense of Article 6 of the ECHR.[278] The 're-nationalisation' of complaints heralded by the newly established emphasis on Article 13 of the ECHR, should create another remedy to be exhausted before individuals resort to addressing the ECrtHR (Article 35 of the ECHR) and therefore, may reduce the number of cases to be heard by the Court itself.[279]

The new interpretation of Article 13 of the ECHR paves the way for legal protection 'against the judge'.[280] It is backed by an overwhelming majority of 16 to 1 of the Court's Great Chamber and was confirmed in subsequent cases.[281] However, it is restricted as to its scope. The Court makes it clear in *Kudła* that the emphasis on Article 13 will only be brought to bear within the realm of reasonable time-cases pursuant to Article 6 of the ECHR.[282]

Does the requirement of an additional remedy in reasonable time-cases mean that State liability for judicial wrongs has become mandatory, at least within the realm of Article 6 of the ECHR? What is the cause of action envisaged by the ECrtHR for the new remedy to be provided under Article 13 of the ECHR? The Court points out that it is not about a new right of appeals on the merits, since a remedy for complaining about the unreasonable length of proceedings does not as such involve a 'determination' of any criminal charge or of civil rights and obligations.[283] The contents of the

---

[277] J. Gundel, 'Neue Anforderungen des EGMR an die Ausgestaltung des nationalen Rechtsschutzsystems – Die Schaffung effektiver Rechtsbehelfe gegen überlange Verfahrensdauer', 119 *DVBl.* (2004) p. 17 at p. 21.

[278] In the year 2000 more than three quarters of all cases disposed of by the ECrtHR concerned the reasonable time-requirement. See V. Vorwerk, 'Kudła gegen Polen – Was kommt danach?', 59 *JZ* (2004) p. 553.

[279] But see J. Meyer-Ladewig, 'Rechtsbehelfe gegen Verzögerungen im gerichtlichen Verfahren – zum Urteil des EGMR Kudła/Polen', 54 *NJW* (2001) p. 2679, who is skeptical as to the potential of a new remedy to facilitate decisions within reasonable time.

[280] Gundel, loc. cit. n. 277, at p. 17.

[281] See for instance ECrtHR, *Holzinger* v. *Austria*, judgment of 30 January 2001, Reports of Judgments and Decisions 2001-I, at paras. 20 et seq., and *van der Kar and Lissaur van West* v. *France*, judgment of 7 November 2000 (unreported), 44952/98, 44953/98.

[282] ECrtHR, *Kudła* v. *Poland*, n. 269 above, at para. 156; see also Meyer-Ladewig, *EMRK Handkommentar* (Baden-Baden, Nomos 2003) commentary on Art. 13 of the ECHR, at mn. 20.

[283] Ibid. at paras. 153 et seq.

remedy to be provided are determined by the principle of effectiveness. Thus the remedy must be effective in practice as well as in law.[284] The notion of effectiveness is to be understood either in the sense of preventing the alleged violation or its continuation, or providing an adequate redress for any violation that had already occurred.[285] Therefore the Court, save from a preventive remedy, has in mind a compensatory device, which is covered by the guarantee of Article 13 of the ECHR. Turning to French law, which in principle requires a serious breach (*faute lourde*) committed by an administrative court as a trigger of State liability, in *Lutz*[286] the Court held it insufficient in regard to providing for a 'specific legal avenue whereby the applicant could complain of the length of the proceedings'.[287] Concerning the point in time when a *compensatory* remedy should be available, the Court clarified in *Mifsud*[288] that it was sufficient for the purposes of Article 13 of the ECHR if an action for damages could be brought during the proceedings, even if it could not speed them up.[289] The judgment in *Kudła* leaves the choice to the Member States, whether or not they opt for preventive or compensatory remedies.[290]

Kudła has paved the way for giving Article 13 a meaning in its own right, when Article 6 is applicable at the same time. This complementary nature of Article 13 is confined to Article 6-cases, where national judges fail to grant justice in connection with rights derived from Community law within reasonable time. To provide for compensation and hence, for State liability for judicial acts, is only one option afforded to the Member States, but, not the only one. There is no obligation to provide for a *compensatory* remedy if a national court fails to do justice within reasonable time. Therefore the tone set by *Kudła* is interesting in requiring legal protection against

[284] Ibid. at para. 157.

[285] Ibid. at paras. 158 et seq.

[286] ECrtHR, *Lutz* v. *France*, judgment of 26 March 2002, 48215/99.

[287] Ibid. at para. 20.

[288] ECrtHR, *Yves Mifsud* v. *France*, judgment of 11 September 2002 (unreported).

[289] Ibid. at para. 17.

[290] ECrtHR, *Kudła* v. *Poland*, n. 269 above, at para. 159; Vorwerk, loc. cit. n. 278, at pp. 556 et seq.; but see also Gundel, loc. cit. n. 277, at pp. 26 et seq., who opines that it was only in *Mifsud* that the Court clarified *Kudła* in terms of the equality of preventive and compensatory remedies. According to this author, this is an unsatisfactory outcome from the viewpoint of comprehensive legal protection.

the judge and in potentially having an impact on national and Community law rules on State liability for judicial acts, without going as far as to *require* a remedy of State liability for judicial wrongs.

2.2 Substantive guarantees – Article 1 of Protocol No. 1

The *Dangeville* judgment[291] of the ECrtHR established a relationship between the unsuccessful claim of damages from the State and the substantive guarantee of Article 1 of Protocol No. 1. In 1986 the applicant, a French insurance company, was denied a tax exemption granted by the Sixth VAT Directive by decision of the *Conseil d'Etat* in the last instance. At the time of deciding, the latter court did not recognise the doctrine of direct effect of directives. France had failed to transpose the said directive into national law within the prescribed time limit. In the course of secondary State liability proceedings, the applicant claimed damages to the amount of the exemption denied. Although, by that time, the direct effect of sufficiently clear and unconditional provisions of directives was already recognised by the *Conseil d'Etat*, this court dismissed the State liability claim essentially on the basis of *res judicata* of its original judgment.

The fact that the damages action had remained unsuccessful was qualified by the ECrtHR as a violation of Article 1 of Protocol No. 1. According to the Court's reasoning, the applicant had a valid claim against the State when it lodged the State liability claim. A claim of that nature constituted an asset and therefore amounted to a 'possession' within the meaning of Article 1 of Protocol No. 1. In any case, there was a legitimate expectation on the part of the applicant of being able to obtain reimbursement.[292]

Despite the obvious relevance of this judgment for the question of State liability for judicial wrongs, the Court's reasoning is intricate and not entirely consistent: Understanding the *Dangeville* judgment is first of all complicated by the fact that the Court fails to distinguish between the scope of primary and secondary proceedings.[293] Thus, the Court argues that the

[291] ECrtHR, *S.A. Dangeville* v. *France*, judgment of 16 April 2002, Reports of Judgments and Decisions 2002-III.

[292] Ibid. at para. 48.

[293] See also M. Breuer, 'Der Europäische Gerichtshof für Menschenrechte als Wächter des Gemeinschaftsrechts', 58 *JZ* (2003) p. 433 at p. 436.

applicant's claim was based on a Community law norm that was perfectly clear, precise and directly applicable. Therefore '[t]hat right did not disappear with the *Conseil d'Etat's* judgment of 1986 and, consequently, survived during the second set of proceedings'.[294] In fact, the second set of proceedings was about something else than the provision at issue having direct effect, since it concerned the issue of State liability, for which direct effect would be a preliminary question only.

In this way, the Court avoids having to deal with the *res judicata*-issue, which motivated the *Conseil d'Etat* to dismiss the applicant's claim. However, this comes at the price of a dogmatically unsatisfactory solution. The Court, in effect arrives via a back-door approach – by stressing the perpetuation of the directly effective right – with a doctrine of State liability for judicial wrongs. It would have been more consistent to actually postulate a principle of State liability for judicial wrongs which then, would be protected by the guarantee of Article 1 of Protocol No. 1.[295] On the other hand, at that stage it was uncertain whether there should be State liability for judicial wrongs in the Community legal order.[296] It therefore, would have been difficult to argue the existence of an asset or a legitimate expectation. Understandingly, the Court did not want to anticipate the subsequent decision by the ECJ, but it anticipated it in regard to its result and set a *fait accompli*, albeit in a disguised manner.

A further element of uncertainty is added by the fact that the Court does not offer a clear distinction between legislative acts and judicial acts either. The failure to observe Article 1 of Protocol No. 1 primarily seems to be imputed to the legislature, which should have brought national law into line with the said directive. Yet in the second instance, the *Conseil d'Etat* failed to give due regard to the effects of the incompatibility of French law with Community law.[297] This focus on the legislature may have been influenced by the submission of the applicant, which had alleged that France was at fault for failing to transpose the said Directive into national law.[298] None-

---

[294] ECrtHR, *S.A. Dangeville* v. *France*, n. 291 above, at para 47.

[295] Gundel, loc. cit. n. 277, at p. 10 (n. 21).

[296] Breuer, loc. cit. n. 293, at p. 437.

[297] ECrtHR, *S.A. Dangeville* v. *France*, n. 291 above, at para 57; Breuer, loc. cit. n. 293, at p. 437.

[298] ECrtHR, *S.A. Dangeville* v. *France*, n. 291 above, at para. 19.

theless, it is apparent that the *Conseil d'Etat,* to the benefit of the applicant could have remedied the failure by providing for direct effect. By failing to do so, it committed an error attributable to it.[299] Therefore, even though the conduct of the *Conseil d'Etat* was instrumental for the Court's finding of a breach,[300] the ECrtHR omits specific reference to the problem of judicial wrongs.

Against this background, it is necessary to answer the question as to whether or not the interpretation of Article 1 of Protocol No. 1 by the ECrtHR brings about a legal obligation on the Member States as well as the Community to provide for State liability for judicial acts. Does the *Dangeville* judgment have to be read as a case in isolation, or does it have further-reaching implications for the Community system of State liability?

It appears that *Dangeville* has to be appraised on its own merits. It has been seen that the notion of direct effect takes an important place in the Court's reasoning and that the subject-matter of the primary and secondary proceedings is equated by means of this doctrine. That the Court chooses the State liability claim as its point of reference is consonant with the logic of the time limit of Article 35(1) of the ECHR. Complaining about the *Conseil d'Etat's* failure to pay tribute to the doctrine of direct effect in 1997, when the secondary proceedings had been concluded and the complaint was filed, would have been precluded.[301] In fact the Court views the State liability proceedings as a prolonged remedy to make good the 'original sin' of denying direct effect. Therefore the Court need not be concerned about the consequence of effectively presuming the existence of State liability for judicial wrongs in France.

A reference to the Community regime of State liability is absent in *Dangeville*. The Court seems only to assume the possibility of obtaining redress in France and therefore arrives at the conclusion of qualifying the applicant's claim as an asset or at least a legitimate expectation. Whereas this result may already be doubtful in the light of restrictive tendencies in

---

[299] Breuer, loc. cit. n. 293, at p. 437.

[300] So the concurrent assessment in the literature on the *Dangeville* judgment. Cf., M. Breuer, 'Staatshaftung für Judikativunrecht vor dem EuGH', *BayVBl* (2003) p. 586 at p. 587; Breuer, loc. cit. n. 293, at p. 437; Gundel, loc. cit. n. 277, at p. 10; P.J. Wattel, 'Köbler, CILFIT and Welthgrove: We can't go on meeting like this', 41 *CML Rev.* (2004) p. 177 at p. 189.

[301] Breuer, loc. cit. n. 293, at p. 436.

French law concerning the liability of the State,[302] it would be an over-stretching of the judgment in *Dangeville*, were one to read into it an obligation for the Community to have in place a system of State liability for judicial wrongs. The undoubtedly innovative reasoning of the ECrtHR resting on an expansive interpretation of Article 1 of Protocol No. 1 would on this reading in the end presuppose something – *Köbler* liability – to be there, which at the time of deciding was not yet there.

On the other hand, the potential *factual* impact of *Dangeville* on the ECJ cannot be denied: The ECJ's *Köbler* decision may also have been motivated by the desire not to fall behind the position of the ECrtHR, which in effect leads to the assumption of State liability for judicial wrongs, even though the judgment in *Dangeville* is not mentioned in *Köbler*.[303] Indeed it would fit uncomfortably with *Dangeville*, if the ECJ had found against a principle of State liability for judicial wrongs. Therefore, it can be stated that *Dangeville* set the tone for *Köbler*, but a legal obligation to this extent flowing from *Dangeville* in connection with Article 6(2) of the EU Treaty cannot be asserted.[304]

2.3 **Conclusion**

Neither procedural nor substantive provisions of the ECHR as interpreted by the ECrtHR make a principle of State liability for judicial acts mandatory in the Community legal order. Nevertheless the judgments in *Kudła* and *Dangeville* can be seen as part of a trend towards making judicial action or inaction reviewable and eventually holding the State liable for judicial conduct. In this sense both judgments paved the way for the recognition of a principle of State liability for judicial wrongs in the Community legal order.

---

302 See ibid. at p. 436.
303 Gundel, loc. cit. n. 277, at pp. 10 et seq. (n. 26).
304 Cf., ibid. at p. 10.

3. Comparative Law-Hypothesis: State Liability for Judicial Acts Is a General Principle Common to the Legal Traditions of the Member States

The comparative law-method, which the Court refers to as an interpretative tool in its task of interpreting the law conferred on it by Article 220 of the EC Treaty,[305] is well-established in the Community legal order. It aims at conferring upon the Community legal order a label of acceptability *vis-à-vis* national legal orders.[306] As has been observed, the case law of the Court exhibits a constant concern to find through the comparative law method the best solution acceptable throughout the Member States.[307] According to the same commentator, the Community courts 'will instinctively seek the right balance' between the interests of Community law and the acceptability of their rulings to the national legal orders. The Community courts will prefer not to impose a solution which would garner insufficient support in some Member States to ensure the uniform and effective application of Community law.[308]

Admittedly, referring to the 'instincts' of the Community courts proper, as advocates of the national legal orders, may seem doubtful from the viewpoint of national judges and give the impression of an overly idealistic account from the viewpoint of a prominent judge of the Court, albeit in his extra-judicial capacity. Nevertheless, express and implicit principles taken from the legal traditions of the Member States inform the general principles of Community law,[309] and in this way contribute to the dialectical relationship between both legal orders. Not least with regard to the implications of *Francovich* liability legitimacy is conferred by bringing in principles of the national legal orders:[310]

---

[305] ECJ, *Brasserie du Pêcheur*, n. 57 above, at para. 27.

[306] Lenaerts, loc. cit. n. 46, at p. 879.

[307] Ibid. at p. 883.

[308] Ibid. at p. 893.

[309] Cf., ECJ, *Brasserie du Pêcheur*, n. 57 above, at paras. 24-30.

[310] It is conspicuous that the Court only in *Brasserie du Pêcheur* supplemented its *Francovich*-reasoning by the comparative-law argument. The development of the principle of State liability should *ex post* be seen to derive from well-established principles of national law rather than from the imagination of the Court. See Craig and de Búrca, op. cit. n. 97, at p. 262.

> 'Since the Treaty contains no provision expressly and specifically governing the consequences of breaches of Community law by Member States, it is for the Court, [...] to rule on such a question in accordance with generally accepted methods of interpretation, in particular by reference to the fundamental principles of the Community legal system and, where necessary, *general principles common to the legal systems of the Member States.*'[311]

At the same time an innovation of the Court's case law, which relies on general principles may have the consequence of heavy inroads into Member States' legal systems,[312] at least for those which do not reflect the general trend. The Court having recognised the non-contractual liability of the Community (Article 288(2) of the EC Treaty) as simply an *expression of the general principle familiar to the legal systems of the Member States* that an unlawful act or omission gives rise to an obligation to make good the damage caused,[313] it needs to be examined to what extent reliance on general principles taken from the national legal orders can serve as additional support for the recognition of a principle of State liability for judicial acts.

3.1 Alleging a general principle

The issue of support in the Member States' legal orders for State liability for judicial acts was touched upon by AG Léger in a cursory and straightforward manner, whereby a purportedly comprehensive analysis of all the Member States' legal orders was conducted in less than 10 paragraphs of the opinion.

Already at the beginning of his examination of national laws AG Léger anticipates its result, namely that, in his understanding, all the Member States accept the principle of State liability for judicial acts.[314] Yet he goes on in the subsequent sentence, to state that Ireland is excluded from the above group.[315] In addition, he explains in the following that the scope of the principle varies in the Member States: So, for instance, would State

---

311 ECJ, *Brasserie du Pêcheur*, n. 57 above, at para. 27.

312 H. Lecheler, 'Der Beitrag der allgemeinen Rechtsgrundsätze zur Europäischen Integration – Rückblick und Ausblick', 6 *ZEuS* (2003) p. 351.

313 ECJ, *Brasserie du Pêcheur*, n. 57 above, at para. 29.

314 Opinion of AG Léger in *Köbler*, n. 1 above, at para. 77.

315 Ibid.

liability for judicial acts in the UK and the Netherlands be limited to claims alleging the breach of a limited number of guarantees of the ECHR.[316] All the other Member States would accept the principle irrespective of the nature of the legal rule infringed; but this would not hold true for Greece, Portugal and France 'where the situation is evolving and more nuanced'.[317] As regards the source of the judgment giving rise to liability, only Austria and Sweden would limit State liability to the decisions of ordinary courts, at the exclusion of acts taken by supreme courts.[318] On the basis of this analysis, AG Léger concludes that a principle of State liability for a judgment of a supreme court in breach of a legal rule is generally acknowledged by the Member States.[319] At least a strong tendency would point in that direction.[320] Finally he refers to the Belgian *De Keyser* case[321] and an Italian case in support of his argument.[322]

The Court takes up the point made by its AG. However, it does so in a much more cautious and open-ended manner:

> 'It should be added that, although considerations to do with observance of the principle of *res judicata* or the independence of the judiciary have caused national legal systems to impose restrictions, which may sometimes be stringent, on the possibility of rendering the State liable for damage caused by mistaken judicial decisions, such considerations have not been such as absolutely to exclude that possibility. Indeed, application of the principle of State liability to judicial decisions has been accepted in one form or another by most of the Member States, as the Advocate General pointed out at paragraphs 77 to 82 of his Opinion, even if subject only to restrictive and varying conditions.'[323]

It is conspicuous that the Court avoids any reference to a general principle of Community law to the extent of an inclusion of national judiciaries for the purposes of State liability.[324] In contrast, this approach had been pro-

---

316 Ibid. at para. 79.
317 Ibid. at para. 80.
318 Ibid. at para. 81.
319 Ibid. at para 82.
320 Ibid.
321 (Belgian) *Cour de Cassation*, De Keyser/Anca, *JT* (1991) p. 141.
322 Opinion of AG Léger in *Köbler*, n. 1 above, at paras. 83 et seq.
323 ECJ, *Köbler*, n. 1 above, at para. 48.
324 Th. von Danwitz, 59 *JZ* (2004) p. 302.

posed by the AG, as far as supreme courts are at issue.[325] The Court restricts itself to adducing the application of the principle of State liability for judicial acts 'in one form or another by most of the Member States' as another factor to be kept in mind when deciding on the question at issue, without attributing the wholesale legitimising force of a general principle of Community law to it. As had been argued by AG Léger, it should not be required to find a particular feature in all the national legal orders in order to be able to speak of a general principle of Community law; in addition, the conditions attached to State liability would not have to be uniform in the various Member States but merely show the existence of common criteria.[326] Thus, neither a minimum or maximum standard approach is in place, but rather a process of *wertende Rechtsvergleichung* restricted by the particular nature of the Community legal order.[327] By contrast, the Court does not seem to be fully convinced of the existence of a general principle in the case at hand, or at least does not pronounce on its existence, presumably in the interest of not upsetting the co-operational relationship between itself and national courts. Indeed the analysis conducted by AG Léger is superficial and cannot live up to the promise made at its outset, namely to demonstrate that the principle is accepted in *all* the Member States. In-depth comparative studies suggest a less clear-cut picture, reflecting a divided or even opposed state of affairs in national legal orders.[328] In fact, the interventions by a great number of governments in *Köbler* reflect well the various legal tradi-

[325] Opinion of AG Léger in *Köbler*, n. 1 above, at para. 85.

[326] Ibid.; see also the opinion of AG Léger in Case C-87/01 P *Commission* v. *CCRE*, at paras. 51 et seq., and W. Kluth, 'Die Haftung der Mitgliedstaaten für gemeinschaftsrechtswidrige höchstrichterliche Entscheidungen – Schlussstein im System der gemeinschaftsrechtlichen Staatshaftung', 119 *DVBl.* (2004) p. 393 at p. 395; cf., also B. Wegener in Calliess and Ruffert, op. cit. n. 167, commentary on Art. 220 of the EC Treaty, at mn. 33, who argues that looking for a general principle of Community law would not involve a schematic search for a common denominator or looking for the majority of legal orders.

[327] M. Breuer, 'State liability for judicial wrongs and Community law: the case of *Gerhard Köbler v Austria*', 29 *EL Rev.* (2004) p. 243 at p. 249.

[328] Cf., G. Vandersanden and M. Dony (eds.), *La Responsabilité des Etats Membres en cas de violation du Droit Communautaire: études de droit communautaire et de droit national comparé* (Brussels, Bruylant 1997); G. Anagnostaras, 'The Principle of State Liability for Judicial Breaches: The Impact of European Community Law', 7 *EPL* (2001) p. 281 at pp. 283 et seq.; H. Toner, 'Thinking the Unthinkable? State Liability for Judicial Acts after Factortame', 16 *YEL* (1997) p. 165 at pp. 170 et seq.

tions and differences in national legal orders,[329] according to which the imposition of State liability for breaches attributed to national courts is heavily restricted or even totally excluded.[330] In the light of these differences, the steadfastness of the views presented by AG Léger appears highly questionable.[331]

To start with, the so-called *Spruchrichterprivileg* (judge's privilege) pursuant to Article 839(2) of the German Civil Code is not even mentioned. *E silentio* Germany is regarded as a Member State with fully-fledged State liability for judicial acts and therefore counts towards 'all the Member States' which would provide for State liability for judicial acts, which the AG refers to. And yet, this very provision entails the factual ruling out of State liability for judicial acts, unless for the highly exceptional case of the breach of law amounting to a criminal act. Article 839(2) encompasses, in particular, perversions of justice,[332] which will be light-years away from a standard breach of Community law. It is clear that German law as it stands – contrary to the AG's silent allegation to this effect – cannot contribute to an alleged general principle of Community law. As was also recognised by AG Léger, the State's liability for its judicial conduct is almost completely ruled out in the United Kingdom[333] and the Netherlands.[334] Very stringent conditions prevail in France, where the existence of a serious breach (*faute lourde*) or of a denial of justice has to be established.[335] Whether judgments once they become final can be the subject of damages actions remains unclear.[336] For Belgium, the judgment of the *Cour de Cassation* in *De*

---

329 Kluth, loc. cit. n. 326, at p. 394.

330 Anagnostaras, loc. cit. n. 328, at p. 281.

331 von Danwitz, loc. cit. n. 324, at p. 302.

332 J. Gundel, 'Gemeinschaftsrechtliche Haftungsvorgaben für judikatives Unrecht – Konsequenzen für die Rechtskraft und das deutsche "Richterprivileg" (§ 839 Abs. 2 BGB)', 15 *EWS* (2004) p. 8.

333 Section 2(5) of the Crown Proceedings Act of 1947; on this provision cf., Toner, loc. cit. n. 328, at p. 168; see also B. Wegener, 'Staatshaftung für die Verletzung von Gemeinschaftsrecht durch nationale Gerichte?', 37 *EuR* (2002) p. 785 at p. 790.

334 Anagnostaras, loc. cit. n. 328, at p. 284.

335 W. van Gerven (ed.), *Tort Law – Scope of Protection* (Oxford, Hart Publishing 1999) p. 381; Vandersanden and Dony, op. cit. n. 328, at pp. 245 et seq.; A. Botella, 'La responsabilité du juge national', 40 *RTDE* (2004) p. 283 at p. 287.

336 Vandersanden and Dony, op. cit. n. 328, at pp. 245 et seq. But see also Botella, loc. cit. n. 335, at pp. 287 et seq., who assumes that State liability is excluded if the serious breach relates to the contents of an already final judgment.

Keyser[337] quoted by Léger has opened the door for a principle of State liability for judicial acts. However, again this is subject to exacting, and in practice, restrictive conditions, namely that

> 'the act in question has, on the grounds of violation of an established legal principle, been removed, amended, annulled or withdrawn by a decision which itself has the authority of *res judicata* and the original act does not itself now have the authority of *res judicata*'.[338]

According to Belgian law the force of *res judicata* thus stands in the way of subsequent State liability proceedings. The legal situation in Italy is characterised by a specifically enacted statute[339] which provides for the possibility of State liability only if the judicial breaches do not constitute criminal acts.[340] Finally, in both Austria and Sweden judgments of supreme courts cannot be the subject of State liability proceedings.[341]

In the light of these factors, one cannot, but have the impression of a divided and differentiated state of affairs in the various Member States. The only common principle which one can possibly deduce seems to be that liability for judicial breaches will only take place in highly exceptional cases.[342] The degree of exceptionality varies from Member State to Member State and ranges from a total exclusion of the judicial function from State liability to a factual ruling-out and acceptance.

3.2 Conclusion

The comparative law-method entails an exercise in 'psycho-diplomacy' for the Community courts.[343] As Lenaerts explains

> '[t]hese courts are constantly divided between the concern "not to give up" when confronting national divergences and that of respecting, in the interest

[337] n. 321 above.
[338] Ibid.
[339] Toner, loc. cit. n. 328, at p. 170.
[340] Anagnostaras, loc. cit. n. 328 at p. 285.
[341] Opinion of AG Léger in *Köbler*, n. 1 above, at para. 81.
[342] Anagnostaras, loc. cit. n. 328, at p. 284.
[343] Lenaerts, loc. cit. n. 46, at p. 906.

> of the "acceptability" of Community law in the domestic legal orders, the national sensitivities and the differences which exist in the legal conceptions and constitutional traditions of the Member States and which, at the same time, constitute the richness of the legal heritage of the Community'.[344]

In *Köbler* the Court opted for a balanced solution in the light of significant divergences in the Member States' legal orders. It refused to find support for a general principle of Community law in the national legal orders, and in the light of significant differences as well as exclusions of State liability for judicial acts in a number of Member States was indeed well-advised to do so. On the other hand, it cannot be denied that the Court had in mind to enhance the legitimacy of its finding when referring to State liability for judicial acts as being recognised, in one form or another, in most Member States. In this way the comparative-law argument was intended to serve as an important justification of the Court's finding of *Francovich* liability extending to the State acting in its judicial capacity. Its effect is comparable to that of proclaiming a general principle of Community law. Nevertheless, if one focuses on the various national laws, whose divergences the Court glosses over, it appears that the argumentative force of the reference to national laws is weak. In fact, the creative function of the Court in the interpretation of the law clearly seems to outweigh the strength of the comparative law-argument.[345]

The Court's exercise in psycho-diplomacy can be exemplified by *Köbler*: Whereas an extension of State liability to judicial acts is in the interest of the effectiveness and supremacy of Community law, Member States' laws on this aspect are far from uniform. Holding a general principle of Community law commensurate with the thrust of *Köbler* would hardly be acceptable to the Member States. Conversely, in order to achieve acceptance in the Member States it is necessary to put flesh on the bones of the arguments derived from international law by referring to national laws. Finding that State liability is recognised in one form or another in most Member States strikes a balance between 'not giving up' and 'acceptability' in the Member States. However, on a strictly legal analysis the Court is in a tenuous position. This reading is further corroborated by taking a look at the conditions

[344] Ibid.
[345] von Danwitz, loc. cit. n. 324, at p. 502.

giving rise to State liability for judicial acts. Instead of drawing inspiration from the alleged common elements of the national legal orders, the ECJ refers to its own autonomous determination of the conditions giving rise to State liability along the lines of *Brasserie du Pêcheur*.[346]

4. Conclusion

As has been seen, the application of international law rules on the attribution to the State is borne out by an apparent analogy between the law of State responsibility and State liability. In addition, the particular features of Community law do not stand in the way of attributing judicial conduct to the States, but on the contrary strongly support this finding. *International Law-Hypothesis I* is consequently sustainable as a basis for a principle of State liability for judicial acts in the Community legal order. By contrast, *International Law-Hypothesis II* does not allow for precise deductions of a principle of State liability for judicial acts in Community law, and cannot be read as imposing an obligation on the Member States or the Community to have in place a system of State liability for judicial wrongs. Nevertheless it sets an interesting trend towards making courts more 'accountable' by means of preventive or compensatory remedies. The factual impact on the Court's ruling in *Köbler* thus cannot be underestimated, even though the Court surprisingly avoids explicit reference to the ECrtHR's case law, in particular to the judgment in *Dangeville*. Finally, the comparative law hypothesis seems delusional. Whereas AG Léger strongly underlined the existence of a general principle common to the Member States' legal orders to the extent of State liability for acts of national supreme courts, the Court refrained from such a bold move. Indeed, national legal orders are characterised by fairly hesitant approaches when it comes to the recognition of State liability for judicial acts. The recognition of this principle in Community law thus can only count on limited support by national law. Nevertheless the Court adduces the existence of State liability for judicial acts in one form or another in most Member States as additional argumentative support for its finding. It is probably here where the creative function

[346] ECJ, *Köbler*, n. 1 above, at paras. 51 et seq.

of the Court in the context of State liability[347] becomes most apparent, which cannot be fully substituted by dogmatic argumentation. The Court is also driven by a political vision which translates into the full effectiveness of Community law. This vision is argumentatively corroborated by dogmatic reasons in support of the Court's finding, which taken in isolation may be too weak to justify the result arrived at. In this sense the Court in *Köbler* takes up the thrust of *Francovich*, where the Court in its reasoning had first and foremost relied on the full effectiveness of Community law for finding a principle of State liability, and then extended this to encompass the judicial function. A *wholly* dogmatic view is therefore doomed to fail, whereas the international law argument transferred into the Community legal order lends strong support to the Court's reasoning.

[347] Cf., Tridimas, op. cit. n. 31, at p. 313.

Chapter IV
RESERVATIONS FOR COMMUNITY LAW

Chapter IV
RESERVATIONS FOR COMMUNITY LAW

1. Grounds Causing Hesitation

That the principle of State liability for judicial acts could not count on the Member States' unlimited approval became clear in the course of the proceedings in *Köbler*. Traditionally, Member States approach the question of State liability for judicial acts restrictively. An inclusion of national judiciaries for the purposes of State liability was thus objected to, by a number of governments on various grounds. These objections relating in particular to the independence and impartiality of national judges, as well as to the doctrine of *res judicata* prompted an answer from the Court. Other reservations were not explicitly raised, and yet are of fundamental importance. Generally, they pertain to the co-operative relationship between the ECJ and national courts, as well as to the argument of national courts and the ECJ being part of the same constitutional structure, which finds support in the Court's case law. It is therefore necessary to examine the relevance of the various grounds for the Court's finding in *Köbler*, as well as their implications.

1.1 Judicial independence

An important objection against a principle of State liability for judicial acts is the independence of the judiciary, a principle which is firmly established in the Member States' legal orders.[348] It is therefore not surprising that in *Köbler* a number of intervening governments[349] pointed to this seminal principle of national law in order to argue against the inclusion of national courts into the Community's State liability regime. In their views acceptance of

[348] On the related and yet distinct problem of judicial independence in international courts and tribunals see R. Mackenzie and Ph. Sands, 'International Courts and Tribunals and the Independence of the International Judge', 44 *Harv. ILJ* (2003) pp. 271 et seq.

[349] This objection was raised by the governments of Germany, the Netherlands, Austria and the United Kingdom.

State liability for judicial acts would be likely to give rise to the risk of questioning the independence of the judiciary.[350]

It is important to stress that judicial independence[351] embraces both institutional as well as personal aspects:[352] The institutional component refers to the legal autonomy of courts from the other State functions and political bodies.[353] By contrast the personal component seeks to preserve the decision-making freedom of judges by shielding them from interference of the legislature and executive.[354] A means to that end is for instance the security of tenure of judges.[355]

Reservations concerning the institutional aspect relate to the fear of too close an entanglement of the executive and the judiciary, if the *State* is to be held liable for judicial conduct. The consequence of judicial independence, namely the fact that the State shall not be held liable for acts over which it has no control, forms the substance of a related objection.[356] As concerns the personal aspect of judicial independence, the availability of a remedy of State liability for judicial acts could exercise at least indirect pressure on judges and their freedom of decision.[357]

Whereas AG Léger had referred to the irrelevance of the independence-argument for both international and Community law,[358] the ECJ in *Köbler* opted for a more subtle reasoning, not denying the relevance of the principle. Instead, it held that given the particular nature of State liability it was simply not affected. The ECJ does not explicitly draw a distinction between the different kinds of judicial independence, but rather comments on the 'independence of the judiciary' by addressing two aspects of the issue, one relating to the personal independence of judges, the other one to the institu-

---

[350] See in particular the intervention of the UK in ECJ, *Köbler*, n. 1 above, at para. 26.

[351] Note that Reisman refers to judicial independence as a myth. See M. Reisman, 'Judge Shigeru Oda: A Tribute to an International Treasure', 16 *LJIL* (2003) p. 57 at p. 59.

[352] Toner, loc. cit. n. 328, at p. 176.

[353] Opinion of AG Geelhoed in *Commission* v. *Italy*, n. 2 above, at para. 56; Alter, op. cit. n. 17, at p. 45.

[354] Anagnostaras, loc. cit. n. 328, at p. 288; Toner, loc. cit. n. 328, at p. 174.

[355] Toner, loc. cit. n. 328, at p. 176.

[356] Anagnostaras, loc. cit. n. 328, at pp. 287 et seq.

[357] Ibid. at p. 288.

[358] Opinion of AG Léger *Köbler*, n. 1 above, at paras. 88 et seq., where he explains that neither under international law nor under Community law a State can rely on the particular characteristics of its constitutional organisation in order to escape liability.

tional dimension of diminishing the authority of courts by subjecting their decisions to State liability.

The Court highlights that State liability for judicial acts is not about the personal liability of the *judge*, but instead of the *State*. Consequently, there would be no particular risk of putting the independence of *courts* in question.[359] In this respect the Court's reasoning suffers from the failure to separate the personal from the institutional aspects of judicial independence. It does not necessarily follow from the impersonal nature of State liability that the independence of *courts* is not put at risk. Despite the brevity of the Court's reasoning, the result is convincing and disposes effectively of the objection concerning judicial independence. It is obvious that a *personal* liability of judges could cast doubts on their independence, since their decision-making freedom could be affected by an imminent liability risk.[360] At the same time, the same cannot be said of a liability of the State.[361] The potentially indirect effect of State liability on judicial independence by for instance affecting the careers of judges seems too remote as to stand in the way of the independent performance of judges. Nevertheless the harmful effects of personal liability of judges could be introduced by the back-door in the form of recoupment actions which again could affect judicial independence.[362] The *Köbler* judgment remains silent on this crucial point, which does not stand in the way of State liability for judicial acts as such. Rather it is a question of national law circumventing this threat to judicial independence. It is thus in the hands of national legislators to provide for adequate safeguards of independence in this respect.

The second aspect in connection with the independence of the judiciary addressed by the Court concerns the risk of a diminution of the authority of a court of last instance by subjecting its decisions to State liability. Unsurprisingly, the Court opts for the qualification of the possibility of claiming damages from the State for erroneous judgments as a virtue of a judicial

---

[359] ECJ, *Köbler*, n. 1 above, at para. 42.

[360] Anagnostaras, loc. cit. n. 328, at p. 288; Toner, loc. cit. n. 328, at p. 174.

[361] Cf., however, the (misleading) title of a colloquium organised by British Institute of International and Comparative Law in London on 19 January 2004: 'Köbler v. Austria: Responsibility of *Judges*' (emphasis added).

[362] Anagnostaras, loc. cit. n. 328, at p. 288; Toner, loc. cit. n. 328, at p. 174; Kluth, loc. cit. n. 326, at p. 398; Wegener, loc. cit. n. 263, at p. 88.

system which is liable to enhance the quality of justice and in the long run the authority of the judiciary.[363]

The Court's qualification of judicial independence as not standing in the way of State liability for judicial acts is commendable.[364] The possibility of claiming damages from the State for acts *iure imperii* is an essential ingredient of the rule of law. By contrast absolutism shielded monarchs and their subjects from liability in the exercise of their functions relying on maxims such as '*princeps legibus solutus*' or 'the king can do no wrong'.[365] Therefore, a maxim of *iudex legibus solutus* cannot be said to reflect the state of the art of modern constitutionalism. It is also noteworthy that on the international plane this responsibility of judges is beyond doubt:

> 'Independence does not however mean absence of responsibility for his own actions. The concept which regards the judge as unrestrained by the law (*legibus solutus*) would end, sooner or later, in protecting, not so much his necessary freedom, as the arbitrariness of his actions.'[366]

Judges are bound to observe the law of the land, which includes Community law. An indirect legality review of their decisions with Community law implications therefore, cannot be said to impinge on their independence, which is confined to the limits of compliance. The situation is comparable to that under the ECHR which provides for a legality review of, *inter alia*, national court decisions in the light of the rights guaranteed by the ECHR.[367] Whereas such a legality review is unobjectionable from the point of view of judicial independence, it is clear that it might go against the self-perceptions of organisational courts of last instance. However, their role as final arbitrators is curtailed by Article 220 of the EC Treaty and the ECJ's role in the interpretation of the Treaties.

The Court did not explicitly deal with the argument that the State should not be liable for the acts of constitutionally independent bodies such as

---

363 ECJ, *Köbler*, n. 1 above, at para. 43.

364 See also Wegener, loc. cit. n. 263, at p. 88; Kluth, loc. cit. n. 326, at p. 398.

365 B.-C. Funk, 'Staatshaftung auf der Grundlage von Gemeinschaftsrecht', 8 *ecolex* (1997) p. 553.

366 UN Social Defence Research Institute and International Association of Judges, *The Role of the Judge in Contemporary Society* (Rome, Palombi 1984) p. 20.

367 Meyer-Ladewig, op. cit. n. 282, commentary on Art. 1 of the ECHR, mn. 4.

courts. However, on the basis of the Court's case law it is clear that this is not a valid objection. As the Court held in *Konle* the Member States are to ensure that individuals obtain reparation for damages caused to them by non-compliance with Community law, regardless of which public authority is responsible for the breach and whichever public authority is in principle, under the law of the Member State concerned, responsible for making reparation.[368] An analogous reasoning applies with regard to the direct effect of non-transposed directives.[369]

1.2 The doctrine of *res judicata*

The main thrust of the doctrine of *res judicata* is the protection of the finality of decisions once they are no longer subject to appeal. Every legal dispute should come to an end once and for all. Once the end has been reached, for the sake of legal certainty and legal peace it should not be possible to reopen the dispute again.[370] As the Court pointed out in *Köbler*, in order to ensure both the stability of the law and legal relations and the sound administration of justice, it is important that judicial decisions which have become definitive after all rights of appeal have been exhausted or after expiry of the time-limits provided for in that connection can no longer be called in question.[371]

In *Köbler* it had been argued by a number of intervening governments, and most forcefully by France and the United Kingdom, that a principle of State liability for judicial acts would be in breach of the doctrine of *res judicata* since it would fail to respect the finality of disputes.[372]

For the purposes of Community law the principle of *res judicata* of national decisions has been explicitly embraced by the ECJ in *Eco Swiss*.[373] In this case Benetton had concluded a licensing agreement with Eco Swiss, which it subsequently terminated before the end of the period originally provided for in the contract. Arbitration proceedings instituted by Eco Swiss led to a first award requiring Benetton to compensate Eco Swiss. As the

---

[368] ECJ, Case C-302/97 *Konle* [1999] ECR 3099, at para. 62.
[369] ECJ, Case 103/88 *Fratelli Costanzo* [1989] ECR 1839, at paras. 30 et seq.
[370] Anagnostaras, loc. cit. n. 328, at p. 289.
[371] ECJ, *Köbler*, n. 1 above, at para. 38.
[372] Ibid. at paras. 20 et seq.
[373] ECJ, *Eco Swiss*, n. 147 above.

parties failed to find agreement on the amount of compensation to be paid, a second arbitral award ordered Benetton to pay 23,75 million USD. The first award had not been challenged by Benetton within the prescribed time-limit. However, in the light of the second award it applied to a Dutch court to stay the enforcement of the final arbitration award. In its submission, Benetton argued that the award was contrary to Dutch public policy, since the original licensing agreement violated Article 81 of the EC Treaty. Amongst other questions, the referring court asked the ECJ whether or not a national court had to set aside a rule of national law providing for the force of *res judicata* of an arbitration award which had not been appealed within a certain period of time. Apparently, reviewing the licensing agreement in the light of Article 81 of the EC Treaty would have necessitated to open-up the final award, which had become incontestable. Examining the prescribed time-limit, the Court found it to be not excessively short in comparison with the legal systems of the other Member States.[374] With regard to the effect of *res judicata* itself which followed from the expiry of the time-limit the Court pronounced as follows:

> '[D]omestic procedural rules which, upon the expiry of that period, restrict the possibility of applying for annulment of a subsequent arbitration award proceeding upon an interim arbitration award which is in the nature of a final award, because it has become *res judicata, are justified by the basic principles of the national judicial system, such as the principle of legal certainty and acceptance of* res judicata, *which is an expression of that principle.*'[375]

The national court was consequently not required to set aside the relevant provision of domestic law.[376]

It is noteworthy that the ECJ here accepted a certain detraction from the effectiveness of Community law, since it follows from its reasoning that the licensing agreement in effect could no longer be assessed in the light of Article 81 of the EC Treaty.[377] On the other hand it pointed out the fundamental importance of the principle of *res judicata* which derives from the principle of legal certainty. It is apparent that the ECJ understands *res judi-*

[374] Ibid. at para. 45.
[375] Ibid. at para. 46 (emphasis added).
[376] Ibid. at para. 47.
[377] Cf., Lenaerts, loc. cit. n. 46, at p. 899.

cata as a basic principle of national judicial systems which when weighed against effectiveness, clearly has to prevail. *Eco Swiss* has to be read as an application of this balancing approach, as set out in *van Schijndel*, which – among others – refers to the importance of a given rule in the context of the national procedure and explicitly mentions the principle of legal certainty as a basic principle of domestic legal systems.[378] It is therefore safe to conclude that the principle of *res judicata* is recognised as a fundamental principle of national procedural law in the Community legal order. Only particular circumstances, such as excessively short time-limits within which a decision may acquire the force of *res judicata*, will justify the setting-aside of a national rule intended to preserve the finality of a judicial or administrative decision.[379]

Whereas the principle of *res judicata* forms part of the Community legal order *qua* reception from the national legal systems, the judgment in *Eco Swiss* has left its exact purport for Community law without definitive contours. Indeed the notion of *res judicata* will have a core meaning in all the Member States, such as the definitive nature of a decision after the exhaustion of all available remedies. Whether it will also extend to bar an indirect reopening of proceedings in the case of State liability for judicial acts, is less clear. Therefore, *res judicata*, as a principle of Community law, was in need of further clarification.

The crucial point of the doctrine of *res judicata* concerns the definition of the dispute which, once settled, should not be opened again. It is undisputed that *res judicata* bars the reopening of the *same* dispute. However, the understanding of what actually is meant by 'the same', depends on whether one applies a formal or a substantive concept of *res judicata*. A distinction between a formal and a substantive concept of *res judicata* can be found in the legal orders of certain Member States.[380] Since it is about the Community law implications of *res judicata* here, a detailed analysis of national laws with regard to *res judicata* is not relevant. Nevertheless, this

---

[378] ECJ, *van Schijndel*, n. 123 above, at para. 19. On the balanced approach in the Court's case law on national procedural rules, which was heralded by this case see Chapter II.2.3 above.

[379] ECJ, *Eco Swiss*, n. 147 above, at para. 45.

[380] So for instance in Germany and Austria. Cf., R. Walter and H. Mayer, *Verwaltungsverfahrensrecht* (Vienna, Manz 1999) mn. 451 et seq.; Ossenbühl, op. cit. n. 163, at p. 102.

distinction, although of national legal provenience, may serve as an analytical tool in scrutinising the Court's jurisprudence with regard to *res judicata*. Whereas a formal concept (*Rechtskraft im formellen Sinn*) takes the same matter in dispute or *Streitgegenstand* as a point of departure, on a substantive understanding *res judicata* seeks to avoid the subsequent entering into force of divergent decisions.[381] In this way, the substantive outcome of the proceedings – and not just the decision in itself as a final legal act – is protected (*Rechtskraft im materiellen Sinn*). It is against this analytical background that the relevance of the principle of *res judicata* in the Community legal order will be dealt with here.

Read in isolation, the *Eco Swiss* case, concerning a single matter that was in dispute, suggests that *res judicata,* as a concept recognised by Community law, at least encompasses a formal understanding. As has been seen, the pertinent question was whether the application of a provision of Community law thus far disregarded should still be possible in the *same* dispute, despite the expiry of a national time-limit. On the basis of *Eco Swiss* it was thus unclear whether *res judicata* would also extend to the substantive limb of the concept.

Applying the formal concept of *res judicata* to the case of State liability for judicial acts, it is obvious that it cannot shield Member States from liability. This is due to the fact that the State liability proceedings as secondary proceedings will necessarily have a different matter in dispute. The *Köbler* case can serve as an illustration in point: The issue in the primary proceedings was whether Mr. Köbler was entitled to a length-of-service increment of his salary as a university professor. By contrast, the subject-matter of the secondary proceedings concerned the question of whether an Austrian court had breached Community law by finding in the negative. A formal conception of *res judicata* as defined above would therefore not stand in the way of a principle of State liability for judicial acts. In the light of this, it becomes apparent that those Member States claiming a violation of the principle of *res judicata* in case of the recognition of State liability for judicial acts by the Court in *Köbler* in fact argued on the basis of a substantive understanding of *res judicata* according to which also an indi-

---

[381] Cf., W. Antoniolli and F. Koja, *Allgemeines Verwaltungsrecht*, 3rd edn. (Vienna, Manz 1996) pp. 581 et seq.; Ossenbühl, op. cit. n. 163, at p. 102.

rect review should be prevented. The question was therefore whether the Court would endorse this understanding.

The Court did not subscribe to this viewpoint. Instead, it made it clear that for the purposes of Community law, and more particularly of the law of State liability, *res judicata* was confined to a formal understanding.[382] The Court started with reiterating the importance of the principle of *res judicata* as held in *Eco Swiss*,[383] which nonetheless, would not stand in the way of the principle of State liability. It explains that '[p]roceedings seeking to render the State liable do not have the same purpose and do not necessarily involve the same parties as the proceedings resulting in the decision which has acquired the status of *res judicata*'.[384] Turning to the legal consequences of a successful State liability action, the Court noted that an applicant would secure an order for reparation of damages which would not necessarily involve a declaration invalidating the original judgment.[385] At the heart of the Court's reasoning lies a resolute distinction between primary and secondary proceedings: State liability would only require making good the damage caused in the form of the *secondary* remedy of reparation, whereas the revision of the judicial decision at the root of the secondary proceedings would not be required.[386] To further bolster its reasoning the Court pointed to Article 41 of the ECHR, according to which the ECrtHR can order a State which has infringed a fundamental right, to provide reparation of the damage resulting from that conduct for the injured party.

That the Court's understanding of *res judicata* is based on a narrow conception has additionally been confirmed in the recent judgment of *Kühne & Heitz*.[387] This case dealt with the question of whether a national administrative body is under an obligation to review a *final* administrative decision which – in the light of the subsequent case law of the ECJ – does not rest on a valid interpretation of Community law. A decision considered final under Dutch law had been challenged in accordance with national law, whereby reliance was placed on the applicability of a different tariff heading for

[382] See also Botella, loc. cit. n. 335, at p. 296.
[383] ECJ, *Köbler*, n. 1 above, at para. 38.
[384] Ibid. at para. 39.
[385] Ibid.
[386] Ibid.
[387] ECJ, *Kühne & Heitz*, n. 3 above.

export refunds (subsidies) for the export of poultry-meat parts to third countries than the one applied by the relevant Dutch authorities. The applicant requested a refund of money unlawfully claimed from him pursuant to the classification proving wrong in the light of a subsequent judgment of the ECJ. Under Dutch law the procedure could be reopened as administrative bodies, in principle, always have the power to reopen a final decision. In certain circumstances this power could even imply an obligation to withdraw a final decision.

The central issue the Court faced in *Kühne & Heitz* concerned the question of whether the obligation of Member State authorities to comply with Community law as interpreted by the Court before and after the decision[388] would also have to be complied with, notwithstanding that a decision had become final before the application for review of that decision in order to take account of a preliminary ruling by the Court had been lodged. In the light of legal certainty, as a general principle of Community law, which, *inter alia*, finds expression in the finality of administrative decisions, the Court held that administrative authorities, as a matter of principle, would not be required to reopen final administrative decisions.[389] However, in the particular circumstances of the case, Article 10 of the EC Treaty would require the review of the decision in the light of Community law as interpreted by the Court.[390] For the Court the following facts constituted the particular circumstances of the case:

---

[388] The legal effects of the Court's preliminary rulings rest on the fiction that the Court, in accordance with Art. 220 of the EC Treaty, only declares what the law is. The interpretation which the Court gives to a rule of Community law clarifies and defines the meaning and scope of that rule as it ought to have been understood and applied from the time of its coming into force. See, e.g., ECJ, *Kühne & Heitz*, n. 3 above, at para. 21; AG Léger in *Köbler*, n. 1 above, at para. 143; and, most recently, ECJ, Case C-209/03 *Bidar*, judgment of 15 March 2005 (nyr), at para. 66. The Court's interpretation is thus only declaratory of existing law. However, the principle of legal certainty should preclude the possibility of State liability for a final judgment, which is contrary to a later judgment of the Court. Cf., Opinion of AG Léger in *Köbler*, n. 1 above, at paras. 142 et seq., and Opinion of AG Léger in *Kühne & Heitz*, n. 3 above, at para. 38. See also Lenaerts and Arts, op. cit. n. 13, at mn. 6-039.

[389] ECJ, *Kühne & Heitz*, n. 3 above, at para. 24.

[390] Ibid. at para. 27.

> 'First, national law confers on the administrative body competence to reopen the decision in question, which has become final. Second, the administrative decision became final only as a result of a judgment of a national court against whose decisions there is no judicial remedy. Third, that judgment was based on an interpretation of Community law which, in the light of a subsequent judgment of the Court, was incorrect and which was adopted without a question being referred to the Court for a preliminary ruling in accordance with the conditions provided for in Article 234 EC. Fourth, the person concerned complained to the administrative body immediately after becoming aware of that judgment of the Court.'[391]

Thus, as a result, the relevant Dutch administrative authority was required to examine the extent to which it was obliged to reopen the case, thereby having due regard to the interests of third parties which should not be adversely affected.[392]

In *Kühne & Heitz* the Court draws a subtle line between legal certainty and the related concept of *res judicata* on the one hand, and the requirement to give full effect to Community law flowing from Article 10 of the EC Treaty on the other. The existence of the principle of legal certainty is not questioned. Nevertheless, in the light of countervailing interests its purport is considerably narrowed down, whereby the Court relies first and foremost on the possibility under national law to reopen the procedure. On an interpretation conforming with Community law, this procedural option under national law would have to be construed, as an obligation for the purposes of Community law.[393] By contrast, AG Léger had advocated that in the given case the principle of legal certainty would have to be set aside *qua* supremacy of Community law.[394]

---

[391] Ibid. at para. 26.

[392] Ibid. at para. 27.

[393] See also W. Frenz, 119 *DVBl.* (2004) p. 375 at p. 376; R. Caranta, 42 *CML Rev.* (2005) p. 179 at p. 183.

[394] Opinon of AG Léger in *Kühne & Heitz*, n. 3 above, at paras. 44 et seq. Only at first sight it would appear that this view can already claim some support from the Court's own case law. The judgment in Case C-224/97 *Ciola* [1999] ECR I-2517 dealt with the question whether Community law would enjoy supremacy even over a final individual administrative decision violating the freedom to provide services. Substantively, the case concerned a prohibition on the operator of a boat harbour, on pain of criminal prosecution, to rent more than a specific quota of moorings to boat-owners resident in another Member State than Austria. The administrative decision had been rendered before Austria's accession to the

The purport of the principle of legal certainty therefore seems to be dependent on the availability of competences of national authorities to reopen their decisions. Where such means exist, *res judicata* possibly cannot prevail and must – with the safeguard of respecting the interests of third parties – give way to Article 10 of the EC Treaty.[395] In spite of the rhetorics of exceptionality underlying *Kühne & Heitz*, national provisions, which provide for retroactive account being taken of new facts or a change of circumstances not known at the time of decision, are a common feature of national procedural laws.[396] In the light of such provisions, the result in *Kühne & Heitz* could have far-reaching effects on the doctrine of *res judicata* which would have to give way to *ex post* interpretative rulings of the Court.[397]

Though, it is noteworthy that the Court expressed several reservations in its ruling, especially in relation to Article 234(3) of the EC Treaty which seems to be of fundamental importance.[398] The competent Dutch court, in deciding at last instance, should have referred the pertinent question to the ECJ and yet failed to do so. Without the Court having recourse to the Article 234(3)-argument, the national authority would have been referred to the benefit of hindsight, which could hardly have justified an exception to

European Union. The Court held that an individual administrative decision conflicting with the freedom to provide services must be disregarded when assessing the validity of a fine imposed for failure to comply with that prohibition after the date of accession. *Ciola* therefore in fact did not concern the legal destiny of the individual administrative decision itself – the issue at hand in *Kühne & Heitz* –, but rather the consequences of its non-compliance for enforcement. This is apparent from para. 25 of the judgment where the Court states 'that the dispute concerns not the fate of the administrative act itself, in this case the decision of 9 August 1990, but the question whether such an act must be disregarded when assessing the validity of a penalty imposed for failure to comply with an obligation thereunder, because of its incompatibility with the principle of freedom to provide services'.

[395] But see also Frenz, loc. cit. n. 393, at p. 376, who questions whether in the light of the direct effect of directives and the principle of State liability it should really be in the hands of the Member States to hinder the effective application of Community law in analogous situations. See also Ruffert, 15 *EuZW* (2004) p. 620 at p. 621, who entertains doubts along the same lines.

[396] A case in point is Article 69(1)(3) of the Austrian General Law on Administrative Procedure *(Allgemeines Verwaltungsverfahrensgesetz)*. See also J. Komárek, 'Federal elements in the Community judicial system: Building coherence in the Community legal order', 42 *CML Rev.* (2005) p. 9 at pp. 19 et seq. with further references.

[397] See also Chapter VII.1 below.

[398] See Ruffert, loc. cit. n. 395, at p. 621.

the principle of *res judicata*. It was only after the national decision that the Court ruled on the applicable head of classification. However, instead of trying to anticipate the Court's decision, the national authority should have referred a question to the Court. As in *Köbler*, where a breach of the obligation to refer was mentioned as one of the instances to be taken into account when ascertaining the existence of a manifest infringement of Community law and therefore grounding State liability,[399] the consequence of the non-referral has a 'punitive' character and requires a reaction on the part of the State, be it in the form of curtailing *res judicata* or making available suitable mechanisms for pursuing State liability claims. Even though an individual has no subjective right to ask for a referral to the Court, the failure of a national court to refer, and the ensuing misinterpretation of Community law, should not be such so as to have negative repercussions for individuals. The principle of *res judicata* thus has to give way to the reopening of the decision, bearing in mind the consequences of the Court's subsequent ruling. In other words, the situation created by the non-referral is such that the interest in justice for an individual litigant clearly prevails over the institutional interest in legal certainty. This reasoning is cautioned by the necessity not to affect interests of third parties involved by lifting the principle of *res judicata*. Lastly, the possibility to challenge final national decisions which contravene Community law is linked to a tight time limit: The applicant who had exhausted all available remedies under national law had complained to the administrative body immediately after becoming aware of that judgment of the Court which was a necessary element for the Court to require the reopening of the final administrative decision.[400]

The judgment in *Kühne & Heitz* therefore is far from sweeping away the principle of *res judicata*, which in *Eco Swiss* had been recognised as a basic principle of the national judicial systems.[401] At the same time it demonstrates that the guarantee of *res judicata* is not of an absolute nature and will at times have to be set aside in the light of prevailing interests, such as

[399] ECJ, *Köbler*, n. 1 above, at para. 55; see also para. 117 of the judgment, which deals with the concrete application to the case at hand and states that the referring court should have maintained its request for a preliminary ruling.

[400] ECJ, *Kühne & Heitz*, n. 3 above, at para. 26.

[401] For a recent confirmation of the recognition of legal certainty as a general principle recognised in the Community legal order see ECJ, Case C-459/02 *Gerekens and Procola*, judgment of 15 July 2004 (nyr), at paras. 22 et seq.

the protection of the individual. *Res judicata* is not an end in itself, but seeks to attain certain objectives which may come into conflict with other objectives, meaning that values underlying the principle of *res judicata* such as legal certainty and legal peace have to then be balanced with competing interests such as justice for individual litigants.[402]

The Court's reasoning with regard to *res judicata* in *Köbler* has been received critically in some quarters. According to some commentators the principle of *res judicata* was essentially ignored by the Court, although the ECJ had paid lip service to its importance.[403] A comparison with the ECHR and the case law of the ECrtHR, most notably the judgment in *Dangeville* where the latter court had equally set aside the principle of *res judicata*,[404] could not hold true since in the field of human rights Member States had expressly submitted themselves to the possibility of State liability for individual damages, including damages caused by national courts. Therefore, an exception to the principle of *res judicata* was covered by the explicit agreement of the States party to the ECHR.[405]

This interpretation rests on the assumption that the Court in effect denies *res judicata* in *Köbler*. However, as has been seen, the Court only applies a formal understanding of *res judicata* which is resonant in the Member States' legal orders. Indeed it has been pointed out that the Court's reasoning is legally correct in detecting two different matters in dispute and – from a formal legal point of view – leaving the decision taken in the course of the primary proceedings unfettered.[406] In this context it has also been stated that the State liability proceedings are dealt with by different courts,[407] one court therefore being not required to overrule its own final judgment.

Regardless of these formal considerations, the factual hollowing-out of the concept of *res judicata* by indirectly reopening a final decision *qua* State liability has been criticised, insofar as, the Court's jurisprudence would show the same disrespect for *res judicata* as would underlie the ECrtHR's ruling in *Dangeville*.[408]

---

[402] Toner, loc. cit. n. 328, at p. 176; Anagnostaras, loc. cit. n. 328, at p. 290.

[403] Wattel, loc. cit. n. 300, at p. 177 and p. 187.

[404] See Chapter III.2.2 above.

[405] Wattel, loc. cit. n. 300, at p. 187.

[406] Kluth, loc. cit. n. 326, at p. 398; Wegener, loc. cit. n. 263, at p. 87; W. Frenz, 118 *DVBl.* (2003) p. 1522 at p. 1523.

[407] Frenz, loc. cit. n. 406, at p. 1523.

[408] Gundel, loc. cit. n. 332, at p. 16.

The latter concerns weigh heavily, and yet, they are not entirely convincing. The initial hesitation which crops up, is that the final word on a particular dispute should have been spoken, once available remedies have been exhausted. However, it remains difficult to see why the negative consequences of a non-compliant judgment should not be alleviated by means of State liability. In this way, the principle of State liability for judicial acts, builds upon the concept of *res judicata* and thus on the enforceability of the primary decision. If this was otherwise, there would be no damage, and a damage claim would have to be rejected. The distinction between the different matters in dispute in primary and secondary proceedings is more than an exercise in legal formalism. It is not the principle of *res judicata* but its consequences when paired with non-compliance which are taken away by State liability for judicial acts. On the other hand, it is also clear that in smoothing out the negative consequences of a judgment *qua* State liability it is necessary to judge the compliance/non-compliance with Community law of the primary judgment. In doing so, the legal question lying at the heart of the initial dispute needs to be reconsidered, the consequence of an instance of ascertained non-compliance, not being, quashing the initial judgment, but rather the grant of compensation. It is possible to discern a certain relativity of the doctrine of *res judicata* here, since the substance of an already final decision is again at the disposal of the State liability court. Nevertheless, at the same time it needs to be stressed that this relativity of *res judicata* is inherent in the very concept of State liability for judicial acts – be it on the national or international level.[409] Therefore it could only be raised against State liability for judicial acts as such, without any specific implications for the Community legal order. However, for Member States without State liability regimes for judicial acts, this must appear to be a most relevant argument.

In the last instance the question is whether or not State liability for judicial acts should be a potential means of review at the disposal of individuals. Once this has been answered in the affirmative – and an affirmative answer is suggested by an analogy with international law as well as in line with recent tendencies in the case law of the ECrtHR –, a certain degree of relativity of the doctrine of *res judicata* is the logical consequence. However, accepting the implications of a formal concept of *res judicata* it would

[409] Kluth, loc. cit. n. 326, at p. 398.

be wrong to see a decisive blow being dealt to the doctrine of *res judicata* which is not an absolute principle, but, at the same time, more than simply subject to the lip service of the Court.

Finally, Classen points to a dilemma, which according to him would amount to the 'central weakness' of the judgment:[410] According to this author, there would be a direct conflict between the court which has dealt with the matter first and the court which deals with State liability in case of an alleged breach of Community law, since all national courts are bound to respect Community law. He concedes that primary and secondary proceedings concern different matters in dispute. However, Classen goes on to state that by means of the doctrine of *res judicata* the judgment in the primary proceedings would have binding effect on the secondary proceedings. Thus, the court in the State liability proceedings would have to consider the first judgment as lawful. The paradoxical consequence would therefore be, the impossibility to obtain redress for damages. The only way out of the dilemma would be a referral to the ECJ.

The objections of Classen can only be understood against the background of German law. The obvious point of departure is the inexistence of State liability for judicial acts, except for the exceptional case where a judgment is characterised by a criminal offence on the part of the judiciary (Article 839(2) of the German Civil Code). Therefore the notion of *res judicata* can take quasi-absolute force, both with regard to its formal and its substantive implications. However, as seen above, the acceptance of State liability for judicial acts necessarily entails a certain relativity of *res judicata*, a phenomenon which is inherent in the notion of State liability for judicial acts as such and not peculiar to Community law. The privileged position of the national judiciary thus has come to an end whenever the non-compliant interpretation of Community law by national courts is at stake.[411] Assuming, that the judgment of the court in primary proceedings would have binding effect on the State liability court, would defeat the very concept of State liability for judicial acts which rests on the possibility of indirect review of the legal reasoning of the court in the primary proceedings. Classen's submission, that this binding effect would also flow from Community law, since all national courts were equally bound to observe Community law, is

---

[410] For the following reasoning see Classen, loc. cit. n. 262, at p. 818.
[411] Frenz, loc. cit. n. 406, at p. 1523; Gundel, loc. cit. n. 332, at p. 16.

not a valid argument. It is true that every national court is required to give effect to Community law, which implies a central role of national courts in the implementation of Community law.[412] Nevertheless this does not mean that every national court decision is compliant. One cannot infer fact from rules or *aus einem Sollen darf man nicht auf ein Sein schließen*. For this very reason, such a binding effect of the judgments of national courts for other national courts cannot exist for the purposes of State liability. Therefore, the dilemma described by Classen does not exist upon the interpretation of *res judicata* as a formal concept which the existence of State liability for judicial acts presupposes.

1.3 **Impartiality of the judiciary**

In *Köbler* a number of intervening governments drew attention to the difficulty in determining competent courts to adjudicate on State liability cases involving judicial acts, which would stand in the way of recognising a principle of State liability for judicial acts.[413] Apart from the already discussed reservations, relating to judicial independence and *res judicata*, this objection boils down to the question of which courts may be competent under national law, without endangering the requirement of an impartial tribunal as mandated by Article 6 of the ECHR. Indeed there seems to be a structural problem related to impartiality, to entrust the national judiciary with determining a breach of Community law, since both the judge and the wrongdoer form part of it.[414]

The Court satisfied itself with a reference to the existence of a national competence to determine the competent courts.[415] The question of which courts can be made competent under national law within the constraints of Community law, as well as how the impartiality of those courts can be ensured will be addressed under VI. below.

---

[412] See Chapter II.2 above.

[413] ECJ, *Köbler*, n. 1 above, at paras. 28 and 44.

[414] Anagnostaras, loc. cit. n. 328, at p. 295; see also AG Léger in *Köbler*, n. 1 above, at para. 107, and F. Chaltiel, 'L'Européanisation de la responsabilité administrative', 47 *RMCUE* (2004) p. 106 at p. 110.

[415] ECJ, *Köbler*, n. 1 above, at para. 45.

1.4 Endangering the spirit of co-operation between the ECJ and national courts?

In the words of the Court, the various provisions of the Community Treaties providing for preliminary rulings (Article 234 of the EC Treaty and Article 150 of the EAEC Treaty) 'all express a twofold need: to ensure the utmost uniformity in the application of Community law and to establish for that purpose effective co-operation between the Court of Justice and national courts'.[416] There is an inherent potential for tension in this twofold need, since the quest for uniformity need not always be in the interest of national courts and thus may have repercussions on their willingness to co-operate with the Court. At the same time the Community judicial system crucially depends on this 'judicial cooperation provided for by that article [Article 234 of the EC Treaty]'.[417] To a large extent, the actual influence of the ECJ is dependent on the preparedness of national courts to refer questions to it.[418]

Empirical political science literature exhibits a persistent interest in this co-operational relationship, the study of which offers a testing field for various models of judicial co-operation.[419] Whereas some authors, in line with neo-institutionalist theory, see both sides as active, strategic and equal partici-

---

416 ECJ, Case C-221/88 *Busseni* [1990] ECR I-495, at para. 13.

417 ECJ, Joined Cases C-515/99, C-519/99 to C-524/99 and C-526/99 to C-540/99 *Reisch and Lassacher* [2002] ECR I-2157, at para. 22.

418 Of the 494 cases decided by the ECJ in 2003, 233 originated from preliminary references, whereas 193 cases concerned direct actions. Not least in quantitative terms the preliminary reference procedure thus continues to be the most important type of procedure before the Court. See ECJ, Annual Report of the Court of Justice of the European Communities (2003) p. 216; see also Streho, loc. cit. n. 157, at pp. 70 et seq.

419 For a recent account see F. Ramos, 'Judicial Cooperation in the European Courts: Testing Three Models of Judicial Behaviour', *GJF* (2002) pp. 1 et seq., who in summing up the literature on legal integration presents the 'Legal Model' ('each judge is a conscientious public official that tries to meet her obligations', ibid. at p. 16), and the 'Bureaucratic Model' ('each judge tries to promote her institutional power and judges compete against each other', ibid. at p. 16). He complements these two models with the 'Team Model' ('judges share the goal of promoting the number of correct decisions', ibid. at p. 16) which after an examination of empirical data on the practice of national courts he describes as most suited to capture the interaction between national courts and the Court of Justice.

pants engaged in the pursuit of their own agendas,[420] others envisage a more harmonious relationship characterised by the goal of maximising the number of legally correct decisions.[421] Despite the variations, both schools of thought claim empirical support for their teachings, and yet give different accounts of the co-operational relationship. The undoubted benefit of these theories lies in their capacity to produce reasons why (or why not) national courts co-operate with the ECJ, while concrete outcomes seem to vary due to political preferences and the different preconceptions of different writers. Nevertheless, this is not the place to conduct a survey of the attempts of political scientists to model the co-operational relationship between the ECJ and national courts in any detail.

Arguably, a dogmatic legal perspective cannot fully capture the relationship between national courts and the ECJ. However, it can offer a yardstick for deciding whether or not the co-operational relationship is in danger in the light of a given ruling of the Court. So, it is a valid assumption that over-intrusive incursions into national (procedural) laws risk upsetting the co-operation with national judges.[422] The preservation of the attitude of co-operation of national courts therefore, depends on the right balance struck between effectiveness of Community law and the compliance by national courts. Losing the support of national courts risks non-compliance with the

---

[420] S. Nyikos, 'The European Court of Justice and National Courts: Strategic Interaction within the EU Judicial Process' (unpublished manuscript on file with the author, 2001) p. 13; according to this view the goals pursued by the ECJ are the favouring of more autonomy and greater integration for the EU without losing the support of national courts. By contrast, the goals of national courts are characterised by preserving the autonomy of the respective national legal system and not excessively losing ground to the ECJ; see also A. Stone Sweet and Th. Brunell, 'The European Court, National Judges, and Legal Integration: A Researcher's Guide to the Data Set on Preliminary References in EC Law, 1958-98', 6 *ELJ* (2000) p. 117 at p. 125; A. Stone Sweet, *Governing with Judges – Constitutional Politics in Europe* (Oxford, Oxford University Press 2000) pp. 164 et seq.; Alter, op. cit. n. 17, at pp. 45 et seq. For country-specific accounts of the co-operational relationship between the ECJ and national courts, with an emphasis on the reception of the doctrines of direct effect and supremacy, see A.-M. Slaughter, et al. (eds.), *The European Courts and National Courts – Doctrine and Jurisprudence – Legal Change in Its Social Context* (Oxford, Oxford University Press 1998) pp. 3 et seq.

[421] Ramos, loc. cit. n. 419, at pp. 10 et seq.

[422] A. Biondi, 'The European Court of Justice and Certain National Procedural Limitations', 36 *CML Rev* (1999) p. 1271 at p. 1272.

looming potential of a judicial rebellion,[423] characterised by open contradictions between the Court's case law and the practice of national courts. Whereas the reaction of political bodies to perceived action of the ECJ, in surpassing its powers, will most likely be subtle, indirect and prospective with a long-term view of changing the Court's attitude, the response of the national judiciary can be far more direct and firmer.[424] Notorious examples include the long-lasting resistance against the doctrine of direct effect by the French *Conseil d'Etat*[425] as well as the confrontational attitude of the German Bundesverfassungsgericht[426] subsequent to the judgment in *Internationale Handelsgesellschaft.*[427] It already becomes clear from these examples that only a country-specific analysis, which takes stock of particular sensitivities as well as of the general propensity of national courts to refer in a given Member State,[428] will produce reliable results.[429]

For a number of reasons the Court's judgment in *Köbler* appears as a carefully balanced decision which, as such, will not give rise to an upheaval of national judiciaries: Firstly, as is the case with other landmark decisions in Community law and beyond, the Court issued a principled judgment,[430] expounding the inclusion of judicial acts for the purposes of

---

[423] Tridimas, loc. cit. n. 42, at p. 37.

[424] Ibid.

[425] (French) *Conseil d'Etat*, judgment of 22 December 1978 (Cohn-Bendit) *RTDE* (1979) p. 175.

[426] Cf., the decisions in *Solange I* (BVerfGE 37/271), *Solange II* (BVerfGE 73/339), and *Brunner* (BVerfGE 89, 155).

[427] ECJ, *Internationale Handelsgesellschaft*, n. 171 above.

[428] There are important variations in the number of references from the various Member States, which obviously cannot be explained by the mere size of population of a given Member State and thus the quantity of litigation before national courts. Whereas in 2001 Germany and Italy requested 53 and 40 preliminary rulings respectively, Austrian courts accounted for 57 references within the same period of time. Cf., the table in Tridimas, loc. cit. n. 42, at p. 50.

[429] But see also Stone Sweet and Brunell, loc. cit. n. 420, at p. 126, who argue that it would make little sense to approach the preliminary reference procedure in strictly national terms, but then explain the high number of references in a given policy area originating from Germany by reference to the protectionist and rigid rules in place likely to generate litigation.

[430] See also C. Tobler, 'Staatshaftung für fehlerhafte höchstrichterliche Rechtsprechung, Rs. C-224/01', *jus & news* (2003) p. 339 at p. 347.

State liability.[431] In the particular case at hand, however, the Court denies the relevance of this principle – to the disadvantage of the individual applicant in the main proceedings – owing to the fairly high liability threshold developed for judicial acts. The barking dog of State liability for judicial acts does not bite in the instant case, which should ensure acceptance in the Member States. Secondly, the Court's judgment is characterised by a give and take attitude: It *takes* away the possibility of Member States to shield themselves for conduct of their courts, and yet *gives* a fairly high liability standard purportedly going beyond the classic test of a sufficiently serious breach, which arguably the Court applies cautiously in the given case, the latter with the aim of preserving the co-operation with national courts.[432] Finally, Member State courts have been prepared gradually for the thrust of the *Köbler* ruling: Already in *Brasserie du Pêcheur,* the Court, *obiter dictum*, made it clear that the principle of State liability would hold good for any breach of Community law, *whatever be the organ of the State* whose act or omission was responsible for the breach.[433] In addition, the very explicit inclusion of the legislature for State liability purposes in *Brasserie du Pêcheur* – a very novel phenomenon for a number of Member States – has not been met with judicial rebellion either.

Indeed *Köbler* implies that particular national courts will have to sit in judgment over decisions of national organisational courts of last instance and is, therefore far-reaching in its implications for all national courts. Nevertheless, it appears that the acceptability of *Köbler* in particular for organisational courts of last instance will depend on the establishment of satisfactory institutional arrangements on the national level for facilitating State liability for judicial acts.[434] Yet the harsh criticism advanced by an Advocate General of the Dutch *Hoge Raad* and thus by a member of a national supreme court against the *Köbler* judgment – albeit in his extra-judicial capacity – could also point into a different direction.[435]

---

[431] See for instance ECJ, *Costa/ENEL*, n. 57 above, but also the decision of the US Supreme Court in *Marbury* v. *Madison*, 5 US 137 (1803).

[432] W. Obwexer, 14 *EuZW* (2003) p. 726 at p. 728.

[433] ECJ, *Brasserie du Pêcheur*, n. 57 above, at paras. 31 et seq.

[434] Cf., the discussion under VI. below.

[435] Wattel, loc. cit. n. 300, *passim*.

1.5 *Litis finiri opportet* or endless litigation within 'reasonable time' (Article 6 of the ECHR)?

On occasions, the finality of litigation and the consequences for national judiciaries, of its weakening, in the case of possible damage actions against the State is submitted as an argument against State liability for judicial acts.[436] In essence, apart from the problem of endangering *res judicata*, proponents of this view envisage the *efficiency* of the national judicial systems being put into jeopardy, once an avalanche of damages actions places additional strains on national courts, and of necessity leads to a reallocation of means, to the detriment of the national courts' ordinary duties. The starting point of this view is that, the recognition of State liability for judicial acts will of itself alone, attract a great number of litigants, willing to make excessive use of an additional remedy at their disposal.[437] The ensuing clogging of national courts would go hand in hand with an increased number of references to the ECJ, leading to backlogs in the Court's docket. In turn, the 'reasonable time' mandated by Article 6 of the ECHR could become of a problem, potentially giving rise to even more litigation: this time before the Strasbourg court.[438] In the end – it has been submitted – '[t]he effectiveness of EC law is beginning to get in the way of the effectiveness of Law itself'.[439]

Clearly the concerns voiced are to be taken seriously. Asking national courts for the acceptance of another remedy in the interest of individual justice, which, in the end has the sole effect of creating turmoil in the national judicial systems, as well as protracted procedures would be a futile enterprise. Yet this objection, no matter how stringently argued it may appear, is not justified since, it takes a questionable assumption as its point of departure. This assumption amounts to taking for granted an avalanche of claims following the acceptance of State liability for judicial acts. On ac-

---

[436] Ibid. at pp. 179 et seq.; for discussions of this argument see also Anagnostaras, loc. cit. n. 328, at pp. 286 et seq., and Toner, loc. cit. n. 328, at p. 175.

[437] Cf., Wattel, loc. cit. n. 300, at p. 180, who succinctly sums up this position by asking whether it would be 'useful or efficient or desirable to solicit an avalanche of (attempts at) claims, going back who knows how many years, in fifteen Member States whose judiciaries were already not bored'.

[438] Ibid. at p. 181.

[439] Ibid. at p. 190.

count of a number of reasons this assumption is refutable, though, as is its consequence of the clogging of national and supra-national systems of judicial review.

Accepting the principle of State liability for judicial acts of itself does not give rise to a significant number of additional litigation. Indeed the preparedness of litigants to have recourse to this remedy will crucially depend on the degree of judicial 'fault' required in order to establish State liability.[440] It stands to reason to take account here, of the particular difficulty of the exercise of the judicial function, which entails deciding on controversial legal disputes, the answer to which may only seem to be clear in the light of the Court's case law. A high liability threshold will have the consequence of deterring litigants who are seeking to protract proceedings. In this context, it is important to remember that already the standard of liability set in *Brasserie du Pêcheur* is fairly exacting, requiring a sufficiently serious breach of Community law which is characterised by a manifest and grave disregard of the limits on the exercise of the Member States' discretionary powers.[441] It has been rightly observed that in the context of normative breaches the notion of seriousness underscores the exceptional character of liability.[442] All the more, this must be true in the light of a further raised liability threshold for judicial acts.[443] Not least for this reason, State liability for judicial acts will be confined to highly exceptional circumstances in which the judiciary has manifestly transgressed its powers, to the detriment of individuals. Also with regard to the criterion of a direct causal link between the breach of Community law and the damage suffered the metaphor of floodgates being opened *qua* recognition of State liability for judicial acts is misconceived.

In addition, the cost and trouble of seeking a remedy against the *State* has to be borne in mind.[444] With the prospect of costly litigation in which the State will in all likelihood exhaust all instances available, applicants will have recourse to this new remedy, only in cases which at least *prima*

---

440 Anagnostarars, loc. cit. n. 328, at p. 287; Toner, loc. cit. n. 328, at p. 175.

441 ECJ, *Brasserie du Pêcheur*, n. 57 above, at para. 55.

442 T. Tridimas, 'Liability for Breach of Community Law: Growing Up and Mellowing Down?', 38 *CML Rev.* (2001) p. 301 at p. 327.

443 See the discussion on the liability threshold under Chapter V below.

444 Toner, loc. cit. n. 328, at p. 175; Anagnostaras, loc. cit. n. 328, at p. 287.

facie stand the chance of successful damages actions. In this way 'frivolous and vexatious' claims will be reduced to a minimum.

Finally, one may refer to the German experience with the *Recht auf den gesetzlichen Richter*. As is the case with State liability for judicial acts, one could suspect an avalanche of litigation challenging the non-referral of courts of last instance in all cases with a Community law-element on the basis of a violation of the *Recht auf den gesetzlichen Richter*. In fact, the number of cases brought so far has been very limited, however.[445]

The danger of the clogging of court systems which may be the potential consequence of the recognition of State liability for judicial acts can thus be contained by the definition of adequate conditions attached to this course of action.

1.6 The parallelism between State liability and the community's extra-contractual liability regime

In *Brasserie du Pêcheur* the ECJ held that the conditions giving rise to the Member States' liability cannot differ from the conditions of the Community's extra-contractual liability pursuant to Article 288(2) of the EC Treaty, in the absence of a particular justification.[446] In spite of this programmatic stance, the *Schöppenstedt*-formula governing the extra-contractual liability of the Community institutions for legislative acts alongside fairly more exacting conditions,[447] continued to co-exist with the newly established conditions for State liability.[448] It was not until the judgment in *Bergaderm*[449] that a fully-fledged unification of the conditions of liability on the basis of a 'sufficiently serious breach' of Community law was provided for. Thereby the door was opened for a cross-fertilisation between the

---

[445] Classen, loc. cit. n. 262, at p. 821.

[446] ECJ, *Brasserie du Pêcheur*, n. 57 above, at para. 42.

[447] According to the rule in *Schöppenstedt*, the Community will be liable only for damages suffered by individuals as a consequence of 'legislative action involving measures of economic policy' where there has occurred 'a sufficiently flagrant violation of a superior rule of law for the protection of the individual'. See ECJ, Case 5/71 *Zuckerfabrik Schöppenstedt* [1971] ECR 975, at para. 11.

[448] Tridimas, loc. cit. n. 442, at pp. 321 et seq.

[449] ECJ, *Bergaderm*, n. 119 above.

two liability regimes.[450] This development was necessitated by the rationale, that the protection of the rights of individuals cannot vary depending on whether a national or a Community authority is responsible for the damage.[451] Community and national institutions are thus viewed as pertaining to the same constitutional order.[452]

It may lead to overstretching the analogy drawn by the Court, to claim that by accepting the application of *Francovich* liability to judicial breaches, the way is *automatically* opened for the imposition of liability on the Community for breaches committed by the ECJ itself pursuant to Article 288(2) of the EC Treaty.[453] Nevertheless, it has to be examined if the analogy drawn by the Court reaches an imminent limitation at this point, or whether it holds true, and thus can eventually operate as an objection against State liability for judicial acts. Indeed, in the course of the proceedings in *Köbler* the Republic of Austria claimed – relying on the Court's no differences-argument in *Brasserie du Pêcheur* – that the State could not incur liability for judicial acts, since the same was precluded for the Community courts proper. Article 288(2) of the EC Treaty could not form the basis of the Community's liability for its courts, since in such a case the Court would be required to determine a question concerning damage which it itself had caused, so as to render it judge and party at the same time.[454] The same point was made by the Government of the United Kingdom, albeit put positively: Again with reliance on the analogy between State liability and the Community's extra-contractual liability, it was argued that if State liability for a mistake by the judiciary could be incurred, the same conditions for the liability of the Community for mistakes by the Community judicature would have to apply.[455]

---

[450] Tridimas, loc. cit. n. 442, at pp. 322 et seq.; B. Hofstötter, 'Außervertragliche Haftung der EG und *Ius Commune*', *ELR* (2000) p. 424 at p. 426.

[451] ECJ, *Brasserie du Pêcheur*, n. 57 above, at para. 42.

[452] Tridimas, loc. cit. n. 442, at p. 332.

[453] But see Anagnostaras, loc. cit. n. 328, at p. 299; see also D. Edward and W. Robinson, 'Is there a Place for Private Law Principles in Community Law?', in T. Heukels and A. McDonnell (eds.), *The Action for Damages in Community Law* (The Hague, Kluwer 1997) p. 339 at p. 343, according to whom the '[p]arallelism becomes logical, as well as being necessitated by the unified source of the underlying principle'.

[454] ECJ, *Köbler*, n. 1 above, at para. 21.

[455] Ibid. at para. 28.

The ECJ can be considered as *primus inter pares* in the Community judicial system, since also national courts – as has been seen – take the function of Community law courts. Is the extension of State liability to judicial acts thus tantamount to accepting the Community's liability for acts of the Community courts proper? On two occasions this issue has been briefly dealt with by AG Léger.[456]

The case in *Baustahlgewebe*[457] concerned the excessive length of proceedings before the CFI (five and a half years elapsed between the lodging of the document instituting proceedings and the date of the judgment of the CFI, and the deliberations lasted for almost 22 months) in the light of Article 6(1) of the ECHR. The central question was which procedural possibilities there were for the applicant to challenge the excessive length. Having dismissed an appeal to the ECJ as an ineffective response,[458] AG Léger turned to the possibility of an action for compensation based on Article 288(2) of the EC Treaty, by which provision in principle also the ECJ is covered.[459] In the light of the CFI´s competence in cases of damage actions brought by individuals and the ensuing partiality-concerns, AG Léger advocated a competence of the ECJ proper to hear such damage claims.[460] The ECJ did not pronounce on the question of the Community's extra-contractual liability in the judgment in *Baustahlgewebe*. However, from the AG's opinion, it becomes clear that it should be possible to hold the Community liable for judicial acts of the CFI. According to AG Léger one means of avoiding the impartiality dilemma created by the involvement of the CFI, which would be called upon to decide *in causa sua*, is the teleological reduction of the provisions grounding competence of the CFI. Consequently the ECJ proper should have competence to decide.

Whereas a liability for acts of the CFI appears not to be ruled out in principle, in *Baustahlgewebe* it remained open whether the Community could also be held liable for acts of the ECJ proper.

---

[456] Opinions of AG Léger in Case C-185/95 P *Baustahlgewebe* [1998] ECR I-8417, at paras. 63 et seq., and in *Köbler*, n. 1 above, at paras. 92 et seq.

[457] ECJ, *Baustahlgewebe*, n. 456 above.

[458] Opinion of AG Léger in *Baustahlgewebe*, n. 456 above, at para. 63.

[459] For this reading of Art. 7(1) of the EC Treaty cf., ECJ, Case C-370/89 *SGEEM* [1992] ECR I-6211, at para. 15.

[460] Opinion of AG Léger in *Baustahlgewebe*, n. 456 above, at paras. 66 et seq.

The latter issue was briefly touched upon by AG Léger in *Köbler*, but the ECJ did not pronounce on it. The AG was firm in discarding the possibility to render the Community liable on account of a decision of the ECJ, since the ECJ was the supreme Court in the Community legal order.[461]

Indeed, his reasoning is entirely convincing. The Community system of judicial review of necessity comes to an end when the highest court of the system has been engaged.[462] Beyond this point a review of judicial decisions, and be it only indirectly in the course of liability proceedings, is unfruitful. The problem of impartiality, whose resolution AG Léger sketched out with regard to the CFI in *Baustahlgewebe*, is no longer resolvable once the ECJ should decide on the legality of one of its decisions. Possibly, one could bring to bear a less stringent concept of impartiality than the one advocated by AG Léger, on which for instance, the Court could decide in a different composition than in the primary judgment. On the other hand, it appears highly unlikely that the Court would ever arrive at a finding that one of its judgments breached Community law. Apart from the impartiality concern, this is associated with the lack of outside control as supreme court of the system, to which national courts, are subjected. Indeed it would mean taking the Community's extra-contractual liability *ad absurdum*, if the authoritative interpreter of Community law was requested for another authoritative interpretation. Obviously, the exit-strategy for the Court, in referring to an incremental development of the case law, or the necessity 'to re-examine and clarify its case-law' on a particular matter[463] would be inherent in the system. However, the situation would be different if the Community were a party to the ECHR and hence subject to the review by the ECrtHR.[464]

What then is the impact of the impossibility of the Community's liability for judicial acts of the ECJ on State liability for judicial acts? As has been

---

[461] Opinion of AG Léger in *Köbler*, n. 1 above, at para. 94.

[462] See also Toner, loc. cit. n. 328, at p. 187.

[463] Cf., ECJ, Joined Cases C-267/91 and C-268/91 *Keck and Mithouard* [1993] ECR I-6097, para. 14.

[464] Opinion of AG Léger in *Köbler*, n. 1 above, at para. 94; see also ECrtHR, *Matthews* v. *UK*, judgment of 18 February 1999, Reports of Judgments and Decisions 1999-I, where the ECrtHR held the Member States jointly responsible for the adoption by the EP of secondary law in contravention of Art. 3 of Protocol 1 to the ECHR. However, given the ECJ's remoteness from direct Member State-influence it seem to be highly unlikely for a *Matthews*-kind of situation to arise in connection with the Community judicature.

seen, the ECJ draws an analogy between the two liability regimes, which should hold 'in the absence of particular justification'.[465] Thus, the analogy is not of an absolute nature, but rather allows for justified deviations. For the said reasons the particular position of the ECJ in the Community judicial architecture suggests a deviation from the analogy. Also AG Léger pointed out the fact that both liability regimes need not develop 'in strict parallel'.[466]

Bearing in mind the relativity of the parallel between the Community's extra-contractual liability and the State liability regime, the impossibility of holding the Community liable for a breach of Community law by the ECJ does not have immediate repercussions on the question of whether States should be liable for their courts. Admittedly, the Court has unified both liability regimes, without however definitively closing the door for justified deviations, which are warranted by conceptual differences between the role of the ECJ and that of national courts. The objection of an alleged fully-fledged parallel between the two liability regimes standing in the way of State liability for judicial acts is therefore not well-founded.

1.7 Undesirable power gain for the ECJ?

It has been argued in post-*Köbler* writing that reading *Köbler* in conjunction with the unrealistically high clarity-threshold in *CILFIT* would lead to a significant increase in the number of cases referred to the Court for a preliminary ruling. In order to avoid the risk of State liability, national courts of last instance would be better off if they were to ask for a preliminary ruling 'in basically every case involving a question of EC law which has not yet been addressed by the ECJ'.[467]

Already by means of the notion of direct effect a shift of power to the ECJ has been effectuated, which was facilitated by the preliminary reference procedure. Establishing national courts as Community law courts at

[465] ECJ, *Brasserie du Pêcheur*, n. 57 above, at para. 42.

[466] Opinion of AG Léger in *Köbler*, n. 1 above, at para. 94; see also the Opinion of AG Léger in Case C-5/94 *Hedley Lomas* [1996] ECR I-2553, at paras. 128 et seq., where he elaborates on structural differences between the extra-contractual liability of the Community and State liability. However, the Court did not take over the line of reasoning of its AG in this case.

[467] Wattel, loc. cit. n. 300, at p. 178.

the disposal of individual applicants, paired with the Article 234-procedure, has lead to a dramatic increase in the number of cases heard by the ECJ and thus has enabled the creation of an effective international rule of law in the European polity.[468] With this in mind, the *Köbler* judgment could be said to further contribute to the effective power of the Court. Indeed, as will be shown in detail under Chapter VI below, the national judiciaries essentially depend on the co-operation with the ECJ when it comes to the determination of the existence of grounds giving rise to State liability for judicial acts. This unsolicited power gain for the ECJ could fuel an objection of judicial policy against the inclusion of the judiciary for the purposes of State liability. An argument raised by the UK government in *Köbler* in connection with the impartiality of national courts echoes this reasoning. So, the UK government entertained doubts as to the impartiality of national courts, in deciding in cases of State liability for judicial acts. These reservations were relevant, *unless those courts were to make references to the Court which would amount to establishing an appeal before the Court, contrary to the wishes of the framers of the EC Treaty.*[469]

Again these fears are countered by the exceptionality of the remedy of State liability for judicial acts. The levels of additional litigation before the ECJ can therefore be expected to remain insignificant, without unduly overstretching the 'balance of power' between the ECJ and national courts. It seems clearly advisable in case of doubt to refer questions to the ECJ in order to minimise the risk of later damage actions,[470] and in this manner, *Köbler* accentuates the duty to refer of courts of last instance. On the other hand – as will still be seen in connection with the standard of liability –, the threshold for liability has been set reasonably high. It is clear that, consistent with the previous case law on liability for the conduct of other State functions, courts acting *bona fide* in the application of Community law will not run a risk of rendering the State liable. As the Court held in *British Telecommunications*[471] in connection with an incorrect transposition of a directive into British law, the relevant provision of the directive was 'im-

---

[468] Alter, op. cit. n. 17, at pp. 21 et seq.

[469] Cf., Opinion of AG Léger in *Köbler*, n. 1 above, at para. 21.

[470] See already C. Beul, 'Kein Richterprivileg bei unterlassener Vorlage gem. Art. 177 EGV', 7 *EuZW* (1996) p. 748 at p. 750.

[471] ECJ, Case C-392/93 *British Telecommunications* [1996] ECR I-1631.

precisely worded and was reasonably capable of bearing, as well as the construction applied to it by the Court in this judgment, the interpretation given to it by the United Kingdom in good faith and on the basis of arguments which are not entirely devoid of substance'.[472] In addition the non-compliant interpretation, which had been shared by other Member States, was not manifestly contrary to the wording of objective of the directive.[473] Guidance from the Court's case law had been absent.[474] A similar line of reasoning with regard to *bona fides* is apparent from the judgment in *Denkavit*.[475]

In the absence of any reasons standing in the way of applying this case law to the judicial function, the exercise of which, is normally characterised by a wide discretion, the fear of a significant power gain of the ECJ appears unfounded. National courts can be sure that a *bona fide*-application of Community law – even if non-compliant in the end – will be sufficient in order to avoid the risk of triggering State liability. By contrast, the referral of questions to the ECJ of *any* question of Community law just for the sake of shielding the State from potential liability claims will not be required. Accepting the principle of State liability for judicial acts in the Community legal order therefore, does not go hand in hand with a *de facto* enrichment of the Court's existing competences.

2. Conclusion

Several arguments against an extension of *Francovich* liability to judicial acts have been submitted in academic writing on the subject, as well as the proceedings in *Köbler*, or can be conceived of. However, none of them is capable of conclusively defeating this extension, or – put differently – of giving reasons for letting individuals bear themselves the financial consequences of unlawful conduct of the State in its judicial capacity. Principles deeply entrenched in national law, such as judicial independence and *res judicata* can be aligned with a principle of State liability for judicial acts.

---

472 Ibid. at para. 42.

473 Ibid. at para. 43.

474 Ibid. at para. 44.

475 ECJ, Joined Cases C-283, 291 and 292/94 *Denkavit* [1996] ECR I-5063, at paras. 51 et seq.

Nevertheless, as has been seen, a certain relativity of *res judicata* is inherent in the recognition of any form of State liability for judicial acts. It remains to be seen to what extent these concerns can be dissolved at the level of the substantive conditions giving rise to liability.[476]

In addition there are few indications that the relationship of co-operation between the ECJ and national courts, which is crucial for the effectiveness of Community law, will be significantly undermined by *Köbler*, although it will only be possible to draw a definitive conclusion in the light of the future reception of this ruling by national courts, and in particular of courts of last instance. As has been seen, due to the exceptional character of the State being held liable in its judicial capacity, there is not much fear of a clogging of the Community judiciary as a whole. In addition, there are good reasons not to view the parallel between State liability and the Community's extra-contractual liability as fully-fledged and therefore as an obstacle to State liability for judicial acts. Finally, the judicial-policy argument of a potential power gain of the ECJ by means of the *Köbler* judgment could not be substantiated to the requisite level.

On the basis of this analysis, it appears rational to also subject the State acting in its judicial capacity to State liability. The peculiarities of the judiciary are not such as to require to reserve that particular remedy to administrative and legislative acts. Nevertheless, the former need to be considered again, in the context of the substantive conditions of State liability for judicial acts.

[476] See Chapter V below.

Chapter V
WHICH STANDARD OF LIABILITY FOR JUDICIAL ACTS?

Chapter V
WHICH STANDARD OF LIABILITY FOR JUDICIAL ACTS?

Apart from the recognition in principle of State liability for judicial acts, its real significance and potential impact hinge on the standard of liability applied. A low standard may attract a great number of additional litigants and place the functioning of the judiciary in jeopardy. By contrast, a too exacting standard may lead to the situation that the exercise of this remedy becomes hypothetical owing to the wholly exceptional character attributed to State liability in this way.

In pre-*Köbler* writing there was agreement that a simple and unqualified breach of Community law by a court should not be enough to trigger the liability of the State.[477] The paralysing effect on the functioning of national and the Community judicial systems of adopting the opposite stance in the end could defeat the ultimate aim of enhancing individual protection. In this context reference was also made to the 'by no means insignificant degree of fault'[478] outlined by the Court in *Brasserie du Pêcheur*, which – if applied to judicial acts – would account for an important obstacle to be taken by potential litigants.[479] It had also been suggested to leave the conditions giving rise to State liability for judicial wrongs to the Member States,[480] a proposal which from the outset seemed to ignore the systematics of the Court's approach in matters of State liability characterised by the intention to provide for a uniform set of minimum conditions giving rise to State liability.

Whereas the Court in *Francovich* referred to a mere *breach* of Community law as being one of the conditions giving rise to State liability for the

---

[477] Anagnostaras, loc. cit. n. 328, at p. 287; Toner, loc. cit. n. 328, at p. 175.

[478] Whereas the notion of a 'sufficiently serious breach' connotes certain aspects which under national law are dealt with under the heading of 'fault', it is to be noted that a criterion of fault going beyond the requirement of the breach being sufficiently serious does not find support in Community law. Cf., ECJ, *Brasserie du Pêcheur*, n. 57 above, at paras. 76 et seq.

[479] Toner, loc. cit. n. 328, at p. 175.

[480] Wegener, loc. cit. n. 333, at pp. 795 et seq.

non-implementation of a directive,[481] the Court seized the opportunity in *Brasserie du Pêcheur* to clarify and qualify the standard of liability: In order to expose the liability of a Member State, a 'sufficiently serious breach' of Community law is required.[482] The decisive test to ascertain the existence of a sufficiently serious breach is whether a Member State has 'manifestly and gravely disregarded the limits on its discretion'.[483] The competent court should thereby, *inter alia*, take into account the clarity and precision of the rule breached, the measures of discretion left by that rule, whether the infringement caused was intentional or involuntary, whether an error of law was excusable or inexcusable, the fact that a Community institution may have contributed towards the omission, and the adoption or retention of national measures or practices contrary to Community law.[484] The Court added that

> '[o]n any view, a breach of Community law will clearly be sufficiently serious if it has persisted despite a judgment finding the infringement in question to be established, or a preliminary ruling or settled case law of the Court on the matter from which it is clear that the conduct in question constituted an infringement.'[485]

The judgment in *Köbler* builds on these well-established concepts, but modifies the standard of a sufficiently serious breach, having regard to the specific nature of the judiciary.

1. The Additional Standard of 'Manifest Infringement' of Community Law

The Court starts with recalling the classic *trias* of conditions giving rise to State liability,[486] which should also govern the liability for damage caused by a decision of a national court of last instance.[487] Therefore, in the case of

---

[481] ECJ, *Francovich*, n. 66 above, at para. 40.
[482] Cf., ECJ, *Brasserie du Pêcheur*, n. 57 above, at para. 51.
[483] Ibid. at para. 55.
[484] Ibid. at para. 56.
[485] Ibid. at para. 57.
[486] ECJ, *Köbler*, n. 1 above, at para. 51.
[487] Ibid. at para. 52.

State liability for judicial acts only a sufficiently serious breach of Community law should give rise to liability. The Court goes on to draw attention to 'the specific nature of the judicial function and to the legitimate requirements of legal certainty', with the declared aim of accommodating the Member States' reservations to this extent.[488] From these particularities the Court concludes as follows:

> '[...] State liability for an infringement of Community law by a decision of a national court adjudicating at last instance *can be incurred only in the exceptional case where the court has manifestly infringed the applicable law.*'[489]

Thus, in the context of judicial acts, the ECJ does not revert to its own definition of a sufficiently serious breach given in *Brasserie du Pêcheur*, namely that the Member State concerned has manifestly and gravely disregarded the limits on its discretion. In contrast, it introduces the novel concept of a manifest infringement of Community law. Furthermore, the Court makes it clear that a manifest infringement shall be taken for granted only in exceptional cases.

It needs to be examined if, and if so to what extent the manifest infringement-formula actually raises the liability threshold as compared to the manifest and grave disregard on Member States' discretion-approach. That the Court intended to provide for a more stringent standard of liability with regard to judicial acts becomes clear from two aspects: Firstly, it is exactly the reference to the exceptional character of a manifest infringement which supports this view. In contrast, a reference to the exceptionality of the State's liability for acts or omissions of its legislature is absent in *Brasserie du Pêcheur* and the subsequent jurisprudence. Secondly, the Court declares that it wants to accommodate the views of the Member State governments voiced against the principle of State liability for judicial acts. Those – as the Court puts it – relate to the specific nature of the judicial function and to the legitimate requirements of legal certainty. Such a concession would however be pointless if a manifest infringement actually amounted to the same as under the *Brasserie*-conditions. Moreover, there would be no need to provide for the new concept of a manifest breach if it was not to create a

[488] Ibid. at para. 53.
[489] Ibid. (emphasis added).

higher threshold, since the 'manifestly and gravely disregarded the limits on its discretion'-formula could also be a prolific concept in connection with judicial acts.[490]

In the post *Köbler* literature, the dominant view that appears is that the Court has raised the threshold for State liability in connection with judicial acts,[491] whereas a minority has pointed out that the standard provided for in *Brasserie* was tailored to the legislative function and, therefore, not suited for judicial acts. That the *Köbler* standard was more stringent could hence not be determined with certainty.[492] However, it does not seem clear why a standard which focuses on discretion should only be adequate for the assessment of legislative acts, but not of judicial conduct. In fact, the judicial function being almost invariably characterised by a wide margin of discretion, could easily be subjected to the *Brasserie*-standard, whereas with regard to the legislative function an exception covering situations of no discretion is required: In such instances the mere breach of Community law will be sufficient in which to ground liability.[493] It can therefore, not be said that the *Brasserie*-standard as such would be inadequate for judicial acts.[494] Objecting to the *Brasserie*-standard when it comes to judicial acts is only viable if one combines this objection with the view that the State should only, under more stringent conditions, be liable for the judiciary.[495]

In determining the sufficiently serious nature of a breach of Community law of the judiciary by reference to a manifest infringement, the Court only partly accepted the view of AG Léger, who had proposed to focus on whether

---

490 See also Botella, loc. cit. n. 335, at pp. 303 et seq.

491 B. Kotschy, 'Responsabilité de l'État – Arrêt Köbler', *RDUE* (2003) p. 763 at p. 765; Wegener, loc. cit. n. 263, at p. 85 et seq. and p. 91; Obwexer, loc. cit. n. 432, at p. 728; B. Hofstötter, 'Härte und Milde für Judikativunrecht vor dem EuGH', *ELR* (2004) p. 60 at p. 64; P. Schwarzenegger, *ZfRV* (2003) p. 236 at p. 237; Breuer, n. 327 above, p. 251 and p. 253.

492 von Danwitz, loc. cit. n. 324, at p. 302.

493 ECJ, Joined Cases C-178/94, C-179/94, C-188/94, C-189/94 and C-190/94 *Dillenkofer* [1996] ECR I-4845, at paras. 21 et seq.

494 See also Tobler, loc. cit. n. 430, at p. 346, who leaves this question unanswered.

495 *Contra* Botella, loc. cit. n. 335, at p. 304, who argues that by disposing of the overtly discretion-based standard the Court emphasises that the mere fact of a breach of Community law is enough to engage State liability. However, this assessment seems to pay too little deference to the Court's list of factors to be taken into account when determining a manifest infringement, which roughly corresponds to that in *Brasserie du Pêcheur*.

or not the error of law committed by a court was excusable.[496] An error of a national supreme court should be deemed inexcusable, if it contravened provisions of Community law whose meaning and scope was clear[497] or, went against the jurisprudence of the ECJ as it stood on the day judgment was given.[498] Finally, State liability for judicial conduct should not be precluded in the case of a supreme court's manifest disregard for its obligation to refer according to Article 234(3) of the EC Treaty, for instance, where there is no case law of the Court.[499]

Even though there is no reference to a standard of excusable judicial errors in the judgment, the two concepts – excusable error of law and manifest infringement – have a common core.[500] Also AG Léger refers to a manifest infringement when explaining what an inexcusable breach of Community law should mean, and, in this way, equates inexcusable error with manifest infringement. However, it is not quite clear if an inexcusable error should *only* cover manifest breaches, which could be inferred from the examples given by AG Léger covering only manifest infringements.[501] In addition, the notion of an inexcusable error implies a requirement of fault as the sole criterion to ascertain a sufficiently serious breach, whereas it is generally recognised that the notion of a sufficiently serious breach extends to both objective and subjective elements.[502] It is, therefore, systematically correct and forthright that the Court – unlike its AG – views the inexcusability as, but an aspect, to be taken into account when assessing the manifest nature of a breach of Community law.[503] In this light it is commendable that the Court opted for the criterion of manifest breach as the

496 Opinion of AG Léger in *Köbler*, n. 1 above, at para. 139.

497 Ibid. at para. 140.

498 Ibid. at para. 141.

499 Ibid. at paras. 144 et seq.

500 But see also Tobler, loc. cit. n. 430, at p. 346, who argues that by requiring a manifest breach the Court implicitly takes over the excusability-criterion proposed by AG Léger, which in the future could possibly become the general standard of liability in the Community legal order. In the light of the observations following here this assessment does not appear to be well-founded, however.

501 Breuer, loc. cit. n. 327, at p. 246.

502 ECJ, *Brasserie du Pêcheur*, n. 57 above, at para. 78.

503 ECJ, *Köbler*, n. 1 above, at para. 55. This is also in line with the conditions for State liability with regard to the other State functions; cf., ECJ, *Brasserie du Pêcheur*, n. 57 above, at para. 56.

more objective standard, which, at the same time, seems to be more precise and less flexible than the criterion proposed by AG Léger.[504]

Finally, the question needs to be addressed whether at all there is a need for a specific standard of liability with regard to judicial acts. Indeed, it has been criticised that from the viewpoint of an individual concerned it would make little difference whether a sufficiently qualified breach of Community law had been committed by the legislative, administrative or judicative branch. A different standard with regard to judicial wrongs would neglect this aspect.[505] Nevertheless, the attribution of a special character to State liability for judicial wrongs seems to be justified by the specific nature of the judiciary, as was pointed out equally by the Court and AG Léger in *Köbler*.[506] It is correct to assume that the Court dispelled reservations, in particular pertaining to the independence of the judiciary and the principle of legal certainty when addressing whether the principle of State liability should extend to judicial wrongs. However, denying a principled difference between the judiciary and the other State functions with regard to the possibility of the remedy of State liability, does not mean that the same standard of liability has to be applied to all three State functions. As has been shown, recognising State liability for judicial wrongs of itself, gives rise to a certain relativity of *res judicata*, understood as a substantive concept. It is clear that this reservation is specific to the judicial function and requires accommodation in a sufficiently qualified standard of liability, which does not lead to a structural setting aside of final judicial decisions. Holding the State liable for its judiciary can be reconciled with a formal reading of *res judicata*. Remaining doubts relating to its substance are not such as to rule out the availability of this remedy, but do justify a particular standard of liability. Not least for this reason the intervening governments in *Köbler* had argued 'in favour of rules governing liability which are specific, restrictive and limited to exceptional, or very exceptional, cases'.[507] It is clear that the ECJ, bearing in mind the acceptability of its decision to the Member States courts, had to take seriously the concerns voiced by the various governments, which underscored the sensitivity of the issue. The Court did

[504] Breuer, loc. cit. n. 327, at p. 250.

[505] Obwexer, loc. cit. n. 432, at p. 728.

[506] ECJ, *Köbler*, n. 1 above, at para. 53; Opinion of AG Léger in *Köbler*, n. 1 above, at paras. 70 and 122.

[507] Cf., Opinion of AG Léger in *Köbler*, n. 1 above, at para. 116.

not hesitate to highlight the specific nature of the judicial function and the legitimate requirements of legal certainty, which both would have to be reflected in a particular standard of liability.[508]

2. Criteria to Be Taken into Account by National Courts

While the Court's intention to raise the standard of liability is apparent from *Köbler*, the exact implications of the new standard of manifest infringement, as of yet, remain imprecise[509] and await further clarification from future jurisprudence. Everything depends on the Court's interpretation of the new concept of a manifest infringement. Despite these uncertainties, it can be presumed that the Court will resort to manifest breaches only within tight limits, having explained the exceptionality of such instances.

It is clear that '[i]n order to determine whether that condition [i.e., the manifest breach] is satisfied, the national court hearing a claim for reparation must take account of all the factors which characterise the situation put before it'.[510] In addition, the Court offers a non-exhaustive list of criteria for the purpose of ascertaining the existence of a manifest breach, thereby giving concrete guidance to the national courts called upon to 'implement' State liability for judicial acts in the first place:

> 'Those factors include, in particular, the degree of clarity and precision of the rule infringed, whether the infringement was intentional, whether the error of law was excusable or inexcusable, the position taken, where applicable, by a Community institution and non-compliance by the court in question with its obligation to make a reference for a preliminary ruling under the third paragraph of Article 234 EC.'[511]

> 'In any event, an infringement of Community law will be sufficiently serious where the decision concerned was made in manifest breach of the case-law of the Court in the matter.'[512]

508 ECJ, *Köbler*, n. 1 above, at para. 53.
509 See also Wegener, loc. cit. n. 263, at p. 90.
510 ECJ, *Köbler*, n. 1 above, at para. 54.
511 Ibid. at para. 55.
512 Ibid. at para. 56.

Whereas most of these criteria are familiar from the Court's judgment in *Brasserie du Pêcheur*,[513] the breach of the duty to refer is tailored to the judicial function and requires closer scrutiny in this context.

2.1 Breach of the duty to refer pursuant to Article 234(3) of the EC Treaty

The Court in *Köbler* mentions the 'non-compliance by the court in question with its obligation to make a reference for a preliminary ruling under the third paragraph of Article 234 EC' as one factor to be taken into account when establishing a manifest infringement by a court, giving rise to State liability. In the light of the requirement of the particular nature of the rule of law infringed, which must be intended to confer rights on individuals,[514] the question needs to be answered whether a breach of the duty to refer, in itself, can give rise to a manifest infringement. Secondly, provided the first question is answered in the negative, it has to be determined what role a breach of the duty to refer can play in qualifying an otherwise simple breach of Community law.

It is common ground that Article 234(3) of the EC Treaty does not confer any subjective right on individuals to have a national court refer a question to the ECJ.[515] Equally, does it not give a direct means of addressing the ECJ in the hands of individuals.[516] The qualification of Article 234(3) as a rule of law intended to confer rights on individuals for the purposes of *Francovich* liability is, consequently, *prima facie* ruled out by its function of securing the uniform interpretation and application of Community law. Consequently, the mere breach of Article 234(3) could not give rise to a damages claim. On the other hand, apart from its primarily institutional character, Article

513 Cf., 3. below.

514 Cf., ECJ, *Brasserie du Pêcheur*, n. 57 above, at para. 51 and its reception in *Köbler*, n. 1 above, at para. 52.

515 Wegener, loc. cit. n. 333, at p. 788; *idem*, loc. cit. n. 263, at p. 90; *idem* in Calliess and Ruffert, op. cit. n. 167, commentary on Article 234 of the EC Treaty, at mn. 11; Solar, op. cit. n. 260, at p. 112; Lenaerts and Arts, op. cit. n. 13, at mn. 2-018.

516 But see also Solar, op. cit. n. 260, at p. 136, who de *lege ferenda* argues in favour of an action for failure to refer ('*Vorlagepflichtverletzungsklage*'), which would give individuals the right to have decisions of national courts of last instance reviewed by the ECJ for compliance with the *CILFIT* criteria.

234(3) also encompasses facilitating the protection of individual rights. As the Court held in *Köbler*

> 'it is, in particular, in order to prevent rights conferred on individuals by Community law from being infringed that under the third paragraph of Article 234 EC, a court against whose decisions there is no judicial remedy under national law is required to make a reference to the Court of Justice'.[517]

It could, therefore, be argued that the fundamental importance of the preliminary references procedure in the protection of individuals renders the mere breach of the duty to refer, sufficient to substantiate an action for damages.[518]

However, it appears from the quoted passage that the Court in fact links Article 234(3) of the EC Treaty with substantive rights of individuals to be protected: The purpose of the duty to refer is, *inter alia*, to secure that *substantive rights* conferred by Community law are not infringed. However, a breach of the duty to refer need not give rise to a breach of substantive rights flowing from Community law. Although State liability can therefore not be the *necessary* consequence of a failure to refer,[519] the breach of the duty to refer will normally go hand in hand with the breach of a substantive norm of Community law.[520] Thus, Article 234(3) becomes part of the effective legal protection of individuals with regard to the relevant substantive right conferred by Community law. Conversely, there is no need for individual protection if a national court of last instance – without respecting its obligation under Article 234(3) – takes a substantively compliant decision. In this case, the failure to refer only touches the institutional aspect of the said provision, but not its individual component. An action for damages, whose function by definition is to secure individual rights in secondary

517 ECJ, *Köbler*, n. 1 above, at para. 35.

518 See Classen, loc. cit. n. 262, at p. 820; see also Botella, loc. cit. n. 335, at p. 306, who opines that '[e]n affirmant que la simple violation de l'obligation résultant de l'article 234 est de nature à engager la responsabilité de l'Etat pour violation du droit communautaire, la Cour élève l'obligation de renvoi préjudiciel au rang d'une obligation de résultat qui ne s'accommode d'aucune considération tenant à une quelconque faute de l'auteur de l'infraction'. See also Komárek, loc. cit. n. 396, at p. 22.

519 But see also Botella, loc. cit. n. 335, at p. 306.

520 Wegener, loc. cit. n. 333, at p. 789; *idem*, loc. cit. n. 263, at p. 90; Beul, loc. cit. n. 470, at p. 749; Solar, op. cit. n. 260, at p. 112.

proceedings, is thus not an appropriate remedy to invoke. Focussing on the issue of damage yields the same result: If a substantively compliant decision has been taken, although without adherence to the duty to refer, there is no damage which would be causally linked to the breach of Article 234(3) of the EC Treaty.[521]

According to the settled case law of the ECrtHR 'it is not completely impossible that, in certain circumstances, refusal by a domestic court trying a case at final instance might infringe the principle of fair trial, as set forth in Article 6(1) of the Convention, in particular where such refusal appears arbitrary',[522] even though the ECrtHR has not yet found a breach in this context. It has been advanced by AG Léger that, in such an instance, that particular manifest infringement of a national court of last instance should in itself be capable of giving rise to State liability.[523] Nevertheless, also in this case it would not be the violation of Article 234(3) of the EC Treaty itself providing the basis for State liability, but only in conjunction with the right to a fair trial as enshrined in Article 6 of the ECHR.[524]

Therefore a mere breach of Article 234(3), viewed in isolation, will not be sufficient in order to give rise to a damages action. Only when paired with the violation of a substantive right conferred by Community law, can liability ensue. By contrast, the view, where a Member State may be liable for *any* breach of Article 234(3) of the EC Treaty,[525] cannot be upheld in the light of the said considerations.

Given this intermediate result, the next question to arise is, what role the breach of the duty to refer can play in determining the nature of the breach of Community law. From the list of criteria given by the Court, it is appar-

---

[521] Beul, loc. cit. n. 470, at p. 749; Classen, loc. cit. n. 262, at p. 820.

[522] ECrtHR, *André Desmots* v. *France* (decision of 23 March 1999 on the admissibility of the application; No. 41358/98), at para. 2; *Peter Moosbrugger* v. *Austria* (decision of 25 January 2000 on the admissibility of the application; No. 44861/98), at para. 2; *Coëme and Others* v. *Belgium*, judgment of 22 June 2000, Reports of Judgments and Decisions 2000-VII, at para. 114; *Nicolas Calena Santiago* v. *Spain* (decision of 4 October 2001 on the admissibility; No. 60350/00), at para. 2; and *Lambert Bakker* v. *Austria* (decision of 13 June 2002 on the admissibility of the application; No 43454/98), at para. 2.

[523] Opinion of AG Léger in *Köbler*, n. 1 above, at para. 148.

[524] Obwexer, loc. cit. n. 432, at p. 727.

[525] B.H. ter Kuile, 'To Refer or not to Refer: About the Last Paragraph of Article 177 of the EC Treaty', in Curtin and Heukels, op. cit. n. 60, p. 381 at p. 389. See also Botella, loc. cit. n. 335, at p. 304 and p. 306, and Komárek, loc. cit. n. 396, at p. 22.

ent that a failure to refer can qualify an otherwise simple breach of Community law as manifest.[526] It has been pointed out that the *CILFIT* formula has done little to clarify the scope of the duty to refer.[527] National judges may thus be left in doubt whether or not they are under an obligation to refer. It is for this reason, that an excusable failure to refer should not add up to a manifest infringement of Community law. The inexcusability criterion suggested by AG Léger and endorsed by the Court as another criterion to be taken into account when determining the manifest nature of a breach of Community law, can serve as a yardstick here. Furthermore, guidance can be gleaned from the requirement of *bona fides* as referred to in *British Telecommunications*.[528] In obvious cases a failure to refer can not be excused. This would comprise cases where a national court of last instance entertains doubts as to the interpretation of a given provision of Community law, and yet fails to refer.[529] This would also include cases in which there is no orientation from the Court's case law yet. The same must be true for a court which deliberately refrains from raising issues of Community law or ignores applicable case law of the Court, and in this way circumvents the duty to refer, when the error of law is inexcusable.[530]

2.2 Conclusion

Köbler slightly accentuates the problems that have always surrounded the application of the *CILFIT* formula by referring to the failure to refer as one of the criteria to adduce a manifest infringement of Community law. Disrespect for the duty to refer may thus be one of the elements triggering State liability. The conclusion that basically every case involving a question of Community law should be referred by a national court of last instance, so as

526 Obwexer, loc. cit. n. 432, at p. 727; Wegener, loc. cit. n. 263, at p. 90; Schwarzenegger, loc. cit. n. 491, at p. 237; cf., Classen, loc. cit. n. 262, at p. 820.

527 Solar, op. cit. n. 260, at p. 114.

528 See Chapter IV.1.7 above.

529 See also Classen, loc. cit. n. 262, at p. 820, who interprets Art. 234(3) of the EC Treaty as including a duty to give a detailed justification for the decision not to make a reference. Failing to observe this duty would give rise to the sufficiently serious nature of the breach.

530 Cf., ECJ, *Köbler*, n. 1 above, at para. 56; Schwarzenegger, loc. cit. n. 491, at p. 237; Solar, op. cit. n. 260, at p. 114.

to avoid the real risk of making the State liable,[531] is nonetheless misplaced. It follows from the Court's explicit logic of State liability as a remedy available only for exceptional cases, that only particularly qualified failures to refer can be sanctioned by means of State liability. The criterion of inexcusability which permeates both the opinion of AG Léger and the Court's judgment can give guidance on which instances to include in this group of cases. What is more, a mere violation of Article 234(3) of the EC Treaty in itself is never sufficient to give rise to State liability. Only when paired with the violation of a substantive right may it become relevant. It can then serve as an element of qualification of a simple breach of Community law. Despite this cautious approach with regard to the duty to refer there can be no doubt about the fact that *Köbler* will act as an incentive for national courts of last instance to live up to the requirements of Article 234(3) of the EC Treaty. Deliberately keeping their eyes shut when confronted with unresolved questions of Community law can no longer work as an unsanctioned defence.

3. The Application of the Standard of Manifest Infringement in *Köbler*

The dispute in *Köbler* concerned a special length-of-service increment to the basic salary after 15 years of employment as a professor at Austrian universities, entitlement to which had been denied to Mr. Köbler by the competent Austrian authorities. Although Mr. Köbler had been working for more than 15 years as a professor at a number of universities, the period of time spent working in Austria was below 15 years. On appeal to the Supreme Administrative Court (*Verwaltungsgerichtshof*), the latter court referred questions to the ECJ in order to find out whether requiring the period of service to be exclusively spent at an Austria university amounted to prohibited discrimination on the basis of nationality. The *Verwaltungsgerichtshof* was directed to the judgment in *Schöning-Kougebetopoulou*[532] by the Registrar of the Court, and in the light of that judgment subsequently decided to withdraw its request. Contrary to its original qualification of the length-of-service increment as a component of salary under the system of career ad-

[531] Cf., Wattel, loc. cit. n. 300, at p. 178.
[532] ECJ, Case C-15/96 *Schöning-Kougebetopoulou* [1998] ECR I-47.

vancement in the request for a preliminary ruling, the *Verwaltungsgerichtshof* now held that it constituted a loyalty bonus which would be in conformity with the rules on the free movement of persons. Hereupon, Mr Köbler brought an action for damages before the *Landesgericht Wien* – the referring court in *Köbler* – against the Republic of Austria for reparation of the loss which he had allegedly suffered as a result of the non-payment to him of the special length-of-service increment. He maintained that the judgment of the *Verwaltungsgerichtshof* infringed directly applicable provisions of Community law, as interpreted by the Court.

Against this factual and legal background the Court based its reasoning on two elements: Firstly, on the *Verwaltungsgerichtshof's* wrongful interpretation of the judgment in *Schöning-Kougebetopoulou*,[533] and secondly, on its failure to uphold its reference, having reviewed and altered the qualification of the length-of-service-increment.[534] Concerning the first element, the Court had not pronounced on the conformity of loyalty bonuses with Community law in *Schöning-Kougebetopoulou*, nor in any other cases. Assuming that it had, the *Verwaltungsgerichtshof* committed an error of law. With regard to the second element, the Court pointed out that the *Verwaltungsgerichtshof* should have afforded the ECJ the possibility to pronounce on the permissibility of loyalty bonuses in Community law.[535] Having replaced the Court's answer with its own reasoning, the *Verwaltungsgerichtshof* had exceeded its mandate under *CILFIT*, since the question at issue could not be considered as clear.

Finding these two breaches of Community law committed by the national court, the ECJ continued its analysis with regard to the manifest character of the infringements. As to the breach of substantive law the Court denied the existence of a manifest infringement. This question had neither been expressly covered by Community law, nor had the Court pronounced on it, and furthermore it was not obvious.[536] Concerning the failure to maintain the preliminary reference, the Court reasoned as follows:

> 'In the present case the *Verwaltungsgerichtshof* had decided to withdraw the request for a preliminary ruling, on the view that the reply to the question of

[533] ECJ, *Köbler*, n. 1 above, at para. 116.
[534] Ibid. at para. 117.
[535] Ibid.
[536] ECJ, *Köbler*, n. 1 above, at para. 122.

> Community law to be resolved had already been given in the judgment in *Schöning-Kougebetopoulou*, cited above. Thus, it was due to its incorrect reading of that judgment that the *Verwaltungsgerichtshof* no longer considered it necessary to refer that question of interpretation to the Court.'[537]

Consequently, the Court did not find a manifest infringement of Community law giving rise to State liability.

That the pattern of conduct of the Austrian court could also be interpreted less benevolently, becomes apparent from the opinion of AG Léger. In his analysis he highlights the substantive element of the breach committed by the *Verwaltungsgerichtshof* and here focuses on the aspect of indirect discrimination. In the light of the Court's case law on Article 39 of the EC Treaty there could be no doubt that 'there is a risk that that condition [i.e., the completion of 15 years of service at Austrian universities] may operate to the particular detriment of migrant workers [...]'.[538] It would therefore be hard to accept that the Austrian court had made an excusable error when qualifying this condition as being justified by the loyalty to one employer, namely the Austrian State.[539] Even if accepting the availability of this particular justification, the court would have ignored the principle of proportionality, whose significance had been pointed out by the ECJ not least in *Schöning-Kougebetopoulou.*[540] In the present case, there would be no doubt that the length-of-service condition went beyond what is necessary to achieve the objective relied on.[541] Turning to the procedural aspect of Article 234(3) of the EC Treaty, the court should have upheld its reference for a preliminary ruling, since in the light of *CILFIT* it could not be convinced of *acte clair*.[542]

Not least, in the light of the fact that differences between the Court and its AGs are exceptional,[543] it is highly conspicuous and weighs heavily that the Court and its AG seem to be in open conflict on the qualification of the

---

537 Ibid. at para. 123.

538 Opinion of AG Léger in *Köbler*, n. 1 above, at para. 169.

539 Ibid. at para. 170.

540 Ibid. at para. 171.

541 Ibid. at para. 172.

542 Ibid. at para. 173.

543 Cf., T. Tridimas, 'The Role of the Advocate General in the Development of Community Law: Some Reflections', 34 *CML Rev.* (1997) p. 1349 at pp. 1373 et seq.

conduct of the Austrian court. The Court chooses a narrow perspective as its point of departure: Before *Köbler* there was no case law on the particular issue of loyalty bonuses under Community law. In the absence of any guidance, the error of law committed by the court thus does not amount to a manifest infringement. By contrast, AG Léger focuses on the more general issues behind loyalty bonuses, namely indirect discrimination and proportionality. On the latter topics, adequate guidance can be gleaned from the Court's case law. Viewed from this perspective the error is manifest, or, in the terms of the AG, inexcusable.

There seems to also be a divide on the qualification of the breach of the *Verwaltungsgerichtshof* in the literature, but with a slight propensity to the view that the Court exercised particular leniency in the case at hand:[544]

It has been pointed out that the result arrived at in *Köbler* suggests that a particularly qualified breach of Community law is required in order to make the State liable for the conduct of one of its courts. In other words, the Court will apply the already high standard of liability set in *Köbler* with the utmost care. Even though this result could be explained by the intention not to upset the co-operational relationship between the ECJ and national courts,[545] it could not be regarded as satisfactory from the point of view of individual protection.[546] Schwarzenegger refers to the judgment in *Schöning-Kougebetopoulou*, where the ECJ had denied the very existence of a loyalty bonus in the case at hand, for reasons which would have deserved consideration by the *Verwaltungsgerichtshof*, and therefore not pronounced on their legality. Thus, the latter court could not assume that the legal situation with regard to loyalty bonuses was clear.[547] On the other hand, it has also been argued that in scholarly writing after *Schöning-Kougebetopoulou* at least occasionally the conformity of loyalty bonuses had been assumed without hesitation. The threshold for an inexcusable error of law should therefore not be set too low.[548] Holding Austria liable in *Köbler* would have sent a wrong signal and would have possibly triggered an enormous flow of

---

[544] Cf., von Danwitz, loc. cit. n. 324, at p. 303; Hofstötter, loc. cit. n. 491, at p. 64; Obwexer, loc. cit. n. 432, at p. 728; Schwarzenegger, loc. cit. n. 491, at p. 237; Frenz, loc. cit. n. 406, at pp. 1523 et seq.; undecided Kluth, loc. cit. n. 326, at p. 399.

[545] See Hofstötter, loc. cit. n. 491, at p. 64; von Danwitz, loc. cit. n. 324, at p. 303.

[546] Obwexer, loc. cit. n. 432, at p. 728.

[547] Schwarzenegger, loc. cit. n. 491, at p. 237.

[548] Breuer, loc. cit. n. 300, at p. 588.

proceedings which would have to be rejected in the interest of legal certainty.[549] Gundel argues along similar lines that the solution adopted by the *Verwaltungsgerichtshof* could not be said to be clearly wrong. In addition, he points out, that withdrawing the reference had been encouraged by the Court sending the judgment in *Schöning-Kougebetopoulou* to the Austrian court.[550] Wattel is unequivocal in claiming that anything else other than the result arrived at by the ECJ would have been a chutzpah.[551]

The fact that the ECJ invited the Austrian court to withdraw its reference is not capable of dispelling State liability, since the qualification of the length-of-service increment had been changed by the *Verwaltungsgerichtshof* after having received the judgment in *Schöning-Kougebetopoulou*, without consulting the ECJ again. Both the Court's reasoning as well as the submissions of its AG are not fully convincing: AG Léger assumes that the legal situation with regard to loyalty bonuses clearly follows from the Court's standing case law on indirect discrimination. In other words, he presupposes the existence of *acte clair* in the case at hand. On the other hand, he considers that the Austrian court should have maintained its reference. However, taking the substantive limb of the AG's argumentation of a clear legal situation seriously, it is difficult to see why in the light of *CILFIT* a reference should still be necessary. Logically, the failure to refer could not play any role in qualifying the breach of Community law committed by the Austrian court. A similar problem is inherent in the Court's reasoning. As has been seen, the ECJ characterises the applicable legal regime as not clear enough to make a breach of it a manifest infringement. Since it is thus not concerned with an *acte clair*,[552] the Court concedes that the *Verwaltungsgerichtshof* should have maintained its reference for a preliminary ruling.[553] Despite the Austrian court's breach of this obligation (in connection with the non-qualified breach of the applicable substantive rules) the Court fails to see a manifest infringement of Community law since the failure to refer is presented as the consequence of the error of law committed by the national court:

---

[549] Ibid. at p. 589; *idem*, loc. cit. n. 327, at p. 251.
[550] Gundel, loc. cit. n. 332, at p. 10 and p. 11 (n. 30).
[551] Wattel, loc. cit. n. 300, at pp. 182 et seq.
[552] ECJ, *Köbler*, n. 1 above, at para. 118.
[553] Ibid. at para. 117.

'In the present case the *Verwaltungsgerichtshof* had decided to withdraw the request for a preliminary ruling, on the view that the reply to the question of Community law to be resolved had already been given in the judgment in *Schöning-Kougebetopoulou*, cited above. Thus, it was owing to its incorrect reading of that judgment that the *Verwaltungsgerichtshof* no longer considered it necessary to refer that question of interpretation to the Court.'[554]

Even so, it seems clear that almost any failure to meet the obligation to refer could be expressed in terms of a mere consecutive error.[555] It is unconvincing that a wrongful interpretation of Community law can serve as an excuse for not making a mandatory reference. The national court should have either upheld its original qualification of the length-of-service-increment in the light of the withdrawal of its reference, or maintained the reference due to the altered qualification.

The problem in the Court's reasoning seems to be that in qualifying the infringement it views both breaches of Community law in isolation.[556] However, taking both aspects together, namely (1) a wrong interpretation of Community law against the background of an unclear legal situation (2) without upholding the reference, these could well amount to a manifest infringement of Community law. By contrast, the Court seeks to avoid this consequence by refraining from addressing both breaches, instead, regarding the failure to refer as the consequence of the error of law.

Despite the recognition, in principle, of State liability for judicial wrongs it is apparent that the Court does not intend to create an insurmountable obstacle to the crucial co-operation with national courts. In this way, it ensures acceptance of the new principle in the Member States and avoids linking failures to make a reference with an all-too strict risk for the Member States to incur liability.[557] Both the high standard of liability set for

[554] Ibid. at para. 123.

[555] Hofstötter, loc. cit. n. 491, at p. 64.

[556] Frenz, loc. cit. n. 406, at p. 1524.

[557] von Danwitz, loc. cit. n. 324, at p. 303. The recent decision of the German *Bundesgericht* in what is apparently one of the first cases after *Köbler* relating to State liability for judicial acts (III ZR 294/03, decision of 28 October 2004) deserves mentioning in the given context. A damages claim of a German tax adviser (*Steuerberater*) having passed the state examinations in law in Germany and being registered as *revisore contabile* (compulsory auditor) in Italy, based on the refusal to be admitted as certified accountant (*Wirtschaftsprüfer*) in Germany without passing an aptitude test, was held to

judicial wrongs, as well as, its lenient application serve to this end. State liability for judicial wrongs clearly remains confined to exceptional cases, with commensurate disadvantages for individuals. This dilemma is well depicted by Kluth:

> 'Wie in den Rechtssachen Francovich und Brasserie du Pêcheur bleibt den Klägern damit in eigener Sache der Erfolg verwährt. Sie können sich nur über die Rechtsfortbildung freuen, zu der sie beigetragen haben.'[558]

However, it should be kept in mind that in national law, holding the State liable for its judiciary is heavily restricted, due to the particular nature of the judicial function. Accepting that Community law, just as national law forms part of 'the law of the land', it would seem that the absence of fully-fledged protection against judicial wrongs in the Community legal order is just as acceptable as it is on the national level. The complete absence of a remedy of State liability for breaches of Community law by national courts, would be deplorable and contribute to different levels of legal protection in the various Member States. Thus, it cannot be denied that the recognition of State liability for judicial acts as such is a major leap forward.

4. Need to Delimit the Judiciary from the Other State Functions

The existence of a particular standard of liability with regard to judicial acts, which raises the threshold in comparison with State liability for legislative or administrative acts, leads to the further problem of delimiting the judiciary from the other State functions.

It may be difficult to attribute a particular breach to one State function only. The following example taken from Anagnostaras is enlightening in this respect:

---

be unfounded given the lack of a sufficiently serious breach of Community law. In the light of secondary Community law and its partial elucidation by the Court, the *Bundesgericht* essentially relied on *acte clair* as well as on the inexistence of a breach of substantive Community law.

[558] Kluth, loc. cit. n. 326, at p. 399 ['Just like in Francovich and Brasserie du Pêcheur the applicants remain unsuccessful with their claims. They may only rejoice in the development of the law, to which they have contributed' – my translation].

> '[A] Member State fails to implement in time Directive 89/48 on the mutual recognition of higher-education diplomas. The public body responsible according to the national legislation for the recognition of the equivalence of degrees acquired in other states to the domestic ones refuses to accept the equivalence of certain degrees meeting the requirements of Directive 89/48. Consequently, the individuals concerned are refused entry to their profession. An action is brought in the highest administrative court for the annulment of that body's decisions. The court rejects the action without even making a reference to the ECJ.'[559]

It is obvious that in such instances a legislative, administrative or judicial breach could form the basis of a damages claim for the loss suffered due to not being able to exercise one's profession. In these cases, it seems advisable not to base one's liability claim on the wrongful judicial conduct, in order to avoid the stricter ramifications of State liability for judicial wrongs. This flexibility in the attribution of a breach of Community law can also be gleaned from the ECrtHR's judgment in *Dangeville*, where the Court chose not to take the French *Conseil d'Etat's* denial of the direct effect of directives, but rather the legislature's failure to transpose the directive at issue in time as point of departure.[560]

It is also conceivable that two or more State functions are jointly responsible for a breach of Community law. In this vein, the Court held in *Commission* v. *Italy* that by failing to amend Article 29(2) of Law No. 428/1990, which is construed and applied by the administrative authorities and a substantial proportion of the courts, including the *Corte suprema di cassazione*, in such a way that the exercise of the right to repayment of charges levied in breach of Community rules is made excessively difficult for the taxpayer, the Italian Republic had failed to fulfil its obligations under the EC Treaty.[561] In such instances, where the conduct at stake cannot be clearly attributed to one particular State function, it is advisable to combine a *Köbler* action with an ordinary *Francovich* action.[562]

---

[559] Anagnostaras, loc. cit. n. 328, at p. 298.

[560] But see also the critique of Breuer, loc. cit. n. 300, at p. 587, who argues that the ECrtHR does not seem to have been aware of the fact of being confronted with a case of judicial wrong.

[561] ECJ, *Commission* v. *Italy*, n. 2 above, at para. 41.

[562] K.J.M. Mortelmans and J.W. van de Gronden, 53 *Ars Aequi* (2004) p. 198 at p. 202.

Even if judicial conduct is combined with that of other State functions, in all these instances it seems necessary to define the notion of 'court' for the purposes of State liability.

4.1 **What is a court for the purposes of State liability?**

Providing for a standard of liability privileging the judiciary, entails the necessity of Community law criteria on the question what a court actually is, for State liability purposes. Member States should not be free to reduce the risk of incurring liability by applying a wide concept of the judiciary and, therefore, benefiting from the stricter standard of liability.

This problem will be approached in the following terms: First it will be determined whether in the light of *Köbler* only national courts of last instance may trigger State liability. An affirmative answer will further require a definition of courts of last instance for the purpose of State liability. The Court's own case law on the meaning of 'court' under Article 234(3) of the EC Treaty may provide guidance on this issue.

4.1.1 *Do only courts of last instance trigger State liability?*

It is clear that the Court in *Köbler* only pronounced on State liability for the decisions of courts of last instance.[563] On the other hand, this result might have been influenced by the logics of the preliminary rulings procedure, since the referring court had only asked about State liability triggered by decisions of a *supreme court*.[564] Thus, it is necessary to consider, if decisions of lower instance courts may also give rise to State liability. This question has occasionally been raised in the legal literature, without, in most instances, offering a conclusive answer.[565]

---

[563] Cf., ECJ, *Köbler*, n. 1 above, at para. 50.

[564] Cf., ECJ, *Köbler*, n. 1 above, at para. 14.

[565] See Wegener, loc. cit. n. 263, at p. 87, who refers to the 'Haftung (allein?) der letztinstanzlichen Gerichte' without going deeper into the subject. Kotschy, loc. cit. n. 491, at p. 765, seems to assume the possibility, in principle, of State liability for the conduct of lower instance courts, but refrains from expressing a definitive stance on this issue: 'Il semble, dès lors, qu'il restera plus difficile d'établir une responsabilité de l'État pour une violation commisse par une juridiction inférieure, dont les décisions sont encore susceptibles de recours'.

Apart from the issue of the framework of the dispute being set by the questions asked by the referring court, the position of the court in the national judicial hierarchy indeed seems important to the ECJ. This follows from paragraph 34 of the *Köbler* judgment where the Court reasons that

> '[i]t must be stressed, in that context, that a court adjudicating at last instance is by definition the last judicial body before which individuals may assert the rights conferred on them by Community law. Since an infringement of those rights by a final decision of such a court cannot thereafter normally be corrected, individuals cannot be deprived of the possibility of rendering the State liable in order in that way to obtain legal protection of their rights.'

Thus, an important line of reasoning in favour of State liability purely for decisions of courts of last instance, is the absence of the possibility of quashing an erroneous judgment. *E contrario*, it is exactly this possibility, which is available with regard to judgments of lower instance courts, and consequently provides a counter argument to the possibility of State liability for the decisions of lower instance courts. In addition, understanding the remedy of State liability as an incentive to compliance with the duty to refer yields the same result, since only courts of last instance are under an obligation to refer. This reasoning is further corroborated by a comparison with public international law. According to Article 44(b) of the ILC Draft Articles on State Responsibility, the responsibility of a State may not be invoked if the claim is one to which the rule of exhaustion of local remedies applies and any available and effective local remedy has not been exhausted. The substantive condition formed by the rule of the exhaustion of local remedies has been circumscribed in the *ELSI* case as the essence of the claim having been 'brought before the competent tribunals and pursued as far as permitted by local law and procedures, and without success'.[566] By way of analogy, this would mean that the Community law-remedy of State liability would not be available, as long as a decision breaching Community law, would still be subject to appeal under national law.

Yet, it is questionable whether this principle of international subsidiarity can be transferred to the Community legal order. The Court has already had the opportunity to clarify that possible reliance on the direct effect of a

---

[566] ICJ, *Elettronica Sicula* [1989] ICJ reports, at para. 59.

provision of Community law in the framework of national procedural rules does not rule out the availability of the remedy of State liability.[567] Therefore, primary and secondary legal protection may go hand in hand,[568] since the Community legal order is characterised by the fact that national remedies and the remedy of State liability[569] sit side by side. Indeed this insight could serve as an argument for the inclusion of national courts of lower instance for the purposes of State liability.

On the other hand, the Court's reasoning in *Köbler* suggests that this complementary nature is superseded when it comes to breaches of Community law by the judiciary which is justified by the specific nature of the judiciary. This follows from the Court's emphasis on the possibility to remedy a breach of Community law by a lower instance court by simply appealing the decision of the latter. The attribution of an exceptional character to the remedy of State liability for judicial wrongs also points into the same direction.[570] Clearly, the remedy of State liability was no longer confined to exceptional cases if the conduct of the large number of national courts of lower instance could also give rise to it.

For these reasons it seems unlikely that the Court will extend its State liability jurisprudence to national courts of lower instance. Instead, the *Köbler* judgment supports the conclusion that State liability for judicial acts is limited to final decisions of national courts of last instance.[571]

4.1.2 *What is a court of last instance for the purposes of State liability?*

Just as the standard of liability applied in connection with judicial wrongs, the answer to the question of which courts qualify as courts of last instance is decisive for the actual scope of State liability for judicial acts. The definition of a court of last instance under Article 234(3) of the EC Treaty afforded by the ECJ's jurisprudence lends itself as a starting point.[572]

---

[567] ECJ, Case C-150/99 *Stockholm Lindöpark* [2001] ECR I-493, at paras. 35 et seq.

[568] Ossenbühl, op. cit. n. 163, at p. 611.

[569] See ECJ, Joined Cases C-192 to 218/95 *Comateb* [1997] ECR I-165, at paras. 31-34, and Case C-66/95 *Eunice Sutton* [1997] ECR I-2163, at paras. 33 et seq.

[570] Kluth, loc. cit. n. 326, at p. 397.

[571] Ibid.; cf., also Classen, loc. cit. n. 262, at p. 819, who writes that 'it would seem that courts of lower instance could not be held liable'. But it is clear that it is not about the liability of a court, but rather of the State for the conduct of its courts.

[572] Like this Wegener, loc. cit. n. 333, at p. 797 (n. 67).

Article 234(3) of the EC Treaty refers to 'a court or tribunal of a Member State against whose decisions there is no judicial remedy under national law' which is obliged to refer questions on the interpretation of Community law to the ECJ. The wording is unclear as to whether a concrete or abstract view should prevail when determining the existence of a court of last instance. Thus, the question whether this obligation would only cover organisational courts of last instance such as supreme courts, or instead also extend to courts, which in a given case, act as a court of last instance due to the absence of further remedies available under national procedural law, cannot be answered on the basis of a merely textual approach. Whereas before the Court's judgment in *Lyckeskog*[573] this issue was arguably unsettled,[574] the latter judgment provided the ECJ with the opportunity to take a clear stance in favour of the concrete approach.[575] The Court held that supreme courts are bound by the obligation to refer, as is any other national court or tribunal against whose decision there is no judicial remedy.[576]

Is this approach also adequate for the purposes of State liability, or should the abstract view prevail here with the result that only courts of last instance, which are designated as supreme courts by national laws on court organisation can act as a trigger of State liability? In order to assess whether this wide conception of national courts of last instance can be transferred to the issue of State liability for judicial wrongs, it is important to keep in mind the objective pursued by it. A comprehensive duty to refer for all national courts deciding at last instance is in the interest of the proper appli-

---

573 ECJ, Case C-99/00 *Lyckeskog* [2002] ECR I-4839.

574 Wegener in Calliess and Ruffert, op. cit. n. 167, commentary on Art. 234 of the EC Treaty, at mn. 19; R. Streinz, *Europarecht*, 5th edn. (Heidelberg, C.F. Müller 2001) mn. 562; B. Hofstötter, 'Neues zu vorlageberechtigten und –verpflichteten Gerichten', *ELR* (2002) p. 249 at p. 251 et seq.; see also Lenaerts and Arts, op. cit. n. 13, at mn. 2-042, and Craig and de Búrca, op. cit. n. 97, at p. 438, who argue that the Court would appear to have answered in favour of the concrete theory already in *Costa/ENEL*, n. 57 above. According to Isaac and Blanquet 'la Cour a toujours admis qu'il [Article 234(3) of the EC Treaty] concerne toutes les jurisdictions de dernier resort, même de niveau subalterne [...]'. G. Isaac and M. Blanquet, *Droit communautaire général*, 8th edn. (Paris, A. Colin 2001) p. 338.

575 Th. Groh, 'Auslegung des Gemeinschaftsrechts und Vorlagepflicht nach Art. 234 EG', 13 *EuZW* (2002) p. 460; Hofstötter, loc. cit. n. 574, at p. 252; R. Streinz, *Europarecht*, 6th edn. (Heidelberg, C.M. Müller 2003) mn. 562.

576 ECJ, *Lyckeskog*, n. 573 above, at para. 15.

cation and uniform interpretation of Community law and is capable of preventing a body of national case law that is not in accordance with Community law.[577] Therefore, the duty to refer shall extend to as many national courts as can be possibly subsumed under the notion of a court or tribunal of a Member State against whose decisions there is no judicial remedy under national law (Article 234(3) of the EC Treaty).

As a starting point, it is apparent that this reasoning can only partly be related to the remedy of State liability for judicial wrongs. A wide concept of 'court of last instance' for the purposes of State liability can not prevent the creation of a national case law deviating from the precepts of Community law since the decision taken in primary proceedings as such remains unfettered by State liability proceedings. On the other hand, the incentive to compliance triggered by the remedy of State liability extending to all courts of last instance would be in the interest of the uniform application of Community law. The congruence between the concept of a court of last instance for the purposes of State liability and under Article 234(3) of the EC Treaty would also be suggested by one of the functions of State liability for judicial wrongs, namely to provide for an effective incentive to abide by the duty to refer.[578]

However, the Court's already discerned restrictive tendency with regard to State liability for judicial acts can be raised against the inclusion of last instance courts which at the same time are not supreme courts. Arguably it could be derived from the Court's emphasis on the exceptionality of *Köbler* liability that only the conduct of the highest courts in the national judicial hierarchy shall be relevant for the purposes of State liability. Unlike the rationale underlying the Court's reliance on the concrete theory in *Lyckeskog*, this argument would point to the fact that only a few courts should be 'answerable' by means of State liability.

In addition, a transfer of the concept under Article 234(3) of the EC Treaty to the realm of State liability could appear to be ruled out by the wording of the relevant passages of the *Köbler* judgment, which only make reference to supreme courts.[579] By contrast, the Court in *Lyckeskog* refers

---

[577] Ibid. at para. 14; cf., also the Opinion of AG Tizzano in *Lyckeskog*, n. 573 above, at para. 36.

[578] With regard to this function see Kluth, loc. cit. n. 326, at p. 398.

[579] ECJ, *Köbler*, n. 1 above, at paras. 34 et seq.

to supreme courts and any other national court against whose decision there is no judicial remedy.[580] On the other hand, the Court in *Köbler* was confronted with the conduct of a supreme court and, consequently, may have seen no need for an *obiter dictum* to the extent of importing the *Lyckeskog* formula.

A further argument against the transfer *telle quelle* of the notion of court developed under Article 234(3) of the EC Treaty could be the particular expertise of supreme court judges. It would again, underline the exceptional character of State liability for judicial wrongs if the State could only be held liable for the conduct of the elite of the national judiciary. On the other hand, individuals concerned have no influence on the availability of remedies to supreme courts. It may be that, for instance, due to the fairly low amount involved in a given case, a court other than a supreme court will be deciding at last instance. However, it would be unreasonable from the viewpoint of an individual whose rights are to be protected, at least indirectly by the remedy of State liability, to be only able to bring a damages action against a non-compliant decision of a supreme court, but not against the decision of another court of last instance.

The conception of State liability for judicial wrongs builds upon the logic that an individual should be able to obtain redress, albeit within restrictive conditions, once another remedy no longer lies against the imputed decision. For this reason, a distinction between supreme courts and other courts of last instances appears artificial. The availability of the remedy of State liability for judicial acts in itself puts an emphasis on the protection of the individual in case of non-compliant judgments. The need for legal relief cannot be devalued when a court of last instance, which is not at the same time a supreme court, has issued a non-compliant judgment. This result is further corroborated by the fact that otherwise it would be possible for the Member States to assign to supreme courts a fairly marginal role in order to reduce the potential instances of State liability for judicial acts.

Consequently, the notion of a court according to Article 234(3) of the EC Treaty can be transferred to the realm of State liability. A judgment of any court of last instance may act as a trigger of State liability.[581] Conversely, if a remedy is still available under national law, and be it only after prior

580 ECJ, *Lyckeskog*, n. 573 above, at para. 15.
581 See also Botella, loc. cit. n. 335, at pp. 293 et seq.

admission by a supreme court,[582] recourse to *Köbler* liability is precluded.

4.2 Conclusion

Both the existing possibility of a non-compliant judgment of a lower instance court being quashed by a court of appeal, as well as the exceptional character of the remedy of State liability for judicial acts which has been emphasised by the Court in *Köbler*, lend strong support to the conclusion that States can be held liable only for the conduct of courts of last instance. The definition of a court of last instance rests on criteria analogous to the Court's case law concerning Article 234(3) of the EC Treaty.

5. Conclusion

With reliance on the specific nature of the judiciary, the judgment in *Köbler* has further raised the already strict standard of liability for the purposes of State liability. Clearly, State liability for judicial acts is devised as an exceptional remedy which is reserved for particularly serious breaches of Community law, namely those which qualify as a manifest infringement of Community law. By setting the standard fairly high, the Court can ensure that the relativity of *res judicata* as a substantive concept is not overstretched. However, the exact implications of the raised standard of liability remain unclear as of yet. In order to determine the existence of a manifest infringement, the Court refers to the criteria familiar from its previous case law, with the exception of the new criterion of a breach of the duty to refer, which is particular to the *judicial* function in the Community legal order. As has been seen, a mere breach of the duty to refer, in itself, will not suffice to give rise to a manifest infringement. However, it may be adduced in order to qualify an otherwise simple breach.

A further element of exceptionality is added by the fact that only courts of last instance may trigger State liability which follows from the Court's reliance on the fact that non-compliant judgments of lower instance courts on appeal may still be quashed. However, judgments of courts of last instance are final by definition, and, as such, are no longer subject to appeal.

---

[582] ECJ, *Lyckeskog*, n. 573 above, at para. 16.

At this stage non-compliance can only be 'remedied' by the subsidiary means of a damages action, which is intended to compensate for the damage suffered. As AG Léger, quoting AG Tesauro in *Brasserie du Pêcheur*,[583] reminds us

> '[...] it is important to bear in mind that, in spite of the considerable advantages which State liability may have for individuals, "reinstating [the] financial content [of the individual's right] is something less, a minimum remedy compared with full substantive reinstatement, which remains the optimum means of protection". Nothing is worth as much as the immediate, direct and substantive protection of the rights which individuals derive from Community law'.[584]

With regard to the concept of a court of last instance it is appropriate to rely on the concrete view developed by the Court in connection with Article 234(3) of the EC Treaty.

On the merits of *Köbler*, the Court underlined its attribution of an exceptional character to the remedy of State liability for judicial wrongs by exhibiting leniency in the application of the standard of manifest infringement. Instead of appraising the two instances of non-compliance inherent in the conduct of the Austrian court taken together, the Court rather chose to assess them in isolation and, consequently, failed to find a manifest infringement.

Setting a high standard of liability, the Court strikes an acceptable balance between the preservation of legal certainty and *res judicata* as its corollary, and individual protection. By contrast, the application of the standard to the case at hand can only be explained by the Court's cautiousness not to upset the co-operational relationship between itself and national courts. As can be gleaned from the remarks by some commentators, holding the State liable in the instant case, bearing all the hallmarks of a landmark case, would have done just that. However, in future cases, when the principle of State liability for judicial wrongs can be regarded as firmly entrenched in the Community legal order, this attitude of leniency may well make place for a more resolute review of national judicial conduct.

---

583 Opinion of AG Tesauro in *Brasserie du Pêcheur*, n. 57 above, at para. 34.

584 Opinion of AG Léger in *Köbler*, n. 1 above, at para. 39.

Chapter VI
NECESSARY INSTITUTIONAL ARRANGEMENTS IN THE MEMBER STATES TO FACILITATE STATE LIABILITY FOR JUDICIAL ACTS – A CASE STUDY ON AUSTRIA

Chapter VI
NECESSARY INSTITUTIONAL ARRANGEMENTS IN THE MEMBER STATES TO FACILITATE STATE LIABILITY FOR JUDICIAL ACTS – A CASE STUDY ON AUSTRIA

In *Köbler*, the Court, in line with its standing case law,[585] leaves it to the Member States to determine the courts competent to hear cases concerning State liability for breaches of Community law.[586] Even though the ruling appears to be unspectacular on this point, it nevertheless leads to a number of intricate legal issues, which the Member States are called upon to resolve. It is beyond the scope of the present work to give a comparative overview of the legal situations with regard to the competent courts in matters of State liability in all of the Member States. Instead, the sensitive choices to be made by national legislatures and, in case of the latter's passivity, by national judges will be illustrated by a case study on the applicable legal regime in Austria, where a comprehensive solution for the competence issues of State liability for judicial acts is yet to be achieved. The issues addressed can be taken as indicative of a set of legal problems which have become particularly prevalent and acute in the aftermath of the *Köbler* judgment and, on a comparable scale, will be faced in the other Member States. The issues discussed in an Austrian legal context can thus *cum grano salis* be transferred to other national legal contexts.

1. Community Law Background

As has been seen, the notion of national procedural autonomy has been confronted with a number of inroads, of various intensity by the ECJ's jurisprudence. Whereas the ECJ has placed heavy reliance on the concept of effectiveness in connection with remedies available in the Member States, its case law on the question of the competent courts and authorities called upon to decide in matters of Community law is characterised by restraint.

[585] See 1. below.
[586] ECJ, *Köbler*, n. 1 above, at para. 59.

The judgment in *Dorsch Consult*[587] is unambiguous in leaving it for the national legal systems to determine which court or tribunal has jurisdiction to hear disputes involving individual rights derived from Community law.[588] At the same time the Court stressed the need for an effective protection of these rights which the Member States must ensure, and reserved to itself a review of effectiveness.[589] Apart from this reservation, the ECJ will not interfere in questions of competence.[590] Thus, a provision of a directive requiring the adoption of national measures ensuring an effective review of decisions in the field of public service contracts, without indicating which national bodies are to have competence, cannot be interpreted as being directly effective in the sense that appeals bodies competent in other areas of public procurement should also have competence in the field of public service contracts.[591] Whereas the judgment in *Dorsch Consult* concerned a *lacuna* in national law with respect to the designation of a body competent for appeals with regard to public service contracts, the *Connect Austria* case[592] was about national law in effect excluding a remedy to a suitable appeals body, which in principle could have been competent. Such a rule of national law – and be it of constitutional rank – will have to be set aside *qua* primacy of Community law.

The dispute in *Connect Austria* involved Article 5a(3) of Directive 90/387/EEC – a provision equal to that at issue in *Dorsch Consult*[593] – according to which Member States are required to provide for suitable appeals mechanisms against decisions of national regulatory authorities in the field of telecommunications. According to Austrian law, the competent national regulatory authority was established as a collegiate authority in the meaning of Article 133(4) of the Austrian Federal Constitutional Law. Pursuant to this very article, the *Verwaltungsgerichtshof* shall have no jurisdiction to review cases decided by collegiate authorities, whose members include at

587 ECJ, Case C-54/96 *Dorsch Consult* [1997] ECR I-4961.
588 Ibid. at para. 40.
589 Ibid.
590 Ibid.
591 Ibid. at paras. 41 to 46.
592 ECJ, Case C-462/99 *Connect Austria* [2003] ECR 5197.
593 Cf., the insofar uncontested submission of the European Commission in the proceedings in *Connect Austria*, which is recited in the opinion of AG Geelhoed in *Connect Austria*, n. 592 above, at para. 31.

least one judge, unless the admissibility of an action before the *Verwaltungsgerichtshof* is expressly stipulated by means of a law. In the absence of measures implementing Article 5a(3) into Austrian law, as well as of an express stipulation to the extent that the *Verwaltungsgerichtshof* would have competence, decisions of the national regulatory authority could only be appealed to the Constitutional Court (*Verfassungsgerichtshof*). While the *Verwaltungsgerichtshof*, according to Austrian law is competent to exercise a *comprehensive* review of decisions of authorities of lower instance, the competences of the *Verfassungsgerichtshof* only cover what is being referred to as '*Sonderverwaltungsgerichtsbarkeit*'.[594] Therefore, pursuant to Article 144 of the Austrian Federal Constitutional Law, applicants challenging a decision of an administrative authority are confined to raising the violation of a right guaranteed by a provision of constitutional law[595] or the violation of a right following the application of an unconstitutional law, an illegal regulation or an illegal international treaty. Apart from these grounds, a comprehensive review of an administrative decision is not possible.

Against this legal background the ECJ held that an appeal to the *Verfassungsgerichtshof* available under Austrian law could not be said to constitute a suitable appeals mechanism in the sense of Article 5a(3) of Directive 90/387/EEC.[596] Subsequently, the Court reiterated the obligation on the Member States including their courts to give full effect to the provisions of a directive, which, if necessary, would include setting aside a provision of national law which could lead to a result contrary to a given directive.[597] In conclusion, the ECJ held that a national court, which would be competent if not prevented by a provision of national law explicitly excluding its competence, is required to set aside this provision of national law.[598]

The distinction between the judgments in *Dorsch Consult* and *Connect Austria* is a very subtle one and, indeed, not free from inconsistencies. In

---

[594] For this notion see T. Öhlinger, *Verfassungsrecht*, 5th edn. (Vienna, WUV 2003) mn. 1049 et seq.

[595] These are subjective rights, which have been conferred on individuals by means of a norm of constitutional rank. See R. Walter and H. Mayer, *Bundesverfassungsrecht*, 9th edn. (Vienna, Manz 2000) mn. 1317 et seq.

[596] ECJ, *Connect Austria*, n. 592 above, at para. 37.

[597] Ibid. at paras. 38 to 40.

[598] Ibid. at para. 41.

Connect Austria the Court starts with exercising the effectiveness-review which it had reserved to itself in *Dorsch Consult*. Stating that the *Verfassungsgerichtshof* would be ill-suited to act as an appeals mechanism as required by the applicable directive, it turns to the issue of primacy of Community law. The underlying assumption is that there is, in fact, a suitable appeals mechanism, namely the *Verwaltungsgerichtshof*, would it not be for the fact that its competence has been expressly ruled out by national law. In the Court's reasoning it is clear and self-evident that the *Verwaltungsgerichtshof* should be competent. In this way the Court substitutes the Member States' freedom to decide on a suitable appeals mechanism, albeit within the constraints of its effectiveness-review, by its own decision.

The supremacy argument raised by the Court presupposes that national law could only be framed in terms of attributing competence to the *Verwaltungsgerichtshof*. A national rule excluding the competence of the latter thus has to be set aside, and here one can detect a flaw in the Court´s reasoning: As long as it has not been assigned competences by the legislature, it is by no means clear that the *Verwaltungsgerichtshof* should be competent. Arguably, in *Connect Austria*, Austrian law on suitable appeals mechanisms was equally silent as German law in *Dorsch Consult*. Even so, the Court in *Connect Austria* took the fact of the mere potential of an appeal to the *Verwaltungsgerichtshof* as a basis for the decision of the legislature, whose freedom in matters of competence it had recognised in *Dorsch Consult*. A more pragmatic reading of the *Connect Austria* case would point to the fact that it is concerned with a particular type of authorities, whose decisions under national law either can or cannot be appealed to the *Verwaltungsgerichtshof*.[599] *Tertium non datur*. By way of contrast, the range of possibilities to attribute review powers in the field of public service contracts in *Dorsch Consult* was potentially open-ended.

It is noteworthy that in *Dorsch Consult* the Court follows a reasoning based on the doctrine of direct effect, whereas in *Connect Austria* it is concerned with supremacy. In both cases the respective provisions lacked direct effect, or as the Commission more precisely had pointed out in the course of the proceedings in *Connect Austria*, Article 5a(3) of Directive 90/387/EEC had direct effect with respect to its content, since individuals could

[599] Art. 133(4) of the Austrian Federal Constitutional Law.

derive a right of appeal. However, as far as its procedural aspects were concerned, it lacked direct effect since it was for the Member States to determine the level of the authorities competent to hear appeals.[600] The lack of direct effect means that a claim cannot be based on the relevant provision of the directive in question by an individual. Positively formulated, an individual may rely on a provision of a directive and, hence, of *Community law* against the authorities of the Community and the Member States.[601] By way of contrast, supremacy entails that a provision of national law has to be set aside, as a result of which a right derived from Community law can be exercised, as a rule within a national procedural context.[602] Obviously, it is inherent in the concept of supremacy that national law also has to give way to Community law if the latter does not fulfil the criteria for direct effect. In a *Connect Austria* or *Dorsch Consult*-like situation these insights put two alternative solutions in the hands of the Court: On the one hand, it may hold the inexistence of direct effect and may hence take recourse to the principle of conform interpretation, and in the last instance to the doctrine of State liability. On the other hand, it can – in the face of the inexistence of direct effect – find in favour of supremacy and thus pave the way for a remedy in principle existing under national law, but being ruled out by a provision of national law.

In his opinion in *Connect Austria*, AG Geelhoed closely followed the *Dorsch Consult* line of reasoning. Having established the non-transposition of Article 5a(3) of Directive 90/387/EEC in Austria[603] as well as the insufficiency of the limited review by the *Verfassungsgerichtshof*,[604] he went on to tackle the issue of direct effect. In the light of the wording of Article 5a(3) as well as the Court's jurisprudence and in particular the judgment in *Dorsch Consult*, according to which it is the Member States' prerogative to designate competent courts, he denied the direct effect of the provision at hand.[605] Examining the possibility of a conform interpretation he hinted at the clear wording of Article 133(4) of the Austrian Federal

---

[600] Opinion of AG Geelhoed in *Connect Austria*, n. 592 above, at para. 31.

[601] Lenaerts and van Nuffel, op. cit. n. 80, at mn. 17-050.

[602] H. Lattenmayer-Latyer, 'Connect-Urteil des EuGH: Anwendungsvorrang von Richtlinien', *ecolex* (2003) p. 722 at p. 723.

[603] Opinion of AG Geelhoed in *Connect Austria*, n. 592 above, at para. 41.

[604] Ibid. at para. 49.

[605] Ibid. at paras. 51 to 53.

Constitution, which would require an express empowerment of the *Verwaltungsgerichtshof* by means of a law; finding in favour of a competence of the *Verwaltungsgerichtshof* in the absence of an empowering provision would thus be an interpretation *contra legem*.[606] As a result, he saw individuals confined to claiming damages from the Member State at fault.[607]

To summarise, it is apparent that the Court has in its arsenal, both a sovereignty-friendly and a more intrusive approach with respect to the issue of the designation of competent courts and authorities in the Member States. The judgment in *Connect Austria* demonstrates a more effectiveness-based approach[608] which goes as far as to impinge on the Member States' discretion, with the benefit of making available a forum on the national level, which otherwise would not have been available. It is evidence of the Court´s preparedness to reign in the Member States' prerogatives, if national law otherwise, would not allow to achieve the result prescribed by a directive. On the other hand, AG Geelhoed in following the *Dorsch Consult* reasoning evinces a different view which is informed by the ambition of leaving unfettered the Member States' room for manoeuvre.

It is important to keep in mind the devices available to the Court, all the more so when discussing the necessary institutional arrangements in the Member States with regard to State liability. Both the *Francovich* and the *Brasserie du Pêcheur* judgments reflect the same idea of the separation of powers between the Community and the Member States as does the ruling in *Dorsch Consult*. Whereas the principle of State liability is rooted in Community law, it is on the basis of the rules of national law on liability that States must make reparation for loss and damage caused.[609] These rules of national law are inclusive of the designation of competent courts.[610] Hence, it is for the Member States to designate competent courts, though subject to potentially more intrusive review of its findings by the ECJ in given cases in the future. As has been seen, in its *Köbler* judgment the Court has reiterated this case law.[611]

---

[606] Ibid. at paras. 54 to 58.
[607] Ibid. at para. 59.
[608] Cf., in particular ibid. at paras. 38 to 41.
[609] ECJ, *Francovich*, n. 66 above, at para. 42.
[610] Ibid. and ECJ, *Brasserie du Pêcheur*, n. 57 above, at para. 41.
[611] ECJ, *Köbler*, n. 1 above, at para. 59.

2. State Liability for Judicial Acts under Austrian Law

2.1 State liability pursuant to the law on official liability (*Amtshaftungsgesetz* – AHG)

According to the predominant view in Austrian legal doctrine,[612] damages claims by individuals against the Republic of Austria based on non-compliant judicial acts are governed by the *Amtshaftungsgesetz*,[613] which apart from referring to the general tort law rules as set out in the Civil Code[614] (Article 1(1)), contains provisions on the competent courts (Article 9). This view finds support in Article 1(2) of the AHG which defines the State organs capable of potentially triggering State liability as any natural person acting 'in the implementation of laws' (*in Vollziehung der Gesetze*). In parenthesis, it is explicitly clarified that this notion covers both the judiciary and the executive. Whereas State liability pursuant to the AHG thus undoubtedly extends to judgments of courts of lower instance, Article 2(3) of the AHG excludes liability for the judgments of *organisational* courts of last instance. Consequently, judgments of the *Verfassungsgerichtshof*, the *Verwaltungsgerichtshof* and the Supreme Court (*Oberster Gerichtshof*) cannot give rise to State liability. However, judgments of *functional* courts of last instance may be the subject of damages actions.

The exclusion of organisational courts of last instance is motivated by a number of rationales. Central to the exception is the maxim of *litis finiri opportet*: There has to be an end to litigation and therefore a potential cascade of actions for damages has to be avoided. Making organisational courts of last instance accountable *qua* State liability would entail that for instance a judgment of the *Oberster Gerichtshof* in secondary proceedings in itself could give rise to a new damages claim, and so forth.[615] In addition, it is said to be in the interest of legal certainty that proceedings should come to

---

[612] Funk, loc. cit. n. 365, at p. 556; A. Lengauer, 'Haftung eines Mitgliedstaates für die Verletzung von EG-Recht', *ÖJZ* (1997) p. 81 at p. 86; and Solar, op. cit. n. 260, at p. 126 and p. 151 with further references.

[613] BGBl. No. 20/1949, as most recently amended by BGBl. I No. 194/1999.

[614] *Allgemeines Bürgerliches Gesetzbuch*, JGS Nr. 946/1811, as most recently amended by BGBl. I No. 91/2003.

[615] B. Jud, 'Staatshaftung für judikatives Unrecht', *ecolex* (2003) p. 385 at p. 386 with further references.

an end when having reached organisational courts of last instance.[616] Finally, and somewhat connected to the latter point, the particular role of organisational courts of last instance, in the procedure should be emphasised by making it impossible to indirectly review their decisions in State liability proceedings.[617]

Excluding organisational courts of last instance for the purpose of State liability openly contradicts the ECJ's ruling in *Köbler* which, considering the potential liability of Austria for a judgment of the *Verwaltungsgerichtshof* and, as a matter of principle although not in the given case, answering in the affirmative, presupposes the possibility of damages actions against the State for non-compliant decisions of its organisational courts of last instance. State liability for judicial acts as a principle of primary Community law, albeit not expressly provided for in the Treaty, takes precedence over national law contrary to it. Consequently, Article 2(3) of the AHG, insofar as it precludes State liability for judgments of organisational courts of last instance, has to be set aside *qua* primacy of Community law, notwithstanding any obligations incumbent on the national legislature to remedy this provision of the AHG contravening Community law.[618]

Setting aside Article 2(3) of the AHG paves the way for State liability for judicial acts of organisational courts of last instance. Damages actions can now be brought, subject to the conditions established by national law, including rules on the competent courts. Pursuant to Article 9(1) of the AHG the competence in matters of State liability comes to lie with the courts of first instance in civil matters (*Landesgerichte*). It will be remembered that also the request for a preliminary ruling in *Köbler* emanated from a *Landesgericht*. The puzzling consequence of the extension of State liability to acts of the judiciary in *Köbler* therefore is that a court of first instance is called upon to decide on the compatibility with Community law of judgments of organisational supreme courts.[619] Quite apart from the specificities of the legal situation in Austria, this will be a typical consequence of the Köbler *judgment*. From a functional perspective a court of first instance

---

[616] Ibid. with further references; Walter and Mayer, op. cit. n. 595, at mn. 531.

[617] Jud, loc. cit. n. 615, at p. 386; Walter and Mayer, op. cit. n. 595, at mn. 531.

[618] See also Solar, op. cit. n. 260, at p. 148; Lengauer, loc. cit. n. 612, at p. 86; Öhlinger, op. cit. n. 594, at mn. 630.

[619] G. Wilhelm, 'Staatshaftung für judikatives Unrecht oder Saturnalien des Schadenersatzes', *ecolex* (2003) p. 733.

is thereby transformed into a supreme court, whenever the question of State liability stemming from an alleged incompatibility of a decision of an organisational court of last instance is at issue. Thus, the national court organisation is fundamentally put into disarray, implying a transfer of powers from national supreme courts to the lower national courts.

However, this natural and yet – viewed from the perspective of the Member States – avoidable[620] consequence of the *Köbler* judgment is less puzzling than it may appear at first sight. In fact it can be conceptualised as part of the ECJ's empowerment strategy of national courts of lower instance, rooted in at least two phenomena.

Firstly, as has already been seen in the discussion of the Court's ruling in *Simmenthal II*,[621] in the interest of supremacy and effectiveness of Community law, a national court of lower instance had to set aside a national rule of constitutional rank. No longer was there a need to await a decision of the *Corte costituzionale* on the unconstitutionality and hence incompatibility with Community law of a national law. Quite to the contrary, a national court of lower instance seized of the case and convinced of the incompatibility with Community law of a national measure had to set aside the latter of its own motion. Viewed from a national perspective, this obviously entailed a significant power drain from a constitutional court to a court of lower instance.

Secondly, the very idea of empowerment of national courts of lower instance is inherent in the spirit of the preliminary reference procedure. It affords courts of lower instance with the possibility of explicitly circumventing decisions of national supreme courts not in conformity with Community law, which they would be bound to observe on account of national law. Instead of paying deference to a decision of a national court of last instance and running the risk of not complying with Community law, courts of lower instance may make use of their limited review powers attributed to them by means of Article 234(2) of the EC Treaty, albeit in the formalised way of asking the ECJ for a preliminary ruling on a given matter. Thus, national courts are afforded the possibility to escape national judicial hierarchies[622] with important consequences for the role of organisational courts of last instance.

---

620 See 2.2 and 2.3 below.

621 Cf., Chapter II.2.2.1 above.

622 Alter, op. cit. n. 17, at p. 47.

Already at an early stage Member States were acutely aware of the 'subversive' potential of the enabling provision of Article 234(2) of the EC Treaty for national rules on court organisation.[623] However, the ECJ was firm in rejecting any attempts to restrict the right of national lower instance courts to refer questions to the ECJ. A ruling of a superior national court, which is binding upon other courts by operation of national law, can not deprive a court of lower instance of its power to refer questions to the ECJ.[624] To be sure, this does not have any bearing on the question of national remedies which may be available against a decision of a court referring a question to the ECJ.[625] Only in the infrequent cases where the decision to refer is appealed to an organisational court of last instance will it be possible to foreclose the referral of a lower instance court. As a consequence, the preliminary reference procedure has had significant constitutional implications on the Member State level and has contributed to a re-allocation of powers within the national judiciaries, from the national courts of last instance to lower national courts.[626]

This re-allocation may have benefited from the different self-conceptions of national courts of last instance and national courts of lower instance respectively. Whereas the former, in a typological abstraction, as final protectors of the respective national legal orders, are particularly sensitive to potentially disruptive influences of Community law, the latter tend to be more concerned with the particular cases which they have to decide, without having to have in mind the 'general good' of their national legal orders.[627] According to Alter this particular self-conception of organisational courts of last instance can also explain their reticence to refer: many supreme courts would only send technical cases to the ECJ and no constitutional court would have ever referred a case to the ECJ.[628] The first

[623] See the subject-matter of the disputes in the *Rheinmühlen* cases: ECJ, Case 166-73 *Rheinmühlen I* [1974] ECR 33 and Case 146-73 *Rheinmühlen II* [1974] ECR 139.

[624] ECJ, *Rheinmühlen I*, n. 623 above, at para. 4 and *Rheinmühlen II*, n. 623 above, at para. 3.

[625] ECJ, *Rheinmühlen II*, n. 623 above, at para. 3.

[626] Tridimas, loc. cit. n. 42, at p. 10.

[627] See Alter, op. cit. n. 17, at pp. 48 et seq. However, caution is due when ascribing a particular set of motives to the various levels of the judiciary. *As a group* judges may indeed represent a typical set of values (ibid. at p. 45), whereas the individual judge may be driven by entirely different motives.

[628] Alter, op. cit. n. 17, at p. 54 et seq.

assumption is at least doubtful in the light of a wealth of cases originating from national supreme courts. In addition, the distinction between technical and non-technical cases cannot hold. Even presuming consensus exists as to what a technical case actually is, cases at face value involving clear-cut technical questions, may have further-reaching implications.[629] As regards the second assumption, recent years have seen references also originate from national constitutional courts.[630] In addition, the attitudes of the German *Bundesverfassungsgericht* and the Austrian *Verfassungsgerichtshof* with regard to the duty to refer as being protected by the right to the *gesetzlicher Richter* is also noteworthy in this respect.[631] Thus, the traditional reservation of organisational courts of last instance to fully co-operate with the ECJ seems, no longer, to be a dogma carved in stone.

The danger of non-compliant rulings by organisational courts of last instance is contained by the obligation to refer (Article 234(3) of the EC Treaty). However, should a court of last instance, despite its obligation, fail to refer and therefore set the tone for courts of lower instance to follow a non-compliant interpretation of Community law, the ability of lower instance courts to control higher-ranking courts by means of the Article 234-procedure still remains intact.

Coming back to the legal situation in Austria, it would eventually be the role of the competent senate of the *Oberster Gerichtshof* to decide in matters of State liability in the last instance.[632] On the national level the problem of a court of lower instance sitting in judgment over an organisational court of last instance is thereby alleviated. At the same time two further problems come to the surface:

On the one hand, it follows from a systematic interpretation of the Austrian Federal Constitutional Law that the three courts of last instance – the

---

[629] The *Connect Austria* case, n. 592 above, may serve as a textbook example in point. Only at face value it concerned a dispute on the allocation of frequencies for mobile communications services.

[630] Cf., the emerging reference-friendly attitude of the Austrian *Verfassungsgerichtshof* finding expression in the references in Case C-143/99 *Adria-Wien Pipeline GmbH* [2001] ECR I-8365, Case C-171/01 *Wählergruppe Gemeinsam Zajedno* [2003] ECR I-4301 and Case C-465/00 *Rechnungshof* [2003] ECR I-4989. See also Botella, loc. cit. n. 335, at p. 305, who notes a similar determination with the French Conseil d'Etat.

[631] See Chapter II.2 above.

[632] Art. 4 of the Act on Jurisdiction (*Jurisdiktionsnorm*), RGBl. No. 111/1895, as most recently amended by BGBl. I No. 114/2003.

Verfassungsgerichtshof, the *Verwaltungsgerichtshof* and the *Oberster Gerichtshof* – are of equal rank.[633] The competence of the *Oberster Gerichtshof* to indirectly review judgments of the *Verfassungsgerichtshof* and the *Verwaltungsgerichtshof* in the last instance, would upset this co-operative relationship between the courts as intended by the Constitution by attributing review powers over the other courts to the *Oberster Gerichtshof*.[634] An amendment to the constitution would thus be required.

On the other hand, the *Oberster Gerichtshof* would have to act as a judge in its own case as soon as a damages action arose which was based on an earlier non-compliant judgment given by itself. With regard to courts of lower instance the aim of the AHG to avoid such instances is clear: Pursuant to Article 9(4) of the AHG a court of first instance shall not hear a State liability-case involving a judgment issued by itself. In such an instance another court of first instance which, under normal circumstances would not be competent *ratione loci,* shall be designated by the competent court of appeals. On a more fundamental level, reservations flow from Article 6(1) of the ECHR,[635] which – among others – requires the impartiality of tribunals adjudicating in civil rights-cases.

It is settled case law that

> 'the existence of impartiality [...] must be determined according to a subjective test, that is, on the basis of the personal conviction of a particular judge in a given case, and also according to an objective test, that is, ascertaining whether the judge offered guarantees sufficient to exclude any legitimate doubt in this respect'.[636]

In assessing the composition and organisation of a tribunal, the ECrtHR will take an objective approach with regard to impartiality, and will exam-

---

[633] Funk, loc. cit. n. 365, at p. 556; in particular with regard to the position of the *Verfassungsgerichtshof* cf., E.-W. Böckenförde, 'Verfassungsgerichtsbarkeit: Strukturfragen, Organisation, Legitimation', 52 *NJW* (1999) p. 9 at p. 14.

[634] Funk, loc. cit. n. 365, at p. 556.

[635] In Austria, the ECHR takes constitutional rank. See Öhlinger, op. cit. n. 594, at mn. 681.

[636] ECrtHR, *Piersack* v. *Belgium*, judgment of 1 October 1982, A.53, at para. 31; *De Cubber* v. *Belgium*, judgment of 26 October 1984, A.86, at para. 26; *Hauschildt* v. *Denmark*, judgment of 24 May 1989, A.154, at para. 46; *McGonnell* v. *United Kingdom*, judgment of 8 February 2000, Reports of Judgments and Decisions 2000-II, at para. 48.

ine whether the fear that a tribunal lacks impartiality is 'objectively justified'.[637] Thus, for instance in the *Piersack*[638] case the president of the tribunal at issue had been involved in an earlier stage of the proceedings as a public prosecutor, which made the tribunal partial. The judgment in *De Cubber*[639] concerned comparable instances of partiality. Finally, in *Procola*[640] involvement in an advisory capacity of judges later acting in a judicial capacity in the same case made the Luxembourg *Conseil d'Etat* partial. Along the same lines the *Verfassungsgerichtshof* held the involvement of only one member of a tribunal in the review of an authorising decision, in whose issuance this member had participated, to be incompatible with Article 6(1) of the ECHR.[641]

With regard to impartiality relating to two different proceedings which are legally distinct although factually connected (as is the case when a non-compliant judgment is indirectly challenged by means of a damages action), there is only limited guidance in the case law of the Strasbourg instances. A purposive interpretation of Article 6(1) of the ECHR would also advise the application of the Court's case law to instances where factually connected proceedings are at stake. A different interpretation would put applicants at a procedural disadvantage, the outcome of the secondary proceedings being overshadowed by a potentially biased court. Consequently, an action for damages could no longer be considered an effective remedy. To solve the ensuing problem of defining what the concept of factually connected proceedings should in fact encompass, would be dispensable at least in the present context, where the same set of facts determine the primary as well as the secondary proceedings. It would, therefore, seem well-founded to transpose the ECrtHR's case law concerning impartiality with respect to different stages of one and the same case, to a situation which involves two legally distinct cases, which are, nonetheless based on the same facts. However, the case of *Masson and van Zon*[642] may be read

[637] P. van Dijk and G. van Hoof, *Theory and Practice of the European Convention on Human Rights*, 3rd edn. (The Hague, Kluwer 1998) pp. 454 et seq.

[638] ECrtHR, *Piersack* v. *Belgium*, n. 636 above, at paras. 30 et seq.

[639] ECrtHR, *De Cubber* v. *Belgium*, n. 636 above, at paras. 29 et seq.

[640] ECrtHR, *Procola* v. *Luxembourg*, judgment of 28 September 1995, A.326, at paras. 45 et seq.

[641] *Verfassungsgerichtshof*, VfSlg. 13.553/1993.

[642] EComHR, *Masson and van Zon* v. *The Netherlands*, decision of 4 July 1994 (B 15346/89).

as a precedent pointing in the opposite direction. In this case the European Commission of Human Rights, as it then was, was not concerned as to whether the impartiality of a judge was placed in jeopardy by the fact that he was sitting on the bench both in a partial acquittal/abandonment of the proceedings and in the subsequent proceedings concerning compensation for wrongful imprisonment. The ECrtHR itself did not have to pronounce on this issue, since it denied the applicability of Article 6 of the ECHR in the given case. However, the main difference between this case and the constellation of interest here, seems to be that in *Masson and van Zon* the judges had to decide on the compensatory corollaries of a *correct* legal decision, the consequence of which was the unlawfulness of prior imprisonment. The judgment holding acquittal/abandonment of the proceedings was not under review, and not even indirectly as is the case in the State liability context under discussion here. In the latter instance, the State liability court, as a preliminary question, will have to answer whether or not a sufficiently serious breach of Community law has been effectuated by the court deciding in the primary proceedings. Hence, the participation of one and the same judge in the primary and secondary proceedings will give rise to doubts as to the impartiality of the tribunal, since an unbiased indirect review of the primary judgment seems to be forestalled by conservative tendencies present on the bench. The situation at hand thus needs to be distinguished from the case in *Masson and van Zon*.

If one accepts the application of the ECrtHR's impartiality-concept to the *Oberster Gerichtshof* deciding in the case allegedly giving rise to State liability, and the State liability case itself, the involvement of judges in the State liability proceedings, who have already sat in the initial phase would be unacceptable. The problem becomes more subtle when one assumes that such double involvements of judges can be avoided. Could one then still entertain doubts as to the impartiality of the *Oberster Gerichtshof*? Having the *Oberster Gerichtshof* sit in both instances has been claimed to be unacceptable.[643] To legally substantiate these concerns on the basis of the ECrtHR's case law is difficult, though. The problem reduces down to the question of whether the 'nobody shall be a judge in his own cause' rule is intended to avoid the involvement of particular objectionable judges, or also the involvement of one and the same court in related proceedings. One

[643] Funk, loc. cit. n. 365, at p. 556.

could argue that already the involvement of the same court could potentially lead to a bias on the part of the judges in the secondary proceedings, who may be concerned with upholding a decision taken by the court of which they are members. Such a potential personal bias (= subjective approach), in itself would not suffice, since the threshold with regard to personal partiality has been set fairly high: The impartiality of a judge will be presumed as long as the contrary has not been proved.[644] To prove conservative tendencies as well as their reflection in the decision-making process will be difficult, if not utterly impossible. With a view to the purpose of Article 6(1) of the ECHR, which is to avoid a biased decision,[645] the institutional setting under review seems at least prone to biased decisions and, therefore, objectionable under this very provision. The court organisation in this point, is such as to *structurally* give rise to doubts about impartiality.[646] It is in this respect that it falls short of Article 6(1) of the ECHR, and thus implicitly, of the Austrian Federal Constitutional Law, of which the ECHR forms part. Therefore in this view, even attributing the competence to decide in the last instance in State liability proceedings to a specialised senate of the *Oberster Gerichtshof* could not satisfactorily resolve the problem that nobody shall be a judge in his own cause.

[644] See for instance ECrtHR, *Piersack* v. *Belgium*, n. 636 above, at paras. 14 et seq.

[645] van Dijk and van Hoof, op. cit. n. 637, at p. 452.

[646] It is noteworthy that a strict conception of impartiality is also advocated by AG Léger in *Baustahlgewebe*. Being confronted with the problem of the CFI having rendered a judgment outside the reasonable time-limit required by Art. 6 of the ECHR and this very same court's simultaneous competence to grant compensation for damages pursuant to Art. 288(2) of the EC Treaty, he reasons as follows: '[I]t is not possible to entrust a judicial body with the task of determining whether its own conduct is wrongful or unlawful. This would unquestionably be contrary to the principle of an impartial tribunal laid down in Article 6(1) of the Convention [the ECHR]. I think it would be difficult to avoid such a conflict by referring the case back to a differently constituted court from that which gave the original judgment because, if we adopt the approach taken by the Strasbourg Court, a change in the constitution of a court may not be enough to remove entirely the impression of partiality which would arise from a judgment concerning the court which it itself delivers'. Cf., Opinion of AG Léger in *Baustahlgewebe*, n. 456 above, at para. 67. For AG Léger this situation is a perfect illustration of the partiality of a court, bearing in mind the ECrtHR's attaching a certain importance even to appearances (ibid. at n. 34).

2.2 State liability pursuant to Article 137 of the Austrian Federal Constitutional Law

Contrary to the mainstream of Austrian judicial practice and the majority of writers' support for the latter, the *Verfassungsgerichtshof* alleges its exclusive competence in cases of State liability involving judicial acts.[647] In this respect it relies on Article 137 of the Austrian Federal Constitutional Law which provides for a *subsidiary* competence of the *Verfassungsgerichtshof*. Therefore, this very article will only apply when neither an ordinary court nor an administrative authority has been attributed competence by the legislature.[648] The *Verfassungsgerichtshof* restrictively construes the provisions of competence of the AHG and relies on the rationale of Article 2(3), from which the absence of competence of ordinary courts would become apparent.[649] Its reasoning has the support of a minority of writers.[650] It is inherent in this solution that Article 2(3) of the AHG can remain unfettered and need not be set aside *qua* primacy, since in this understanding it only restricts the competence of *ordinary* courts with regard to non-compliant judicial acts of organisational courts of last instance, but does not exclude their review as such. *Mutatis mutandis,* just as the *Oberster Gerichtshof*, the *Verfassungsgerichtshof* would face the problem of impartiality, once it is concerned with a State liability claim based on its own prior judgment. Since there is no review of the decisions of the *Verfassungsgerichtshof*, its decisions are final.

---

[647] Cf., *Verfassungsgerichtshof*, judgment of 10 October 2003, A 36/00.

[648] Cf., the wording of Art. 137 of the Austrian Federal Constitution: 'Der Verfassungsgerichtshof erkennt über vermögensrechtliche Ansprüche an den Bund, die Länder, die Bezirke, die Gemeinden und Gemeindeverbände, *die weder im ordentlichen Rechtsweg auszutragen, noch durch Bescheid einer Verwaltungsbehörde zu erledigen sind*'. ['The Constitutional Court pronounces on pecuniary claims of the Federation, the States, the Districts, the Counties and County Associations *which cannot be settled by ordinary legal process nor be liquidated by the ruling of an administrative authority*' – my translation] (emphasis added), as well as H. Mayer, *Das österreichische Bundes-Verfassungsrecht*, 3rd edn. (Vienna, Manz 2002) p. 411.

[649] *Verfassungsgerichtshof*, judgment of 10 October 2003, A 36/00, under II.3.

[650] So for instance Öhlinger, op. cit. n. 594, at mn. 676; T. Öhlinger and M. Potacs, *Gemeinschaftsrecht und staatliches Recht*, 2nd edn. (Vienna, Orac 2001) p. 176; see also Walter and Mayer, op. cit. n. 595, at mn. 1316/1, who assume a competence of the *Verfassungsgerichtshof*, acknowledging at the same time the practice of ordinary Austrian courts to take for granted their competence.

2.3 Concluding assessment

As has become apparent, the *Köbler* judgment in conjunction with the competence of ordinary courts in matters of State liability in a given Member State leads to an empowerment of national courts of lower instance to sit in judgment over judicial pronouncements of organisational courts of last instance. On the other hand, this is not a necessary consequence, since, in line with the judgment in *Dorsch Consult*, the Member States remain free to designate alternative fora to settle disputes with regard to non-compliant judgments of organisational courts of last instance. So for example, an organisational court of last instance itself may be given competence to decide. At any rate, national institutional arrangements have to comply with the proviso of effectiveness and in this respect the judgment in *Connect Austria* can be read as a shot across the bows. The current legal situation in Austria is characterised by relative uncertainty with regard to competences, which, on the national level, gives rise to concerns over legal certainty.

In addressing the problem of competent courts for State liability for judicial acts issued by organisational courts of last instance, Member States face a basic legislative choice: Either they may confer competences on ordinary courts, or on organisational courts of last instance. The following is a discussion of the pros and cons of these two alternatives.

Having courts of lower instance sit in judgment over organisational courts of last instance can give rise to constitutional problems. However, from a national perspective the legitimacy of the decisions of the former courts can be enhanced by means of the preliminary reference procedure.[651] *In fact*, it would then be for the ECJ to decide, while the national court of lower instance would only implement its ruling.[652] On the other hand, Article 234(2) of the EC Treaty only *authorises* national courts of lower instance to refer questions to the ECJ, without there being a requirement to do so. Thus, the legitimating effect of this very procedure hinges on the preparedness of national courts to refer. On the Community level nothing sug-

[651] Cf., the Opinion of AG Léger in *Köbler*, n. 1 above, who argues at para. 111 that a guarantee of impartiality could be identified in the mechanism of judicial co-operation provided for by the preliminary reference procedure.

[652] On the binding effect of preliminary rulings on the referring court, which coincides with the binding effect of the Community law provisions interpreted by the Court, see Lenaerts and Arts, op. cit. n. 13, at mn. 6-036.

gests extending the duty to refer to national courts of lower instance in this particular situation *praeter legem*.[653] However, *qua* national law, national courts could be required to refer to the ECJ in order to attenuate the fact that national courts of lower instance decide on the compliance or non-compliance of the decisions of organisational supreme courts.

Yet, another problem may arise in connection with the empowerment of national courts of lower instance which relates to the length of proceedings: In general, questions for a preliminary ruling should be addressed to the Court at as early a stage as possible in order to avoid an unwarranted delay in the proceedings.[654] All the more this must be true in the framework of secondary proceedings concerning State liability which will possibly involve the referral for a second preliminary ruling as to the conformity with Community law of the ruling in the primary proceedings. Currently, the average waiting time to obtain a preliminary ruling from the ECJ amounts to roughly 2 years.[655] Indeed the ECrtHR has served the Community a 'clean bill of health' with regard to the system of preliminary rulings: The period of time during which a case is pending in preliminary rulings proceedings with the ECJ shall not be taken into consideration for assessing the reasonableness of the time of proceedings according to Article 6 of the ECHR.[656] The level of scrutiny may have to be increased in the light of two related references for a preliminary rulings which are introduced at a late

[653] Cf., the views of AG Léger in *Köbler*, n. 1 above, who states at para. 112 that '[i]t is not a question of making a reference for a preliminary ruling automatic, but rather of pointing out that such a reference is possible. I do not regard this type of reference as anything other than the expression of a mechanism of judicial cooperation founded on the logic of dialogue and mutual trust between courts'. Note however the Court's preparedness to expand the duty to refer when otherwise the uniformity of Community law, and in particular its uniform validity, would be put in jeopardy. See ECJ, *Foto Frost*, n. 37 above, at paras. 13 et seq.

[654] ECJ, Information note on references by national courts for preliminary rulings, para. 7 (retrieved from <http://www.curia.eu.int/en/instit/txtdocfr/autrestxts/txt8.pdf> – visited on 2 April 2005).

[655] In 2003 the average duration of proceedings in preliminary reference cases amounted to 25.5 months. Since 1999 (21.2 months) there has been a slight but continuous increase in the time required to dispose of preliminary references, which can be explained by a backlog in the docket of the Court. Cf., Annual Report of the European Court of Justice 2003, Annex A, p. 222 and p. 215.

[656] ECrtHR, *Pafitis* v. *Greece*, judgment of 26 February 1998, Reports 1998-I, at para. 95.

stage of the national proceedings. At the same time, the 'chilling effect' of a long procedure before the ECJ for the willingness of national courts to refer cannot be underestimated.[657]

Once proceedings have reached an organisational court of last instance, the problem of impartiality comes to the fore. Again the preliminary reference procedure can act as a device to smooth out this problem by *in fact* delegating the decision to the ECJ.[658]

Turning to the second alternative, namely the reliance on an organisational court of last instance, the very same problem of impartiality, as well as its resolution apply.[659] An obvious advantage of this policy choice would be the obligation *qua* Community law to refer of the organisational court of last instance. In this way, it could be ensured that questions to the ECJ are already put at an early stage with the result of an expeditious procedure. To avoid lengthy litigation would be in the interest of the parties and at the same time of the effective application of Community law. The downside of this alternative is, that an appeal against the decision of the national court would not be available. This problem would become particularly acute if the competent national court fails to observe its duty to refer and issues a non-compliant decision. With regard to the alleged competence of the *Verfassungsgerichtshof* in Austria, the relative reluctance of national constitutional courts to refer also needs to be kept in mind.[660] The only remedy available then would be yet another damages action, which would run contrary to, and even defeat the aim of having a speedy procedure with regard to State liability.

It therefore seems that entrusting organisational courts of last instance, cannot offer sufficient guarantees as to an expeditious procedure. The advantage of having a national system of judicial review in place in the case of the competence of ordinary courts outweighs the mere potentiality of speeding up proceedings in the case of the competence of an organisational court of last instance. At the same time suitable measures should be taken on the national level to encourage courts of lower instance to refer to the ECJ at as early a stage as possible.

---

[657] Tridimas, loc. cit. n. 42, at p. 17 with further references.
[658] See Solar, op. cit. n. 260, at pp. 154 et seq.
[659] Cf., *Verfassungsgerichtshof*, judgment of 10 October 2003, A 36/00, under II.3.
[660] But see also n. 630 under Chapter VI.2.1.

More so, the preliminary reference procedure is a crucial device to ensure the legitimacy of decisions taken. Having the ECJ *de facto* decide in the case of competence of ordinary national courts, from a national perspective evades the problem of circumventing the national court organisation. With regard to the issue of *nemo iudex in causa sua* this very procedure offers a way out of an irresolvable dilemma. In neither of the alternatives discussed the problem of impartiality can be avoided. Even establishing a specialised court of last instance with exclusive competence to hear State liability cases in connection with judicial conduct could not solve this problem. Quite apart from the political unlikeliness of establishing new organisational courts of last instance in the Member States, which would have to coexist with the already existing supreme courts, such a court's judgments could again be made the subject of a new State liability claim, this time directed against the potentially wrongful decision of this very court. Again it would be this very court to decide, this time in *causa sua*. However, *de facto* delegating the decision on State liability to the ECJ would subtract from the acuteness of the problem in all the alternatives discussed. Paraphrasing the ECrtHR's case law, the situation would no longer be such as to create doubts, neither on the basis of the objective nor of the subjective test, about a potential bias of the competent court.

On a more abstract level, this co-operation strategy in the matters of State liability for non-compliant court decisions is probably the most ingenious and effective pull to compliance one could possibly think of: Due to the peculiarities of the national court organisations as well as the *nemo iudex in causa sua*-problem, the legitimacy of the decisions of national courts crucially depends on the legitimising effect of the ECJ's rulings. Thus, in order to achieve a satisfactory resolution of the question of competent courts on the national level, the national legal orders depend on the input from the supra-national level. The interest of the Member States to have in place a constitutionally sound system of indirect review, which complies with international commitments such as the ECHR, in effect converges with the ECJ's interest in compliant national courts, and overall with the effectiveness of Community law. This convergence induced by the Court's *Köbler* judgment comes at the price of factually giving away national powers to the ECJ, albeit within the tight limits set by the exceptional character of the remedy. Whether this device will bear fruit depends on the actual willingness of national courts to refer, as well as, on the Court's preparedness to dispose efficiently of preliminary references.[661]

[661] Indeed excessive reliance on the Article 234-procedure gives rise to a number of efficiency-related doubts. See Tridimas, loc. cit. n. 42, at pp. 16 et seq.; see also J.H.H. Weiler, 'Epilogue: The Judicial Après Nice', in G. de Búrca and J.H.H. Weiler (eds.), *The European Court of Justice* (Oxford, Oxford University Press 2001) p. 215 at pp. 219 et seq., who refers to the preliminary reference-procedure as one of the most remarkable and successful dimensions of the European legal order and European Constitutionalism, which however has come with a number of costs, mostly related to the Court's workload and the ensuing problems of backlog and delays of proceedings ('justice delayed is justice denied') as well as the quality of justice. Against this background Weiler speaks about the ECJ as 'a judicial giant which has successfully positioned itself at the constitutional centre of Europe, a Europe in which national legal orders suddenly feel under threat. In this respect the Court is a (lucky) victim of its own spectacular success' (ibid. at p. 218). In this context cf., also the suggestions *de lege ferenda* of AG Jacobs, who advocates the idea of giving more freedom to the national courts in the application of general principles to which the ECJ should limit itself in answering preliminary references. Opinion of AG Jacobs in Case C-338/95 *Wiener* [1997] ECR I-6495.

Chapter VII
ALTERNATIVE REMEDIES

Chapter VII
ALTERNATIVE REMEDIES

1. *Kühne & Heitz* and an Approach of 'Try Again'?

Whereas the principle of legal certainty as well as its corollary of *res judicata* are recognised in the Community legal order, the judgment in *Kühne & Heitz* has accentuated the relativity of *res judicata*, which may have to give way to the overriding individual interest in a compliant solution of a legal dispute.[662] Given this relativity, it is necessary to consider to what extent it can give rise to an alternative remedy, which can avoid the high standard of liability as set out in *Köbler* by relying on a reopening of the primary proceedings. That there can be another legal avenue apart from State liability is apparent from the case of *Kühne & Heitz* itself. However, to what degree, can reliance be placed on this precedent?

The key to the answer is to be found in the conditions attached to a reopening of the dispute. As has already been discussed in more detail,[663] these are four-pronged: (1) An administrative authority erring in law has the power to reopen the decision; (2) the administrative decision in question has become final as a result of a judgment of a national court ruling at last instance; (3) that judgment is, in the light of a decision given by the Court subsequent to it, based on a misinterpretation of Community law which was adopted without a question being referred for a preliminary ruling under Article 234(3) of the EC Treaty; and (4) the person concerned complained to the administrative body immediately after becoming aware of that decision of the Court.

Whereas the Court seems inclined to confine its ruling to 'the circumstances of the main case',[664] it is apparent that the conditions for reopening the dispute as formulated in *Kühne & Heitz* can have far-reaching implications. True, *Kühne & Heitz* in the first place is about a mistake of an administrative authority, whose decision, has subsequently been confirmed by a

---

[662] See Chapter IV.1.2 above.
[663] See Chapter IV.1.2 above.
[664] ECJ, *Kühne & Heitz*, n. 3 above, at para. 26.

court with the result of attaching the force of *res judicata* to the matter in dispute. In this sense *Kühne & Heitz* is concerned with judicial non-compliance and thus amenable to provide a further remedy against non-compliant judicial conduct.

It has already been observed that the possibility of an extraordinary review of final administrative decisions, as required by the first element of the *Kühne & Heitz*-test is a standard feature of national legal orders.[665] As concerns elements (2) and (3) of the test, both of them are fulfilled in a *Köbler*-like situation:[666] A matter in dispute has become final by means of a decision of a national court of last instance, which – in the light of subsequent case law – proves to be non-compliant. Satisfying element (4), i.e., approaching the competent administrative authority immediately after becoming aware of the Court's judgment, Mr. Köbler could obtain the length-of-service increment.

The Court leaves the back-door open in *Kühne & Heitz* by referring to the requirement that reopening the procedure must not adversely affect the interests of third parties.[667] In doing so the Court demonstrates that what it has in mind, is not an unlimited review of final decisions but rather, a carefully balanced solution for cases where the institutional guarantee of *res judicata* is not in the best interest of the applicant. Typically, there will be no interests of third parties at stake in purely vertical relationships. In such instances 'trying again' in line with the conditions sketched out in *Kühne & Heitz* may be preferable to seeking compensatory justice by attempting to establish a manifest breach of Community law in State liability proceedings before a national court. Nevertheless, the approach in *Kühne & Heitz* presupposes the existence of a judgment of the ECJ, which proves wrong the original interpretation of the national authorities. It is here that the real problem lies in the *Kühne & Heitz*-approach, since it is beyond an individual's reach, as to whether or not there will be a judgment of the ECJ on the same subject-matter. In this sense, the arrival of a judgment is accidental and dependent on parallel litigation on the same subject-matter before national courts as well as on the latters' preparedness to refer. Against

[665] See Chapter IV.1.2 above.

[666] See Komárek, loc. cit. n. 396, at p. 20 et seq., who apparently was the first one to draw attention to this connection between *Köbler* and *Kühne & Heitz*.

[667] ECJ, *Kühne & Heitz*, n. 3 above, at para. 27.

this background opening up primary proceedings will remain simply a hypothetical remedy in many instances.

2. The Action for Infringement

The enforcement of Community law can adequately be depicted by the 'dual vigilance' model: One element of this is the European Commission's concern with the supra-national enforcement of Community law. The other strand of this model is represented by private enforcement before national courts and the ECJ, the latter in exceptional cases only.[668] Whereas private enforcement is effectuated by the doctrines of direct effect and *Francovich* liability, the Commission can enforce Community law by means of the action for infringement.

It has been clear for a long time that, 'the liability of a Member State under Article 169 [now Article 226] arises whatever agency of the State whose action or inaction is the cause of the failure to fulfil its obligations, even in the case of a constitutionally independent institution'.[669] In spite of this *dictum* the practice of the Commission exhibits the utmost hesitance to start infringement proceedings by reason of the fact that a court has breached Community law. AG Tizzano even went so far as to refer to the action for infringement in connection with judicial acts as of a theoretical nature only.[670] Until fairly recently, there have only been two occasions when proceedings have been commenced, which, have subsequently come to a halt before reaching the ECJ.[671] Thus, no case of a judicial infringement of Community law had been decided by the ECJ until late 2003. The case in *Commission* v. *Italy*[672] is the first occasion in which the Court dealt with the question of judicial wrongs in the framework of an Article 226 procedure. It illustrates that the action for infringement can gain practical significance in connection with judicial acts, albeit in narrowly defined instances.

---

[668] Weatherill, loc. cit. n. 27, at p. 89; see also Chapter II above.

[669] ECJ, Case 77/69 *Commission* v. *Belgium* [1970] ECR 237, at para. 15; Case 8/70 *Commission* v. *Italy* [1970] ECR 961, at para. 9.

[670] Opinion of AG Tizzano in *Lyckeskog*, n. 573 above, at para. 65.

[671] For details see Anagnostaras, loc. cit. n. 328, at p. 295; Mortelmans and van de Gronden, loc. cit. n. 562, at pp. 198 et seq.; Solar, op. cit. n. 260, at pp. 107 et seq.

[672] ECJ, *Commission* v. *Italy*, n. 2 above.

2.1 Deficiencies

The action for infringement is objective in nature. Its sole aim is to determine whether or not the defendant Member State has failed to fulfil an obligation under the Treaty.[673] Consequently, it is not in the first place, intended to ensure the protection of individual rights and interests.[674] Individuals have no standing in the Article 226 procedure and are confined to national avenues of contesting non-compliant State conduct, which eventually may reach the ECJ via Article 234 of the EC Treaty. Whereas individuals may bring a complaint before the Commission, the Commission is afforded full discretion whether or not to act upon a complaint.[675] The minor role of individuals is further exacerbated by the structural lack of sufficient investigatory powers of the Commission.[676] Finally, a judgment finding an infringement is purely declaratory of the infringement. Article 228 provides for enforcement options, but these require a second set of proceedings and therefore account for the lapse of a long period between the actual existence of an infringement and the entering into effect of adequate sanctions. Admittedly, the ECrtHR's case law may provide for another pull to compliance: Thus, the Strasbourg court held in *Hornsby* that the omission of a Member State to implement a ruling of the ECJ given in an infringement procedure amounted to a violation of Article 6 of the ECHR.[677] In this way individuals may gain ground in the State-centred action for infringement.

Nevertheless, for the mentioned reasons the action for infringement has rightly been labelled a long and insufficient procedure.[678]

With regard to infringement proceedings concerning breaches of Community law by national courts, there are yet other objections which may be

[673] See Art. 226 of the EC Treaty; Lenaerts and Arts, op. cit. n. 13, at mn. 5-001.

[674] C.W.A. Timmermans, 'Judicial Protection against the Member States: Articles 169 and 177 Revisited', in Curtin and Heukels, op. cit. n. 60, p. 391 at p. 397.

[675] Lenaerts and Arts, op. cit. n. 13, at mn. 5-023.

[676] Timmermans, loc. cit. n. 674, at p. 399.

[677] ECrtHR, *Hornsby* v. *Greece*, judgment of 19 March 1997, Reports 1997-II, paras. 44-45.

[678] Cf., Alter, op. cit. n. 17, at p. 15; D. Waelbrock, 'Treaty Violations and Liability of Member States and the European Community: Convergence or Divergence?', in Curtin and Heukels, op. cit. n. 60, p. 467 at p. 472.

raised. For instance, the judicial co-operation between national courts and the ECJ could be put at risk by the Commission making use of the Article 226-mechanism.[679] Nevertheless, this is more concerned with the delicate balance that has to be struck between compliance and co-operation, by the Commission and the ECJ rather than a principled impossibility to ever have recourse to the action for infringement in connection with judicial conduct. On a more fundamental level, one may feel ill at ease with a largely unaccountable international legal body with weak democratic legitimacy, the European Commission, starting infringement proceedings against a Member State for the conduct of constitutionally independent courts.[680] Yet, similar reservations could be levelled against overturning national laws passed by democratic means, which by now undeniably, is a standard feature of the action for infringement. In this respect the judicial function differs little from the legislature, and both are subject to compliance with Community law.

The deficiencies of the action for infringement in terms of the protection of individual interests have lead to reinforcing their direct enforcement powers in *Francovich*,[681] as well as with regard to judicial wrongs, in *Köbler*. Thus, it may appear surprising to again have recourse to an insufficient procedure in this context. However, the signalling function of a judgment holding that something within the national judiciary is structurally wrong cannot be underestimated and may be of indirect relevance to individuals. The recent judgment in *Commission* v. *Italy* is a first test case in this respect.[682]

2.2 *Commission* v. *Italy*

The legal and factual background in *Commission* v. *Italy* can be summarised as follows. In 1990 an Italian law was passed according to which customs import duties or other taxes levied in contravention of Community law were to be reimbursed only if the corresponding burden had not been passed on

---

[679] P. Kapteyn and P. VerLoren van Themaat, *Introduction to the Law of the European Communities*, 3rd edn. (The Hague, Kluwer 1998) p. 456.

[680] Cf., Hofstötter, loc. cit. n. 491, at p. 65.

[681] Waelbrock, loc. cit. n. 678, at pp. 472 et seq.

[682] Cf., Botella, loc. cit. n. 335, at p. 308.

to third parties. The legal situation prior to this law provided for a legal presumption with regard to commercial entities that the burden had been passed on to third parties, which could only be refuted on the production of specific documents. This presumption led to a reversal of the burden of proof from the national authorities to the taxpayers. On two occasions the ECJ had declared the latter law as incompatible with Community law.[683] Hereupon the legal presumption was withdrawn by the Italian legislator. However, the interpretation of the new legal situation by national authorities and courts, including the Italian Supreme Court, perpetuated the old regime and *de facto* continued to entail a reversal of the burden of proof.

It has been argued by Breuer that, *Commission* v. *Italy* only concerned a judicial infringement of Community law at first sight. In fact, the Commission had not started proceedings directly against the jurisprudence of the *Corte suprema di cassazione*, but rather against the Italian legislature maintaining a provision which – as exhibited by the practice of national courts – facilitated non-compliant interpretations. Therefore, according to this author, this case deals with a legislative infringement of Community law which is activated by the legislature's failure to reign in the illegal interpretation of national courts, including the supreme court.[684] This view finds partial support in the opinion of AG Geelhoed[685] as well as in the operative part of the judgment which refers to the infringement of the Italian State as a failure to amend the law which can give rise to non-compliant interpretations by national courts.

Nevertheless the judgment is full of indications that the Court in essence deals with judicial conduct and in this way for the very first time holds responsible a Member State for an infringement committed by its judiciary, albeit in the guise of a legislative breach.

In paragraph 29 of the judgment the Court stresses, that even the conduct of *constitutionally independent institutions* may give rise to a finding of an infringement pursuant to Article 226 of the EC Treaty. The Court goes on to declare the *interpretations of national courts* relevant for the assess-

---

683 ECJ, Case 199/82 *San Giorgio* [1983] ECR 3595 and Case 104/86 *Commission* v. *Italy* [1988] ECR 1799.

684 M. Breuer, 'Urteile mitgliedstaatlicher Gerichte als möglicher Gegenstand eines Vertragsverletzungsverfahrens gem. Art. 226?', 15 *EuZW* (2004) p. 199.

685 Opinion of AG Geelhoed in *Commission* v. *Italy*, n. 2 above, at para. 117.

ment of the scope of national laws.[686] In this context, it is worthwhile mentioning that the Court refers to the provision of Italian law at issue as 'in itself neutral'.[687] 'Its effect must be determined in the light of the *construction which the national courts give it*'.[688] What is required for finding an infringement, is a systematic and structural practice of non-compliance, whereas isolated or numerically insignificant judicial decisions, as well as interpretations subsequently quashed by the national supreme court, do not give rise to an infringement under Article 226 of the EC Treaty.[689] Conversely, only eminent interpretations confirmed by the national supreme court may lead to finding an infringement.[690] In addition, it is noteworthy that also AG Geelhoed dedicates a number of paragraphs to the possibility of a '[s]chending van verdragsplichten *door nationale rechtspraak*'.[691]

In his interpretation of the judgment, Breuer relies to a large extent on the Court requiring not just isolated or numerically insignificant judicial decisions in order to find an infringement, but instead, 'a widely-held judicial construction which has not been disowned by the supreme court, but rather confirmed by it'.[692] In this requirement he finds confirmation of his point that *Commission* v. *Italy* in fact concerns a legislative breach of Community law. If it was about the judiciary, any breach – and not just a systematic pattern – would have to give rise to finding an infringement. On the other hand, the legislature could not be required to interfere in isolated incidences of judicial non-compliance. Consequently, according to Breuer, by stressing the existence of a structural problem, the Court must be referring to an omission of the legislature.[693]

Indeed, the judgment in *Commission* v. *Italy* is also amenable to another interpretation, which can better reconcile the apparent tension between legislative and judicial conduct in the judgment. The key to understanding the judgment lies in the co-operational relationship between national courts

---

[686] ECJ, *Commission* v. *Italy*, n. 2 above, at para. 30.
[687] Ibid. at para. 31.
[688] Ibid.
[689] Ibid at para. 32.
[690] Ibid.
[691] Opinion of AG Geelhoed in *Commission* v. *Italy*, n. 2 above, at paras. 48 et seq. (emphasis added).
[692] ECJ, *Commission* v. *Italy*, n. 2 above, at para. 32.
[693] Breuer, loc. cit. n. 684, at pp. 200 et seq.

and the ECJ. Both the Commission's submission and the Court's pronouncement appear to pay tribute to this seminal principle, which lies at the heart of the Community judicial system. The starting point of this reading of *Commission* v. *Italy* is the neutrality of the national rule at issue. As the Court concedes[694] the rule as such does nothing to infringe Community law. It already becomes apparent from this fact, that the conduct of the judiciary is crucial for finding an infringement in the case at hand. As concerns a possible interference by the legislature in instances of systematic non-compliance of national courts, the leeway of the national legislator is limited, all the more so in the light of an already amended rule cancelling from a legislative point of view, the former situation of non-compliance. In addition, it is clear that such an intervention would rest on the fact of a judicial failure to comply with Community law. Given the availability of an action for infringement against the conduct of national courts, from a legal point of view it remains questionable why it should be necessary to attribute a separate omission to the legislature. Therefore, *Commission* v. *Italy* also has to be read as a political ruling which is motivated by the desire not to impinge excessively on the co-operational relationship between national courts and the ECJ. This aim is achieved in two ways.

Firstly, both State functions – the judicature and the legislature – are adduced in order to argue the infringement in both the Commission's submission as well as in the Court's judgment. In this way, objections against the new phenomenon of imputing an infringement to the judiciary can be countered. In addition, referring to the legislature avoids another serious problem, namely, how to remedy judicial non-compliance once an infringement has been declared by the Court. Clearly, quashing the great number of final non-compliant judgments making up the systematic pattern required by the Court would be impossible without impinging on the fundamental principle of legal certainty as well as the legitimate expectations of third parties. To hold instead the national legislature accountable for having failed to change the law in the light of a practice of judicial non-compliance circumvents this problem, since the course of action required from the infringing Member State then becomes a simple change of the law. Astute as this move may seem, relying on the exact conditioning of judicial conduct by means of national laws is delusive and problematic. No longer can

[694] ECJ, *Commission* v. *Italy*, n. 2 above, at para. 31.

Montesquieu's idea of courts as 'the mouthpiece of the law' claim validity. Overestimating the virtues of the law's language and at the same time curtailing judicial discretion touches upon the very nature of the judicial function. Nevertheless this is not the necessary consequence of the Court's bold move in *Commission* v. *Italy*. Nor is it necessary to involve the legislature in cases of judicial non-compliance, nor to require the quashing of final judgments. There is a third alternative pointing to future judicial conduct: Non-compliant interpretations in analogous cases shall be ruled out *pro futuro*. Departing from a notion of the State which is inclusive of the judiciary, it is clear that a finding of an infringement entails the obligation on the part of the judiciary to bring instances of non-compliance to a halt. Whether national courts will act accordingly on the conviction of their Member State will be dependent on their will to comply, as is the case with the other State functions. Eventually, they may be confronted with interventions from the executive branch, enforcing the Court's finding.

Secondly, just as in *Köbler*, the standard of liability had been slightly raised, similarly, the threshold for finding an infringement of the judicial branch has also been elevated.[695] It will take a systematic practice of non-compliance, which involves the highest courts, in order to hold a State responsible for an infringement committed by its judiciary. It is true that in international law a single judgment in breach of international law would be sufficient in order to make a State responsible.[696] However, transferring this rule to the Community legal order is not adequate, since it would place in jeopardy the successful co-operation between national courts and the ECJ. In this context it is noteworthy that already in scholarly writing predating *Commission* v. *Italy* it had been argued that an ordinary judicial error in all likelihood was not sufficient in order to find an infringement.[697] This view is confirmed by the Commission's policy with regard to infringements emanating from the judiciary: Despite the possibility in principle, not even grave and yet isolated instances such as the *Solange I* decision of the German *Bundesverfassungsgericht* have given rise to infringement proceedings, but have only triggered an informal warning.[698]

[695] Mortelmans and van de Gronden, loc. cit. n. 562, at p. 201.
[696] Cf., Art. 4 of the ILC Draft Articles on the Responsibility of States.
[697] Lenaerts and Arts, op. cit. n. 13, at mn. 5-032.
[698] Response of the Commission to question 414/74 by Cousté [1975] OJ C 54/1.

In spite of the Court's cautious approach in *Commission* v. *Italy*, a tendency towards holding Member States accountable for their judiciaries emerges, albeit within more stringent conditions than associated hitherto with the action for infringement. Apart from a stricter standard for finding an infringement, an attempt at disguising the judicial wrong by involving other State functions is apparent.

2.3 Relationship between *Köbler* liability and the action for infringement

The remedy of State liability for judicial wrongs and the action for infringement represent the two different strands of the 'dual vigilance' model.[699] *Köbler* opens the door for individual redress, whereas *Commission* v. *Italy* stands for the more institutional approach, which as such does little to remedy the unlawful situation for aggrieved individuals. The consequence of a successful action for infringement will be a judgment declaratory of the infringement, without, as such conferring any rights on individuals.[700] The finding of a failure to fulfil obligations may give rise to State liability if the infringement amounts to a 'manifest infringement' in the meaning of *Köbler*. However, the finding of an infringement in proceedings according to Article 226 of the EC Treaty in itself is not sufficient, but merely one of the factors to be taken into account.[701]

It follows from these observations that both State liability and an action for infringement may be available in one and the same case. Could traders, affected by the practice of Italian courts at issue in *Commission* v. *Italy*, claim damages from the Italian State? Bearing in mind that the rule of Italian law on the reversed burden of proof had already been found incompatible with Community law suggests an affirmative answer. The interpretation given by a dominant strand in the Italian jurisprudence on a basically 'neutral' rule, which would yield the same result as the abandoned rule could, therefore, not have been deemed to be in conformity with Community law by Italian courts. The prior rulings of the ECJ on the reimbursement of

[699] Kilpatrick, loc. cit. n. 130, at pp. 2 et seq.; Weatherill, loc. cit. n. 27, at p. 89; Timmermans, loc. cit. n. 674, at p. 393.

[700] Lenaerts and Arts, op. cit. n. 13, at mn. 5-061 and mn. 5-063.

[701] Ibid. at mn. 5-064.

undue taxes are clear and unambiguous with regard to the prohibition of a reversal of the burden of proof.[702] The non-compliant interpretation by Italian courts must therefore be held to be inexcusable. Consequently, the standard of 'manifest infringement' of Community law would not amount to an insurmountable obstacle for affected traders and an action for damages would probably be successful, despite the stringency of the conditions for *Köbler* liability.

3. The Residuary Role of the ECrtHR

According to Article 1 of the ECHR the contracting parties shall secure, for everyone within their jurisdiction, the rights and freedoms defined in Section I of the Convention. The notion of a contracting party thereby extends to all institutions of the State, be they of an executive, legislative or judicial nature. Consequently, the State is also responsible for the conduct of its courts, even though they are independent of the executive branch.[703] In this way the conduct of national courts is, in principle, amenable to the review exercised by the ECrtHR. Therefore, it is necessary to address the issue, whether the non-compliant application of *Community law* by national courts can also engage the responsibility of a Member State under the ECHR.

Due to the fact that the EU is not a party to the ECHR, it is not possible for the ECrtHR to directly review acts of the Community institutions.[704] However, the situation is different, with regard to the application of Community law in the Member States. As has been already observed in connection with the judgment in *Dangeville*, the ECrtHR does not refrain from considering the Community law obligations of the Member States when assessing their conduct in the light of the ECHR. Therefore, the failure to recognise the direct effect of certain provisions of a directive was relevant for finding a breach of Article 1 of Protocol No. 1. The dogmatic foundation of this approach lies in Article 32 of the ECHR, according to which, the jurisdiction of the Court shall extend to all matters concerning the interpre-

[702] ECJ, *San Giorgio*, n. 683 above, at paras. 6 et seq., and Case C-343/96 *Dilexport* [1999] ECR I-579, at paras. 52 et seq.

[703] See Meyer-Ladewig, op. cit. n. 282, commentary on Art. 1 of the ECHR, at mn. 4.

[704] ECrtHR, *Matthews* v. *UK*, n. 464 above, at para. 32.

tation and application of the Convention and the protocols thereto. The interpretation of other international treaties, just as the interpretation of Community law is to be regarded as a preliminary question which can determine the result of the interpretation and application of the Convention, and consequently falls under the scope of Article 32 of the ECHR.[705] The application of Community law by national authorities is thus viewed as falling under the jurisdiction of the ECrtHR.[706] What is at stake here, is an autonomous conduct of a Member State violating the Convention without there being a conflict between Community law and the ECHR.[707] From the point of view of the ECHR, Community law as applied by national authorities is to be treated as if part of the national legal order. Against this background, it is logical that the ECrtHR will frequently refer to Community law, including the jurisprudence of the ECJ.[708]

The possibility of addressing the ECrtHR after the exhaustion of national remedies puts an effective remedy in the hands of individuals, in particular in cases of failures to refer by national courts of last instance. In the latter instance individuals will not have to accept the finality of national decisions, which – in the absence of suitable remedies such as an action for breach of the duty to refer[709] – they cannot appeal to the ECJ. Instead, they can file an individual complaint with the ECrtHR, if one of the guarantees of the ECHR has been violated. Given the predominantly economic impli-

---

[705] G. Ress, 'Das Europarecht vor dem Europäischen Gerichtshof für Menschenrechte in Strassburg', *Forum Constitutionis Europae* (2002) p. 1.

[706] Cf., ECrtHR, *Cantoni* v. *France*, judgment of 15 November 1996, Reports 1996-V; see also Ress, loc. cit. n. 705, at p. 10 and B. Conforti, 'Community Law and European Convention on Human Rights: A Quest for Coordination', in L. Chand Vorah, et al. (eds.), *Man's Inhumanity to Man – Essays on International Law in Honour of Antonio Cassese* (The Hague, Kluwer 2003) p. 221 at p. 225.

[707] Cf., Conforti, ibid. at p. 226.

[708] Apart from the judgment in *Dangeville*, n. 291 above, see for instance *Pellegrin* v. *France*, judgment of 8 December 1999, Reports of Judgments and Decisions 1999-VIII; *Kress* v. *France*, judgment of 7 June 2001, Reports of Judgments and Decisions 2001-VI; *Stes Colas Est et autres* v. *France*, judgment of 16 April 2002, Reports of Judgments and Decisions 2002-III; *Meftah et autres* v. *France*, judgment of 26 July 2002, Reports of Judgments and Decisions 2002-VII; *Goodwin* v. *UK*, judgment of 11 July 2002, Reports of Judgments and Decisions 2002-VI; *Posti and Rahko* v. *Finland*, judgment of 24 September 2002, Reports of Judgments and Decisions 2002-VII.

[709] Cf., on this action *de lege ferenda* Solar, op. cit. n. 260, at pp. 136 et seq.; see also Ress, loc. cit. n. 705, at n. 50.

cations of rights granted by Community law, Article 1 of Protocol No. 1 will often be applicable, especially when bearing in mind the relatively wide interpretation of 'possession' and 'legitimate expectation' by the ECrtHR.[710] Apart from that, Article 6 of the ECHR may qualify as a procedural basis for a complaint before the ECrtHR, for instance with regard to failures to refer.[711]

4. Conclusion

In a recent article Puissochet, who also served as judge rapporteur in *Commission* v. *Italy*, laments that the action for infringement has become a mere automatism even in minor cases, which is characterised by the Commission turning mechanically to the Luxembourg judges whenever there are indications of an infringement.[712] In the light of this state of affairs he concludes that

> '[i]l est temps de redonner à cette voie de droit la place qui lui revient, et d'éviter que sa practique quotidienne ne donne trop souvent l'impression d'un relatif enlisement dans les litiges mineurs où ne peuvent être invoqués que des arguments juridiques stéréotypes.'[713]

Commission v. *Italy* is an obvious step into this direction and a straightforward signal that the Commission takes seriously its role as guardian of the

[710] Cf., ECrtHR, *S.A. Dangeville* v. *France*, n. 291 above, at paras. 44 et seq., where in contradistinction to the standing case law a claim which was not yet 'sufficiently established to be enforceable' (cf., for instance ECrtHR, *Stran Greek Refineries* v. *Greece*, judgment of 9 December 1994) was considered to be covered by Art. 1 of Protocol No. 1.

[711] It corresponds to the standing case law of the ECrtHR to hold that 'it is not completely impossible that, in certain circumstances, refusal by a domestic court trying a case at final instance might infringe the principle of fair trial, as set forth in Article 6(1) of the Convention, in particular where such refusal appears arbitrary'. See for instance *Peter Moosbrugger* v. *Austria* (decision of 25 January 2000 on the admissibility of the application; No. 44861/98), at para. 2; *Coëme and Others* v. *Belgium*, judgment of 22 June 2000, Reports of Judgments and Decisions 2000-VII, at para. 114; *Nicolas Calena Santiago* v. *Spain* (decision of 4 October 2001 on the admissibility; No. 60350/00), at para. 2.

[712] J.-P. Puissochet, 'L'action en manquement peut-elle encore se parer de ses justes vertus?', in Colneric, et al. (eds.), *Une communauté de droit – Festschrift für Gil Carlos Rodríguez Iglesias* (Berlin, BWV 2003) p. 569 at p. 571 et seq.

[713] Ibid. at p. 580.

Treaties. This involves changing its hitherto lenient practice with regard to infringements by national courts, when there are indications of a systematic and significant practice of national courts going against Community law. At the same time the Commission seems to want to enhance the legitimacy of such proceedings by trying to establish a link between the infringement at issue and State functions other than the judiciary. Even though artificial and unnecessary in cases such as *Commission* v. *Italy*, this move is driven by the desire to render subsequent rulings of the ECJ acceptable to the Member States and to avoid upsetting the pivotal co-operational relationship between national courts and the ECJ. On the other hand, the Commission's recent start of the pre-litigation stage pursuant to Article 226 of the EC Treaty in the case of an apparently isolated breach by the Dutch *Hoge Raad* may bear witness of a bolder approach,[714] which, appears unlikely to be underwritten by the Court though.[715]

It seems unlikely that Member States will frequently be confronted with successful actions for infringement based on the conduct of national courts in the future. Firstly, despite the Court's programmatic *dictum*, whereas a Member State's failure to fulfil obligations may, in principle, be established under Article 226 of the EC Treaty whatever the agency of that State whose action or inaction is the cause of the failure to fulfil its obligations, even in the case of a constitutionally independent institution,[716] the judgment in *Commission* v. *Italy* exhibits a great degree of caution in attributing an infringement to the judiciary. Where the attribution to another State function seems conceivable, the Commission will make use of this possibility. Secondly, an isolated infringement of a national court will not be sufficient for declaring an infringement pursuant to Article 226 of the EC Treaty. Instead it takes a systematic failure to observe Community law by the national judiciaries, which only can give rise to finding an infringement. Thirdly, and somehow connected to the second point, the rulings of national courts of last instance assume a large significance when determining the existence of an infringement. At the same time it is in their hands to put lower instance

[714] See European Commission, Press Release IP/04/178 of 9 February 2004 ('Posted workers: Commission takes action against the Netherlands').

[715] See also Komárek, loc. cit. n. 396, at p. 26, who hints at the deterrent potential of the mere opening of infringement proceedings, regardless of the Court's stance on the matter.

[716] ECJ, Case 77/69 *Commission* v. *Belgium*, n. 669 above, at para. 15.

courts, which err, on track again, by quashing their non-compliant interpretations.[717] Finally, the Commission's annual reports on the application of Community law take the function of an early warning system, informing Member States of systematic problems in the application of Community law by national courts. Only if an early warning remains unheard and does not trigger a change in the interpretative practice will the need arise for an intervention by means of the Article 226-procedure.[718] It seems likely that the Commission, given the piecemeal character of its enforcement, will confine itself to setting precedents in particular grave instances of breaches of Community law by national supreme courts.

A potential alternative course of action to State liability proceedings has been opened up by the Court's judgment in *Kühne & Heitz*. Putting national administrative authorities under an *obligation* to review final primary proceedings upon a clarifying judgment of the Court, where such a *possibility* exists in national law, may mean that individuals can address administrative authorities, whose non-compliant interpretation of Community law has been confirmed by a national court of last instance, and thereby avoid having recourse to the compensatory remedy of State liability, which is coupled with a high liability threshold.

As far as the ECrtHR is concerned, it has shown no hesitation, thus far, to subject the application of Community law in the Member States to scrutiny in the light of the ECHR. In cases of non-compliant national judgments exhibiting human rights implications, individuals may thus turn to the Strasbourg court and apply for compensation.

---

[717] Cf., Opinion of AG Geelhoed in *Commission* v. *Italy*, n. 2 above, at para. 57.
[718] Mortelmans and van de Gronden, loc. cit. n. 562, at p. 204.

Chapter VIII
EPILOGUE

Chapter VIII
EPILOGUE

With the judgment in *Köbler*, the ECJ has laid the cap stone of the edifice of State liability, which it has progressively constructed over the years, starting with the landmark case of *Francovich*. At the same time *Köbler* has brought to an end speculations in scholarly writing as to whether, and to what extent the principle of State liability as devised under Community law could also be of relevance to the judicial function. This is not a judicial revolution, since already *Brasserie du Pêcheur* had set the tone for an all-embracing State concept for State liability purposes. Nevertheless, in its explicitness, *Köbler* forms an important building block in the protection of individual interests in the Community legal order.

It is legitimate to ask what purpose a remedy, available only in exceptional circumstances, can serve. Who can benefit from a remedy that introduces a stringent standard of liability, which the ECJ additionally seems to apply only leniently? Is it really necessary and worth the trouble to subject the final judgments of national courts of last instance to an indirect *ex post*-control of compliance, possibly exercised by lower instance courts? Would it not appear sounder to accept isolated instances of non-compliance than to subject the national judiciary to the overt and constant danger of making their State liable?

Article 234(3) of the EC Treaty is a *lex imperfecta* in not providing for any sanctions for failures to discharge the duty to refer. In the end, the functioning of the co-operational relationship between the ECJ and national courts (of last instance) is thus dependent on the goodwill of the latter. That the preliminary reference procedure has become a tremendous success, with preliminary references accounting for the hub of cases before the Court bears witness to the fact that national courts are indeed prepared to co-operate and do not eschew the logics of subordination, which the Court's monopoly in authoritatively interpreting the Treaties implies. Empirical evidence suggests that, it is in particular, lower instance courts which make use of the full potential of the Article 234-procedure, whereas traditionally national supreme courts exhibit an attitude of avoidance of the ECJ. Occasionally avoidance turns into defiance. The self-perception of national supreme courts as the *highest* courts of their relevant systems fits uneasily with the existence of a supreme court for the Community legal order, the ECJ.

Against this background the Court's move towards the inclusion of the judiciary for State liability purposes becomes understandable. Both the failure to respect the duty to refer and substantively non-compliant outcomes of the national judicial process shall be relevant in the context of State liability.

Due to the crucial position of national courts in the enforcement of Community law, and in particular, of national courts of last instance which are called upon to achieve a final settlement of disputes, isolated instances of non-compliance by national supreme courts may have a detrimental impact on the uniformity of Community law as well, and in addition set the tone for lower instance courts, which more often than not will follow the reasoning of the national supreme court rather than referring a question to the Court. Apart from this institutional aspect, it would appear inequitable to have individuals incurring damages, by reason of the fact that a national supreme court is minded to go astray, actually bearing the damage. Both an institutional and an individual perspective, point to the necessity of making available an action for damages in case of particularly qualified breaches of Community law committed by last instance courts. Although this new remedy has been confined to exceptional cases it closes an important gap in the Community judicial system, since instances of non-compliance by national supreme courts as such are exceptional.

The *Köbler* judgment is also informative in terms of the relativity of juridical wisdom. What may appear to be unthinkable, under national law at a given time, may turn out to be feasible, provided that certain safeguards are attached. A principle of State liability for judicial wrongs is not impossible *per se* but can be reconciled with legitimate concerns. 'Insurmountable' obstacles such as the finality of decisions of national courts of last instance, which amount to conventional wisdom carved out in stone, become surmountable after a paradigm shift. The Court's stake in provoking a rethinking of national legal dogmas thus cannot be denied.

This preparedness, to counter non-compliant conduct of national courts more actively is also apparent from the judgment in *Commission* v. *Italy*. Whereas the Commission's practice was hitherto characterised by self-restraint, in spite of the possibility, in principle, to sanction non-compliant judicial conduct by means of an action for infringement, this judgment sends an important signal to national courts and stresses that the other strand of the 'dual vigilance'-model may be of relevance to judicial conduct as well, again albeit within limited and particular circumstances.

The findings of the present work can be summarised as follows:

1. By means of the doctrine of direct effect national courts have been transformed into Community law courts and are thus characterised by a *dédoublement fonctionnel*. Whereas this phenomenon has been unprecedented in scope in the Community legal order, as such it was not unknown to international law before the ECJ's ruling in *van Gend & Loos*.

2. Article 234 of the EC Treaty provides for a formalised and channelled dialogue whose interlocutors are the ECJ and national courts. The uniform application of Community law is secured by the duty to refer of national courts of last instance.

3. In the absence of a general Community competence to harmonise procedural laws, harmonisation of procedural rules by means of secondary Community legislation has remained piecemeal. Member States in principle enjoy national procedural competence, which is commonly referred to as 'national procedural autonomy'.

4. The ECJ has taken an active role in shaping national procedural laws. An initial minimum interference approach has occasionally given way to a more effectiveness-oriented behaviour, which has ultimately led to the creation of new remedies as well as spelling out harmonised minimum conditions for their exercise. The remedy of State liability is the progeny of this approach. Recent years have also seen the arrival of a more balanced approach, being concerned about a context-specific assessment of the national rules in question.

5. The benefits of legal certainty and enhanced individual protection associated with the establishment of the remedy of State liability have come at the price of severe inroads into the concept of national procedural competence, which nowadays appears as a shallow concept.

6. In *Köbler*, the principle of State liability, by now firmly entrenched in the Community legal order, has been extended to also cover judicial acts. Whereas this result had been prepared by an *obiter dictum* in *Brasserie du Pêcheur*, *Köbler* concerns the first instance of a judicial breach of Community law before the ECJ.

7. In its reasoning the Court places emphasis on the full effectiveness of Community law, in particular, in the light of the pivotal role of national courts in the Community legal order, as well as on an analogy with public international law.

8. State liability can be conceptualised as a refined form of State responsibility which is tailored to the individualising nature of the Community legal order. Unlike public international law, Community law emphasised the full involvement of individuals from its very inception. Putting the remedy of State liability in the hands of individuals reflects this structural difference between the subjects of the two legal orders, whilst the compensatory function of State responsibility and State liability is the same.

9. The ECJ refers to international law with regard to the attribution of the conduct of national courts to the State. Public international law on this issue is characterised by a long-standing and, almost uniform, practice insofar as concerns the attribution of judicial conduct to the State. Most recently this has been confirmed by Article 4 of the ILC Draft Articles on State Responsibility.

10. The rationale behind the international law rules on the attribution of judicial conduct apply with equal strength to the Community legal order. No reason for not applying those rules in Community law is apparent. Furthermore, the particular features of Community law, such as its full effectiveness, its supremacy, as well as the crucial role given to national courts in the implementation of Community law require a notion of the State which is inclusive of the judiciary. In *Köbler*, the Court stresses this analogy between Community law and public international law.

11. The case law of the ECrtHR exhibits a clear tendency towards more accountability of national courts. In *Kudła*, in contrast to its standing case law, the Court gave Article 13 of the ECHR a meaning in its own right when paired with Article 6 of the ECHR. Following *Kudła*, the former provision requires States parties to provide for a remedy directed against courts failing to decide within reasonable time. This remedy may also be compensatory. In *Dangeville* the Court, in effect, recognised a principle of State liability for judicial acts, albeit not in a very outspoken manner. Even though a direct obligation on the part of the Community to follow suit does not ensue from either of these judgments, the *Dangeville* ruling sets an important factual precedent of relevance to the Community legal order.

12. Looking at the laws of the Member States with regard to State liability for judicial acts, this comparative law-approach unearths a disparate picture which does not allow for precise deductions. Obviously, the Court wants to put flesh on the bones of the doctrine of State liability for judicial acts by referring to national laws, without going as far as its AG did, in assuming a general principle common to the Member States' legal orders to this effect.

13. A number of reservations exist, which *prima facie* reason against the inclusion of the judiciary for the purposes of State liability, some of which have been pleaded in the proceedings in *Köbler*. The argument of putting judicial independence at risk can be countered by the fact that it is about the liability of *States*, and not of individual judges. Moreover, State liability is about an indirect *control of legality*, which as such is not alien to the judicial function.

14. A formal conception of *res judicata* clearly does not stand in the way of State liability for judicial wrongs, as primary and secondary proceedings are concerned with different matters in dispute. On the other hand, a certain relativity of a substantive notion of *res judicata* is the unavoidable consequence of a principle of State liability for judicial acts, be it in national legal orders, be it in Community law.

15. The judgment in *Kühne & Heitz* underscores the Court´s narrow conception of *res judicata*: as a consequence of a failure to refer, national courts of last instance may be required to set aside final national judgments, which have turned out to be non-compliant in light of the ECJ's subsequent case law.

16. The danger of putting at risk the co-operational relationship between national courts and the ECJ can be contained by setting the standard of liability reasonably high. In this respect, *Köbler* scores well as a balanced judgment which presumably will not lead to judicial rebellion in the Member States. Similarly, concerns relating to the efficiency of the national judiciary can be countered by providing for adequate substantive conditions giving rise to liability in order to avoid vexatious litigation. A clogging of the system of judicial review can thereby be prevented.

17. The ECJ recognises a parallelism between the extra-contractual liability of the Community and State liability. It is clear that the judicial conduct of the ECJ proper as the ultimate arbitrator of the system cannot trigger the liability of the Community, since at this stage there are no longer any means available to dispose satisfactorily of the *nemo iudex in causa sua*-problem. Nevertheless, this does not stand in the way of the recognition of State liability for judicial acts, since as the Court explained in *Brasserie du Pêcheur*, the parallelism only applies in the absence of particular justification. It is exactly the particular position of the ECJ proper in the Community judicial system which justifies an exception to the parallelism.

18. A significant power gain for the ECJ is not in sight, given the exceptionality of State liability for judicial acts. National courts of last instance are not compelled to refer in any case involving questions of Community law as a precautionary measure so as to make their Member States escape the risk of liability. By contrast, by way of analogy to *British Telecommunications* a non-compliant *bona fide* interpretation will not trigger liability.

19. By introducing the concept of a 'manifest infringement', the Court has set the standard of liability reasonably high, stressing at the same time the exceptional character of State liability for judicial acts. The already exacting standard of *Brasserie du Pêcheur* has consequently further been raised. In this way the Court successfully accommodates the reservations of a number of Member States, in particular with regard to the relativity of *res judicata*.

20. The exact implications of the standard of 'manifest infringement' await further clarification from the Court's case law.

21. The higher standard as compared with the one applicable to the other State functions is justified by the specific nature of the judiciary, which most prominently finds expression in the principle of *res judicata*.

22. The breach of the duty to refer is one criterion, which is to be taken into account when assessing the manifest character of an infringement. Since no individual right can be derived from Article 234 of the EC Treaty, the breach of the duty to refer, in itself is not sufficient, to give rise to State liability. By contrast it can serve as a qualification of an otherwise simple breach. However, not every breach of the duty to refer will make an otherwise simple breach of Community law a 'manifest infringement'. Clearly, if a court deliberately refrains from making a reference in spite of the ascertained need to do so, this will be sufficient in order to make an otherwise simple breach a manifest infringement.

23. In the application of the new standard to the facts of *Köbler*, the Court exhibits particular leniency by viewing the two breaches at issue in isolation. It seems plausible that the Court, in this way, intended to ensure the acceptability of its judgment in the Member States. In the future, once the principle of State liability for judicial wrongs is firmly entrenched in the Community legal order, the Court will probably bring to bear a more robust attitude.

24. The separate standard of liability for the judicial function necessitates the delimitation of the judiciary from the other State functions.

25. In the light of the logics of the duty to refer which only extends to national courts of last instance, as well as the fact that judgments still subject to appeal can be quashed at next instance it seems unlikely that the Court will extend the principle of State liability for judicial acts to lower instance courts. Equally, the Court's insistence on the exceptionality of *Köbler* liability supports this result.

26. With regard to the notion of a national court of last instance, recourse can be had to the case law of the Court in connection with Article 234(3) of the EC Treaty. The prevailing concrete theory, which builds on a differentiation between supreme courts and other courts of last instance, can be transferred to the question of State liability, since from the viewpoint of an individual concerned it makes no difference whether a judgment has become final by reason of the decision of a supreme court or of any other court of last instance.

27. As is apparent from *Dorsch Consult*, the designation of competent courts and authorities for the implementation of Community law is clearly an issue falling under the heading of national procedural autonomy. However, the Court has reserved to itself an effectiveness-review which can, at times, go as far as to require the competence of a particular court or authority such as in *Connect Austria*.

28. Under the Austrian Law on Official Liability, State liability for organisational courts of last instance is precluded. In the light of the Court's judgment in *Köbler* this rule has to be set aside *qua* supremacy of Community law.

29. According to the relevant provisions of the Austrian Law on Official Liability it is ordinary courts of first instance which are competent in matters of State liability. The competence of lower instance courts to indirectly review the judgments of courts of last instance will be a typical consequence of *Köbler*.

30. Although problematic from the viewpoint of national court organisation, the empowerment of national courts is a standard feature of Community law, as can be gleaned from the Court's judgment in *Simmenthal* as well as the preliminary reference procedure, which equips lower instance courts with limited review powers of non-compliant decisions of national courts of last instance.

31. The fact that courts deciding at last instance in State liability matters may also issue non-compliant judgments gives rise to the problem of impartiality. Even if a special court is created only for State liability purposes, the risk that this court will have to decide *in causa sua* cannot be avoided. On the national level this problem cannot be solved.

32. A minority view in Austria assumes a competence of the *Verfassungsgerichtshof* when State liability for judicial conduct is at issue. This solution can avoid the unease in regard to having a court of first instance indirectly review a judgment of a supreme court. However, again the aforementioned impartiality-concerns will apply.

33. Both the problems of ordinary courts sitting in judgment over decisions of national courts of last instance and the impartiality dilemma can be resolved by involving the ECJ via the Article 234-procedure. At least, *de facto*, it will then be for the ECJ to decide. In this manner, the legitimacy of judgments of ordinary courts can be increased. Equally, the issue of impartiality loses its acuteness since referring courts are bound by the ECJ's preliminary ruling and thus can bring to bear no bias on the decision taken.

34. *Commission* v. *Italy* is an initial test case for the application of the action for infringement to judicial conduct. Adducing a legislative omission alongside judicial conduct seems motivated by the desire to enhance the acceptability of this ruling in the Member States. At the same time, the strong reliance on the necessary interference of the legislature in cases of non-compliant judicial conduct is unconvincing and cannot live up to the realities of the judicial function.

35. As in *Köbler* the Court raises the standard required to find an infringement in the sense of a systematic pattern of non-compliance which includes approval by national supreme courts.

36. A judgment finding an infringement will require the defaulting courts to remedy the unlawful situation *pro futuro*, and take all necessary measures to comply with the judgment. Continuing non-compliance may put them under pressure from the executive.

37. There are no indications that the Commission will successfully have recourse to the action for infringement more frequently in the near future. Instead, the action for infringement in connection with judicial conduct seems to be governed by the logics of exceptionality.

38. The same factual circumstances may give rise to *Köbler* liability and to an action for infringement at the same time. In addition, following the reasoning in *Kühne & Heitz*, under given circumstances, individuals may open up administrative proceedings, which have become final by means of a judgment of a national court of last instance, by relying on a subsequent different judgment of the ECJ before the competent administrative authorities.

39. The application of Community law by national courts is subject to the review exercised by the ECrtHR.

40. Issues of non-compliance with ECHR-implications, such as a violation of Article 1 of Protocol No. 1 by denying an enforceable right derived from Community law, may be raised by means of an individual complaint to the ECrtHR.

BIBLIOGRAPHY

ALTER, K., *Establishing the Supremacy of European Community Law – The Making of an International Rule of Law in Europe* (Oxford, Oxford University Press 2001).

ANTONIOLLI, W./KOJA, F., *Allgemeines Verwaltungsrecht*, 3rd edn. (Vienna, Manz 1996).

ANAGNOSTARAS, G., 'The Principle of State Liability for Judicial Breaches: The Impact of European Community Law', 7 *EPL* (2001) pp. 281 et seq.

ARNULL, A., 'Private Applicants and the Action for Annulment since *Codorniu*', 38 *CML Rev.* (2001) pp. 7 et seq.

BARAV, A., 'Omnipotent Courts', in Curtin/Heukels (eds.), *Institutional Dynamics of European Integration* (1994) pp. 265 et seq.

BEAUMONT, P., et al. (eds.), *Convergence and Divergence in European Public Law* (Oxford, Oxford University Press 2002).

BEUL, C.R., 'Kein Richterprivileg bei unterlassener Vorlage gem. Art. 177 EGV', 7 *EuZW* (1996) pp. 748 et seq.

BIONDI, A., 'The European Court of Justice and Certain National Procedural Limitations: Not Such a Tough Relationship', 36 *CML Rev.* (1999) pp. 1271 et seq.

BÖCKENFÖRDE, E.-W., 'Verfassungsgerichtsbarkeit: Strukturfragen, Organisation, Legitimation', 52 *NJW* (1999) pp. 9 et seq.

BOTELLA, A.-S., 'La responsabilité du juge national', 40 *RTDE* (2004) pp. 283 et seq.

BREUER, M., 'State liability for judicial wrongs and Community law: the case of *Gerhard Köbler v Austria*', 29 *EL Rev.* (2004) pp. 243 et seq.

—, 'Urteile mitgliedstaatlicher Gerichte als möglicher Gegenstand eines Vertragsverletzungsverfahrens gem. Art. 226 EG?', 15 *EuZW* (2004) pp. 199 et seq.

—, 'Staatshaftung für Judikativunrecht', (2003) *BayVBl* pp. 586 et seq.

—, 'Der Europäische Gerichtshof für Menschenrechte als Wächter des europäischen Gemeinschaftsrechts', 58 *JZ* (2003) pp. 433 et seq.

BRING, O./MAHMOUDI, S. (eds.), *Current International Law Issues – Nordic Perspectives – Essays in Honour of Jerzy Sztucki* (Dordrecht, M. Nijhoff 1994).

BROWNLIE, I., *Principles of Public International Law*, 6th edn. (Oxford, Oxford University Press 2003).

DE BÚRCA, G./WEILER, J.H.H. (eds.), *The European Court of Justice* (Oxford, Oxford University Press 2001).

CALLIESS, C./RUFFERT, M. (eds.), *Kommentar zu EU-Vertrag und EG-Vertrag*, 2nd edn. (Neuwied, Luchterhand 2002).

CARANTA, R., Case note on ECJ, Case C-453/00 *Kühne & Heitz*, 42 *CML Rev.* (2005) pp. 375 et seq.

CASSESE, A., *International Law* (Oxford, Oxford University Press 2001).

CHALTIEL, F., 'L'Européanisation de la responsabilité administrative – À propos de l'ârret du Conseil d'État du 30 juillet 2003, Association pour le développement de l'aquaculture en région Centre et autres', 47 *RMCUE* (2004) pp. 106 et seq.

CHAND VOHRAH, L., et al. (eds.), *Man's Inhumanity to Man – Essays on International Law in Honour of Antonio Cassese* (The Hague, Kluwer 2003).

CLASSEN, C.D., Case note on ECJ, Case C-224/01 *Köbler*, 41 *CML Rev.* (2004) pp. 813 et seq.

COLNERIC, N., et al. (eds.), *Une communauté de droit – Festschrift für Gil Carlos Rodríguez Iglesias* (Berlin, BWV 2003).

CONFORTI, B., 'Community Law and European Convention on Human Rights: A Quest for Coordination', in Chand Vorah, et al. (eds.), *Man's Inhumanity to Man – Essays on International Law in Honour of Antonio Cassese* (2003) pp. 221 et seq.

CRAIG, P./DE BÚRCA, G., *EU Law – Text, Cases and Materials*, 3rd edn. (Oxford, Oxford University Press 2003).

CRAWFORD, J., *The International Law Commission's Articles on State Responsibility – Introduction, Text and Commentaries* (Cambridge, Cambridge University Press 2002).

—/OLLESON, S., 'The nature and forms of international responsibility', in Evans (ed.), *International Law* (2004) pp. 445 et seq.

CURTIN, D./HEUKELS, T. (eds.), *Institutional Dynamics of European Integration – Essays in Honour of Henry G. Schermers* (Dordrecht, M. Nijhoff 1994).

VON DANWITZ, TH., Case note on ECJ, Case C-224/01 *Köbler*, 59 *JZ* (2004) pp. 301 et seq.

DETTER, I., The Concept of International Law, 2nd edn. (Stockholm, Norstedts Juridik 1993).

DOEHRING, K., *Völkerrecht*, 2nd edn. (Heidelberg, C.F. Müller 2004).

DUE, O. et al. (eds.), *Festschrift für Ulrich Everling*, Vol. 2 (Baden-Baden, Nomos 1995).

VAN DIJK, P./VAN HOOF, G.J.H., *Theory and Practice of the European Convention on Human Rights*, 3rd edn. (The Hague, Kluwer 1998).

EDWARD, D./ROBINSON, W., 'Is there a Place for Private Law Principles in Community Law?', in Heukels/McDonnell (eds.), *The Action for Damages in Community Law* (1997) pp. 339 et seq.

EPINEY, A./SOLLBERGER, K., *Verwaltungsgerichtlicher Rechtsschutz in Umweltangelegenheiten* (Berne, Stämpfli 2003).

ECJ, Annual Report of the Court of Justice of the European Communities (Luxembourg, 2003).
EVANS, M.D. (ed.), *International Law* (Oxford, Oxford University Press 2004).
FLYNN, L., 'Whatever Happened to Emmott? The Perfecting of Community Rules on National Time-Limits', in Kilpatrick, et al. (eds.), *The Future of Remedies in Europe* (2000) pp. 51 et seq.
FRENZ, W., Case note on ECJ, Case C-453/00 *Kühne & Heitz*, 119 *DVBl.* (2004) pp. 375 et seq.
—, Case note on ECJ, Case C-224/01 *Köbler*, 118 *DVBl.* (2003) pp. 1522 et seq.
FUNK, B.C., 'Staatshaftung auf Grundlage von Gemeinschaftsrecht', (1997) *ecolex* pp. 553 et seq.
VAN GERVEN, W., general ed., *Cases, Materials and Text on National, Supranational and International Tort Law – Scope of Protection* (Oxford, Hart Publishing 2000).
—, 'Of Rights, Remedies and Procedures', 37 *CML Rev.* (2000) pp. 501 et seq.
—, general ed., *Tort Law – Scope of Protection* (Oxford, Hart Publishing 1999).
—, 'Bridging the Gap between Community and National Laws: Towards a Principle of Homogeneity in the Field of Legal Remedies?', 32 *CML Rev.* (1995) pp. 679 et seq.
GROH, TH., 'Auslegung des Gemeinschaftsrechts und Vorlagepflicht nach Art. 234 EG', 13 *EuZW* (2002) pp. 460 et seq.
GROTIUS, H., *De Iure Belli ac Pacis Libri tres* (Paris 1625).
GRUSSMANN, W.-D., 'Europäische Regulierungsschwerpunkte für den Bereich der elektronischen Kommunikation im Jahr 2003', (2003) *wbl* pp. 306 et seq.
GUNDEL, J., 'Gemeinschaftsrechtliche Haftungsvorgaben für judikatives Unrecht – Konsequenzen für die Rechtskraft und das deutsche "Richterprivileg" (§ 839 Abs. 2 BGB)', 15 *EWS* (2004) pp. 8 et seq.
—, 'Neue Anforderungen des EGMR an die Ausgestaltung des nationalen Rechtsschutzsystems – Die Schaffung effektiver Rechtsbehelfe gegen überlange Verfahrensdauer', 119 *DVBl.* (2004) pp. 17 et seq.
HALTERN, U., 'Integration Through Law', in Wiener/Diez (eds.), *European Integration Theory* (Oxford, Oxford University Press 2004) pp. 177 et seq.
HENKIN, L., et al., *International Law – Cases and Materials*, 3rd edn. (St. Paul, West Publishing 1993).
HEUKELS, T./MCDONNELL, A. (eds.), *The Action for Damages in Community Law* (The Hague, Kluwer 1997).
—/TIB, J., 'Towards Homogeneity in the Field of Legal Remedies: Convergence and Divergence', in Beaumont, et al. (eds.), *Convergence and Divergence in European Public Law* (2002) pp. 111 et seq.
HIGGINS, R., *Problems and Process – International Law and How We Use it* (Oxford, Oxford University Press 1994).

HIMSWORTH, C., 'Convergence and Divergence in Administrative Law', in Beaumont, et al. (eds.), *Convergence and Divergence in European Public Law* (2002) pp. 99 et seq.

HOFSTÖTTER, B., 'Härte und Milde für Judikativunrecht vor dem EuGH', (2004) *ELR* pp. 60 et seq.

—, 'Neues zu vorlageberechtigten und –verpflichteten Gerichten', (2002) *ELR* pp. 249 et seq.

—, 'Außervertragliche Haftung der EG und *Ius Commune*', (2000) *ELR* pp. 424 et seq.

ISAAC, G./BLANQUET, M., *Droit communautaire général*, 8th edn. (Paris, A. Colin 2001).

JUD, B., 'Staatshaftung für judikatives Unrecht', (2003) *ecolex* pp. 385 et seq.

KAMMERHOFER, J., 'The Binding Nature of Provisional Measures of the International Court of Justice: the "Settlement" of the Issue in the *LaGrand* Case', 16 *LJIL* (2003) pp. 67 et seq.

KAKOURIS, C.N., 'Do the Member States Possess Judicial Procedural "Autonomy"?', 34 *CML Rev.* (1997) pp. 1389 et seq.

KAPTEYN, P.G.G./VERLOREN VAN THEMAAT, P. (GORMLEY, L. (ed.)), *Introduction to the Law of the European Communities*, 3rd edn. (The Hague, Kluwer 1998).

KEVILLE, C., 'The principle of effectiveness and the development of remedies at European Community law', in Lucey/Keville (eds.), *Irish Perspectives on EC Law* (2003) pp. 1 et seq.

KILPATRICK, C., et al. (eds.), *The Future of Remedies in Europe* (Oxford, Hart Publishing 2000).

—, 'The Future of Remedies in Europe', in Kilpatrick, et al. (eds.), *The Future of Remedies in Europe* (2000) pp. 1 et seq.

KLUTH, W., 'Die Haftung der Mitgliedstaaten für gemeinschaftsrechtswidrige höchstrichterliche Entscheidungen – Schlussstein im System der gemeinschaftsrechtlichen Staatshaftung – Zugleich ein Plädoyer für eine zeitgemäße Reform des deutschen Staatshaftungsrechts', 119 *DVBl.* (2004) pp. 393 et seq.

KOKOTT, J., 'Der Grundrechtsschutz im europäischen Gemeinschaftsrecht', 121 AöR (1996) pp. 599 et seq.

KOMÁREK, J., 'Federal elements in the Community judicial system: Building coherence in the Community legal order', 42 *CML Rev.* (2005) pp. 9 et seq.

KOSKENNIEMI, M., 'What is international law for?', in Evans (ed.), *International Law* (2004) pp. 89 et seq.

—, *The Gentle Civilizer of Nations – The Rise and Fall of International Law 1870-1960* (Cambridge, Cambridge University Press 2001).

—, *From Apology to Utopia: the structure of international legal argument* (Helsinki, Lakimiesliiton Kustannus 1989).

KOTSCHY, B., 'Responsabilité de l'État – Arrêt Köbler', (2003) *RDUE* pp. 763 et seq.

Lattenmayer-Latyer, H., 'Connect-Urteil des EuGH: Anwendungsvorrang von Richtlinien', (2003) *ecolex* pp. 722 et seq.

Lauterpacht, E., 'Implementation of Decisions of International Organizations through National Courts', in Schwebel (ed.), *The Effectiveness of International Decisions* (1971) pp. 57 et seq.

Lauterpacht, H., *International Law and Human Rights* (London, Stevens 1950).

Lecheler, H., 'Der Beitrag der allgemeinen Rechtsgrundsätze zur Europäischen Integration – Rückblick und Ausblick', 6 *ZEuS* (2003) pp. 351 et seq.

Lee, I.B., 'In Search of a Theory of State Liability in the European Union', *Harvard Jean Monnet Working Paper* 9/99 (retrieved from <http://www.jeanmonnet program.org/papers/99/990901.html> – visited on 18 April 2005).

da Legnano, G., *Tractatus De Bello, De Represaliis et De Duello* (Bologna, ca. 1360), modern edn. by Th.E. Holland (Oxford, Oxford University Press 1917).

Lenaerts, K., 'Interlocking legal orders in the European Union and Comparative law', 52 *ICLQ* (2003) pp. 873 et seq.

—/Arts, D., *Europees Procesrecht*, 3rd edn. (Antwerp, Maklu 2003).

—/Arts, D., *Procedural Law of the European Union* (London, Sweet & Maxwell 1999).

—/van Nuffel, P., *Constitutional Law of the European Union*, 2nd edn. (London, Sweet & Maxwell 2005).

Lengauer, A., 'Haftung eines Mitgliedstaates für die Verletzung von EG-Recht', (1997) *ÖJZ* pp. 81 et seq.

Lissitzyn, O.J., 'The Meaning of the Term Denial of Justice in International Law', 30 *AJIL* (1936) pp. 632 et seq.

Lonbay, J./Biondi, A. (eds.), *Remedies for Breach of EC Law* (Chichester, J. Wiley & Sons 1997).

Lucey, M.C./Keville C. (eds.), *Irish Perspectives on EC Law* (Dublin, Round Hall 2003).

Mackenzie, R./Sands, P., 'International Courts and Tribunals and the Independence of the International Judge', 44 *Harv. ILJ* (2003) pp. 271 et seq.

Mancini, F./Keeling, D.T., 'From *CILFIT* to *ERT*: The Constitutional Challenge Facing the European Court', 11 *YEL* (1991) pp. 1 et seq.

Marschik, A., *Subsysteme im Völkerrecht – Ist die Europäische Union ein 'Self-Contained Regime'?* (Berlin, Duncker & Humblot 1997).

Mayer, F., 'Individualrechtsschutz im Europäischen Verfassungsrecht', 119 *DVBl.* (2004) pp. 606 et seq.

Mayer, H., *Das österreichische Bundes-Verfassungsrecht – Kurzkommentar*, 3rd edn. (Vienna, Manz 2002).

McNair, A.D., *The Law of Treaties*, reprint of the 1st edn. of 1961 (Oxford, Clarendon 1998).

Merkl, A.J., *Die Lehre von der Rechtskraft entwickelt aus dem Rechtsbegriff: eine rechtstheoretische Untersuchung* (Leipzig, Deuticke 1923).

Meyer-Ladewig, J., *Konvention zum Schutz der Menschenrechte und Grundfreiheiten – Handkommentar* (Baden-Baden, Nomos 2003).

—, 'Rechtsbehelfe gegen Verzögerungen im gerichtlichen Verfahren – zum Urteil des EGMR Kudła/Polen', 54 *NJW* (2001) pp. 2679 et seq.

Mortelmans, K.J.M./van de Gronden, J.W., Case note on Case C-224/01 *Köbler*, 53 *Ars Aequi* (2004) pp. 198 et seq.

Neuhold, H., et al. (eds.), *Österreichisches Handbuch des Völkerrechts*, 4th edn. (Vienna, Manz 2004).

Nyikos, S.A., 'The European Court of Justice and National Courts: Strategic Interaction within the EU Judicial Process' (2001) unpublished manuscript (retrieved from <http://law.wustl.edu/igls/Conconfpapers/Nyikos.pdf> – visited on 11 January 2005).

Obwexer, W., Case note on ECJ, Case C-224/01 *Köbler*, 15 *EuZW* (2003) pp. 726 et seq.

Öhlinger, Th.,Verfassungsrecht, 5th edn. (Vienna, WUV 2003).

—/Potacs, M., *Gemeinschaftsrecht und staatliches Recht*, 2nd edn. (Vienna, Orac 2001).

Ossenbühl, F., *Staatshaftungsrecht*, 5th edn. (Munich, C.H. Beck 1998).

Pfander, J.E., 'Government Accountability in Europe: A Comparative Assessment', 35 *GeoWashIL Rev.* (2003) pp. 611 et seq.

Politis, N., *Les nouvelles tendences du droit international* (Paris, Hachette 1927).

Prechal, S., 'Community Law in National Courts: The Lessons from Van Schijndel', 35 *CML Rev.* (1998) pp. 681 et seq.

—, 'EC Requirements for an Effective Remedy', in Lonbay/Biondi (eds.), *Remedies for Breach of EC Law* (1997) pp. 3 et seq.

Puissochet, J.-P., 'L'action en manquement peut-elle encore se parer de ses justes vertus?', in Colneric, et al. (eds.), *Une communauté de droit – Festschrift für Gil Carlos Rodríguez Iglesias* (2003) pp. 569 et seq.

Ramos, F., 'Judicial Cooperation in the European Courts: Testing Three Models of Judicial Behaviour', 2 *GJF* (2002) pp. 1 et seq.

Rasmussen, H., 'The European Court´s Acte Clair Strategy in CILFIT', 9 *EL Rev.* (1984) pp. 242 et seq.

Reisman, M., 'Judge Shigeru Oda: A Tribute to an International Treasure', 16 *LJIL* (2003) pp. 57 et seq.

Ress, G., 'Das Europarecht vor dem Europäischen Gerichtshof für Menschenrechte in Strassburg', *Forum Constitutionis Europae* nr. 2/02 (retrieved from <http://www.rewi.hu-berlin.de/WHI/deutsch/fce/fce202/ress.pdf> – visited on 18 April 2005).

Rosas, A., 'State Responsibility and Liability under Civil Liability Regimes', in Bring/Mahmoudi (eds.), *Current International Law Issues – Nordic Perspectives* (1994) pp. 161 et seq.

Ruffert, M., Case note on Case C-453/00 *Kühne & Heitz*, 59 *JZ* (2004) pp. 620 et seq.

Scelle, G., 'Théorie du gouvernement international', (1935) *AIIDP* pp. 41 et seq.

Schermers, H.G./Waelbrock, D.F., *Judicial Protection in the European Union*, 6th edn. (The Hague, Kluwer 2001).

Schröder, M., 'Verantwortlichkeit, Völkerstrafrecht, Streitbeilegung und Sanktionen', in Graf Vitzthum (ed.), *Völkerrecht*, 3rd edn. (Berlin, De Gruyter 2004) pp. 535 et seq.

Schübel-Pfister, I., *Sprache und Gemeinschaftsrecht – Die Auslegung der mehrsprachig verbindlichen Rechtstexte durch den Europäischen Gerichtshof* (Berlin, Duncker & Humblot 2004).

Schwarzenegger, P., Case note on Case C-224/01 *Köbler*, (2003) *ZfRV* pp. 236 et seq.

Schwebel, S.M. (ed.), *The Effectiveness of International Decisions* (Leiden, Sijthoff 1971).

Seidl-Hohenveldern, I./Stein, T., *Völkerrecht*, 10th edn. (Cologne, Heymanns 2000).

Shaw, M.N., *International Law*, 5th edn. (Cambridge, Cambridge University Press 2003).

Slaughter, A.-M., 'A Global Community of Courts', 44 *Harv. IL J* (2003) pp. 191 et seq.

— et al. (eds.), *The European Courts and National Courts – Doctrine and Jurisprudence – Legal Change in Its Social Context* (Oxford, Oxford University Press 1998).

Solar, N., *Vorlagepflichtverletzung mitgliedstaatlicher Gerichte und ihre Sanierung* (Vienna, Neuer Wissenschaftlicher Verlag 2004).

Spiegel, H.W., 'Origin and Development of Denial of Justice', 30 *AJIL* (1936) pp. 62 et seq.

Spiermann, O., 'The Other Side of the Story: An Unpopular Essay on the Making of the European Community Legal Order', 10 *EJIL* (1999) pp. 763 et seq.

Steiner, J., 'From direct effects to Francovich: shifting means of enforcement of Community Law', 18 *EL Rev.* (1993) pp. 11 et seq.

Stone Sweet, A., *Governing with Judges – Constitutional Politics in Europe* (Oxford, Oxford University Press 2000).

—/Brunell, Th.L., 'The European Court, National Judges, and Legal Integration: A Researcher's Guide to the Data Set on Preliminary References in EC Law, 1958-98', 6 *ELJ* (2000) pp. 117 et seq.

STREHO, I., 'Regional Organizations' Judicial System Compared: Is the European Model Transposable and Should It Be?', 27 *Review of Asian and Pacific Studies* (2004) pp. 57 et seq.

STREINZ, R., *Europarecht*, 5th edn. (Heidelberg, C.F. Müller 2001).

—, *Europarecht*, 6th edn. (Heidelberg, C.F. Müller 2003).

TER KUILE, B.H., 'To Refer or not to Refer: About the Last Paragraph of Article 177 of the EC Treaty', in Curtin/Heukels (eds.), *Institutional Dynamics of European Integration* (1994) pp. 381 et seq.

TIMMERMANS, C.W.A., 'The European Union's Judicial System', 41 *CML Rev.* (2004) pp. 393 et seq.

—, 'Judicial Protection against the Member States: Articles 169 and 177 Revisited', in Curtin/Heukels (eds.), *Institutional Dynamics of European Integration* (1994) pp. 391 et seq.

TOBLER, C., 'Staatshaftung für fehlerhafte höchstrichterliche Rechtsprechung, Rs. C-224/01', (2003) *jus & news* pp. 339 et seq.

TOMUSCHAT, C., 'Das Francovich-Urteil des EuGH – Ein Lehrstück zum Europarecht', in Due, et al. (eds.), *Festschrift für Ulrich Everling*, Vol. 2 (Baden-Baden, Nomos 1995) pp. 1585 et seq.

TONER, H., 'Thinking the Unthinkable? State Liability for Judicial Acts after Factortame (III)', (1997) *YEL* pp. 165 et seq.

TRIDIMAS, T., 'Knocking on Heaven's Door: Fragmentation, Efficiency and Defiance in the Preliminary Reference Procedure', 40 *CML Rev.* (2003) pp. 9 et seq.

—, 'Liability for Breach of Community Law: Growing Up and Mellowing Down?', 38 *CML Rev.* (2001) pp. 301 et seq.

—, 'Enforcing Community Rights in National Courts: Some Recent Developments', in Kilpatrick, et al. (eds.), *The Future of Remedies in Europe* (2000) pp. 35 et seq.

—, *The General Principles of EC Law* (Oxford, Oxford University Press 1999).

—, 'The Role of the Advocate General in the Development of Community Law: Some Reflections', 34 *CML Rev.* (1997) pp. 1349 et seq.

UN SOCIAL DEFENCE RESEARCH INSTITUTE/INTERNATIONAL ASSOCIATION OF JUDGES, *The Role of the Judge in Contemporary Society* (Rome, Palombi 1984).

VANDERSANDEN, G./DONY, M., La Responsabilité des Etats Membres en cas de violation du Droit Communautaire: études de droit communautaire et de droit national comparé (Brussels, Bruylant 1997).

GRAF VITZTHUM, W. (ed.), *Völkerrecht*, 3rd edn. (Berlin, De Gruyter 2004).

VORWERK, V., 'Kudła gegen Polen – Was kommt danach?', 59 *JZ* (2004) pp. 553.

WAELBROECK, D.F., 'Treaty Violations and Liability of Member States and the European Community: Convergence or Divergence?', in Curtin/Heukels (eds.), *Institutional Dynamics of European Integration* (1994) pp. 467 et seq.

WALTER, R./MAYER, H., *Bundesverfassungsrecht*, 9th edn. (Vienna, Manz 2000).
—, *Verwaltungsverfahrensrecht*, 7th edn. (Vienna, Manz 1999).
WARD, A., *Judicial Review and the Rights of Private Parties in EC Law* (Oxford, Oxford University Press 2000).
—, 'The Limits of the Uniform Application of Community Law and Effective Judicial Review: A Look Post-Amsterdam', in Kilpatrick, et al. (eds.), *The Future of Remedies in Europe* (2000) pp. 213 et seq.
WATTEL, P.J., 'Köbler, CILFIT and Welthgrove: We can't go on meeting like this', 41 *CML Rev.* (2004) pp. 177 et seq.
WEATHERILL, S., 'Addressing Problems of Imbalanced Implementation in EC Law: Remedies in an Institutional Perspective', in Kilpatrick, et al. (eds.), *The Future of Remedies in Europe* (2000) pp. 87 et seq.
WEGENER, B.W., '(Fehl-)Urteilsverantwortung und Richterspruchprivileg in der Haftung der Mitgliedstaaten für die Verletzung von Gemeinschaftsrecht', 39 *EuR* (2004) pp. 84 et seq.
—, 'Staatshaftung für die Verletzung von Gemeinschaftsrecht durch nationale Gerichte?', 37 *EuR* (2002) pp. 785 et seq.
WEILER, J.H.H., 'Epilogue: The Judicial Après Nice', in de Búrca/Weiler (eds.), *The European Court of Justice* (2001) pp. 215 et seq.
—, *The Constitution of Europe – 'Do the New Clothes have an Emperor?' and other Essays on European Integration* (Oxford, Oxford University Press 1999).
—, 'The Transformation of Europe', in Weiler, *The Constitution of Europe – 'Do the New Clothes have an Emperor?' and other Essays on European Integration* (1999) pp. 10 et seq. [reprint of 100 *YLJ* (1991) pp. 2403 et seq.]
WIENER, A./DIEZ, TH. (eds.), *European Integration Theory* (Oxford, Oxford University Press 2004).
WILHELM, G., 'Staatshaftung für judikatives Unrecht oder Saturnalien des Schadenersatzes', (2003) *ecolex* p. 733.
ZEMANEK, K., et al., 'Die völkerrechtliche Verantwortlichkeit und die Sanktionen des Völkerrechts', in Neuhold, et al. (eds.), *Österreichisches Handbuch des Völkerrechts*, 4th edn. (Vienna, Manz 2004) mn. 2682 et seq.

TABLE OF CASES

European Court of Justice & Court of First Instance

Adria-Wien Pipeline GmbH (Case C-143/99) [2001] ECR I-8365 ... 165

Antillean Rice Mills (Cases T-480 and T-483/93) [1995] ECR II-2305 ... 11

Baustahlgewebe (Case C-185/95 P) [1998] ECR I-8417 ... 116-117, 169

Bergaderm (Case C-352/98 P) [2000] ECR I-5291 ... 32, 114-115

Bidar (Case C-209/03), judgment of 15 March 2005 (nyr) ... 100

Borelli (Case C-97/91) [1992] ECR I-6330 ... 29

Brasserie du pêcheur (Cases C-46/93 and C-48/93) [1996] ECR I-1029 ... 21, 32, 33, 47, 49-51, 67, 79-80, 86, 111, 113-115, 118, 125-129, 132, 142, 151, 160, 197, 200, 202, 203

British Telecommunications (Case C-392/93) [1996] ECR I-1631 ... 119-120, 135, 202

Busseni (Case C-221/88) [1990] ECR I-495 ... 108

CILFIT (Case 283/81) [1982] ECR 3415 ... 17-19, 39, 42, 118, 132, 135, 137-138, 140

Ciola (Case C-224/97) [1999] ECR I-2517 ... 101, 102

Codorniu (Case C-309/89) [1994] ECR I-1853 ... 11

Comateb (Cases C-192 to 218/95) [1997] ECR I-165 ... 146

Comet (Case 45/76) [1976] ECR 2043 ... 23

Commission v. *Belgium* (Case 239/85) [1986] ECR 3645 ... 67

Commission v. *Belgium* (Case 77/69) [1970] ECR 237 ... 181, 192

Commission v. *CCRE* (Case C-87/01) P, ECR [2003] I-7617 ... 82

Commission v. *Italy* (Case 104/86) [1988] ECR 1799 ... 184

Commission v. *Italy* (Case 39/72) [1973] ECR 101 ... 31

Commission v. *Italy* (Case 8/70) [1970] ECR 961 ... 181

Commission v. *Italy* (Case C-129/00) [2003] ECR I-14637 ... 3, 5, 92, 143, 181, 183-188, 191-193, 198- 199, 205

Connect Austria (Case C-462/99) [2003] ECR I-5197 ... 156-160, 165, 171, 204

Costa/ENEL (Case 6/64) [1964] ECR 585 ... 21, 111, 147

Da Costa & Schaake (Cases 28 to 30/62) [1963] ECR 31 ... 39, 42

Denkavit (Cases C-283, 291 and 292/94) [1996] ECR I-5063 ... 120

Dilexport (Case C-343/96) [1999] ECR I-579 ... 189

Dillenkofer (Cases C-178/94, C-179/94, C-188/94, C-189/94 and C-190/94) [1996] ECR I-4845 ... 128

Dorsch Consult (Case C-54/96) [1997] ECR I-4961 ... 156-160, 171, 204

Eco Swiss (Case C-126/97) [1999] ECR I-3055 ... 37, 95-99, 103

Emmott (Case C-208/90) [1991] ECR I-4269 ... 24, 35-36, 38

Eunice Sutton (Case C-66/95) [1997] ECR I-2163 ... 146

Factortame (Case C-213/89) [1990] ECR I-2433 ... 30, 31

Fantask (Case C-188/95) [1997] ECR I-6783 ... 21, 36

Fazenda Pública (Case C-446/98) [2000] ECR I-11435 ... 37

FMC plc (Case C-212/94) [1996] ECR I-389 ... 34

Foreningen af Jernskibs- og Maskinbyggerier i Danmark (Case T-266/94) [1996] ECR II-1339 ... 10

Foto Frost (Case 314/85) [1987] ECR 4199 ... 17, 21, 172

Francovich (Cases C-6/90 and C-9/90) [1991] ECR I-5357 ... 18, 23, 26, 30-32, 47, 50, 67, 68, 79, 85, 87, 115, 125-126, 142, 160, 181, 183, 197

Fratelli Costanzo (Case 103/88) [1989] ECR 1839 ... 95

Gerekens and Procola (Case C-459/02), judgment of 15 July 2004 (nyr) ... 103

Hedley Lomas (Case C-5/94) [1996] ECR I-2553 ... 118

Intermodal Transports (C-495/03) [2004] OJ C 21/23 – pending ... 19

Internationale Handelsgesellschaft (Case 11/70) [1970] ECR 1125 ... 49, 110

Jégo-Quéré (Case C-263/02 P), judgment of 1 April 2004 (nyr) ... 10

Jégo-Quéré (Case T-177/01) [2002] ECR II-2365 ... 10

Johnson (Case C-410/92) [1994] ECR I-5483 ... 35

Johnston (Case 222/84) [1986] ECR 1651 ... 28-30

Keck and Mithouard (Cases C-267/91 and C-268/91) [1993] ECR I-6097 ... 117

Köbler (Case C-224/01) [2003] ECR I-10239 ... 3, 15-16, 40, 48, 51, 66-70, 71, 78, 80-86, 87, 91-95, 98-99, 100, 103, 104, 107, 110-111, 115-121, 125-151, 155, 160, 162, 163, 171-175, 179, 180, 183, 187, 188-189, 197, 198, 200-204, 206

Konle (Case C-302/97) [1999] ECR I-3099 ... 95

Kraaijeveld (Case C-72/95) [1996] ECR I-5403 ... 37

Kühne & Heitz (Case C-453/00) [2004] ECR I-837 ... 3, 99-104, 179-181, 193, 202, 206

Les Verts (Case 294/83) [1986] ECR 1339 ... 69

Lyckeskog (Case C-99/00) [2002] ECR I-4839 ... 147-150, 181

Nold (Case 4/73) [1974] ECR 491 ... 49

Océano Grupo (Cases C-240 to 244/98) [2000] ECR I-4491 ... 37

Palmisani (Case C-261/95) [1997] ECR I-4025 ... 24, 32

Peterbroeck (Case C-312/93) [1995] ECR I-4599 ... 33, 36-37

Plaumann (Case 25/62) [1963] ECR 107 ... 10

Rechnungshof (Case C-465/00) [2003] ECR I-4989 ... 165

Reisch and Lassacher (Cases C-515/99, C-519/99 to C-524/99 and C-526/99 to C-540/99) [2002] ECR I-2157 ... 108

Rewe (Case 33/76) [1976] ECR 1989 ... 23-26, 28, 29, 34, 35

Rewe v. *Hauptzollamt Kiel* (Case 158/80) [1981] ECR 1805 ... 25

Rheinmühlen I (Case 166-73) [1974] ECR 33 ... 164

Rheinmühlen II (Case 146-73) [1974] ECR 139 ... 164

Salamander (Cases T-172/98 and 175-177/98) [2000] ECR II-2487 ... 11-12

San Giorgio (Case 199/82) [1983] ECR 3595 ... 184, 189

Schöning-Kougebetopoulou (Case C-15/96) [1998] ECR I-47 ... 136-141

SGEEM (Case C-370/89) [1992] ECR I-6211 ... 116

Shingara and Radiom (Cases C-65 and C-111/95) [1997] ECR I-3343 ... 24

Simmenthal I (Case 35/76) [1976] ECR 1871 ... 27

Simmenthal II (Case 106/77) [1978] ECR 629 ... 27, 28, 163, 205

Steenhorst-Neerings (Case C-338/91) [1993] ECR I-5475 ... 35

Stockholm Lindöpark (Case C-150/99) [2001] ECR I-493 ... 146

UEAPME v. *Council* (Case T-135/96) [1998] ECR II-2335 ... 11

UNECTEF v. *Heylens* (Case 222/84) [1987] ECR 4097 ... 29-30

Unión de Pequeños Agricultores (Case C-50/00 P) [2002] ECR I-6677 ... 10

van Gend & Loos (Case 26/62) [1963] ECR 1 ... 9, 12-15, 32, 53, 65, 69, 199

van Schijndel (Cases C-430-431/93) [1995] ECR I-4705 ... 33-34, 36, 37, 97

Wählergruppe Gemeinsam Zajedno (Case C-171/01) [2003] ECR I-4301 ... 165

Wiener (Case C-338/95) [1997] ECR I-6495 ... 175

Zuckerfabrik Schöppenstedt (Case 5/71) [1971] ECR 975 ... 114

Zuckerfabrik Süderdithmarschen (Cases C-143/88 and 92/89) [1991] ECR I-415 ... 21, 31

European Court and Commission of Human Rights

BAT v. *The Netherlands*, judgment of 20 November 1995, No. A.331 ... 72

Brualla Gómez de la Torre v. *Spain*, judgment of 19 December 1997, Reports 1997-VIII ... 72

Calena Santiago v. *Spain*, decision of 4 October 2001 (on the admissibility), App. No. 60350/00 ... 134, 191

Cantoni v. *France*, judgment of 15 November 1996, Reports 1996-V ... 190

Coëme and Others v. *Belgium*, judgment of 22 June 2000, Reports of Judgments and Decisions 2000-VII ... 134, 191

De Cubber v. *Belgium*, judgment of 26 October 1984, No. A.86 ... 166, 167

de Geouffre de la Pradelle v. *France*, judgment of 16 December 1992, No. A.253-B ... 72

Desmots v. *France*, decision of 23 March 1999 (on the admissibility), App. No. 41358/98 ... 134

Goodwin v. *UK*, judgment of 11 July 2002, Reports of Judgments and Decisions 2002-VI ... 190

Hauschildt v. *Denmark*, judgment of 24 May 1989, No. A.154 ... 166

Holzinger v. *Austria*, judgment of 30 January 2001, Reports of Judgments and Decisions 2001-I ... 73

Hornsby v. *Greece*, judgment of 19 March 1997, Reports 1997-II ... 182

Kress v. *France*, judgment of 7 June 2001, Reports of Judgments and Decisions 2001-VI ... 190

Kudła v. *Poland*, judgment of 26 October 2000, Reports of Judgments and Decisions 2000-XI ... 71-75, 78, 201

Lambert Bakker v. *Austria*, decision of 13 June 2002 (on the admissibility), App. No. 43454/98 ... 134

Lingens v. *Austria*, judgment of 8 July 1986, No. A.103 ... 54

Lutz v. *France*, judgment of 26 March 2002, App. No. 48215/99 ... 74

Masson and van Zon v. *The Netherlands*, decision of 4 July 1994, App. No. B 15346/89 ... 167-168

Matthews v. *UK*, judgment of 18 February 1999, Reports of Judgments and Decisions 1999-I ... 117, 189

McGonnell v. *United Kingdom*, judgment of 8 February 2000, Reports of Judgments and Decisions 2000-II ... 166

Meftah et autres v. *France*, judgment of 26 July 2002, Reports of Judgments and Decisions 2002-VII ... 190

Mifsud v. *France*, judgment of 11 September 2002, Reports of Judgments and Decisions 2002-VIII ... 74

Moosbrugger v. *Austria*, decision of 25 January 2000 (on the admissibility), App. No. 44861/98 ... 134, 191

Pafitis v. *Greece*, judgment of 26 February 1998, Reports 1998-I ... 172

Pellegrin v. *France*, judgment of 8 December 1999, Reports of Judgments and Decisions 1999-VIII ... 190

Piersack v. *Belgium*, judgment of 1 October 1982, No. A.53 ... 166-167, 169

Posti and Rahko v. *Finland*, judgment of 24 September 2002, Reports of Judgments and Decisions 2002-VII ... 190

Procola v. *Luxembourg*, judgment of 28 September 1995, No. A.326 ... 167

S.A. Dangeville v. *France*, judgment of 16 April 2002, Reports of Judgments and Decisions 2002-III ... 75-78, 86, 104, 143, 189-191, 201

Sporrong and Lönnroth v. *Sweden*, judgment of 23 September 1982, No. A.52 ... 72

Stes Colas Est et autres v. *France*, judgment of 16 April 2002, Reports of Judgments and Decisions 2002-III ... 190

Stran Greek Refineries v. *Greece*, judgment of 9 December 1994, No. A 301-B ... 191

van der Kar and Lissaur van West v. *France*, judgment of 7 November 2000, App. No. 44952/98, 44953/98 ... 73

Zimmermann and Steiner v. *Switzerland*, judgment of 13 July 1983, No. A.66 ... 54

International Court of Justice

Difference relating to Immunity from Legal Process of a Special Rapporteur of the Commission of Human Rights (Advisory Opinion) [1999] ICJ Reports, p. 3 ... 59, 61-62

Diplomatic and Consular Staff [1980] ICJ Reports, p. 3 ... 61

Elettronica Sicula [1989] ICJ reports, p. 15 ... 145

LaGrand (Provisional Measures) [1999] ICJ Reports, p. 466 ... 62-63

Legality of the Threat or Use of Nuclear Weapons (Advisory Opinion) [1996] ICJ Reports, p. 226 ... 42

Permanent Court of International Justice

Certain German Interests in Polish Upper Silesia (Merits), 1926, Series A, No. 7, p. 3 ... 61

Jurisdiction of the Courts of Danzig (Advisory Opinion), 1928, Series B, No. 15, p. 3 ... 12-15, 52, 61

Lotus, 1927, Series A, No. 10, p. 3 ... 61

Cases from Other Jurisdictions

Austria

Verfassungsgerichtshof, VfSlg. 13.553/93 ... 167

Verfassungsgerichtshof, judgment of 10 June 1999, B 1809-1811/97 ... 19

Verfassungsgerichtshof, judgment of 10 October 2003, A 36/00 ... 170, 173

Belgium

Cour de Cassation, De Keyser/Anca, judgment of 19 December 1991, *JT* (1991) p. 141 ... 81, 83-84

France

Conseil d'Etat, Cohn-Bendit, judgment of 22 December 1978, *RTDE* (1979) p. 175 ... 17, 110

Germany

Bundesverfassungsgericht, Solange I, BVerfGE 37/271 ... 110, 187

Bundesverfassungsgericht, Solange II, BVerfGE 73/339 ... 110

Bundesverfassungsgericht, Brunner v. *The European Union Treaty,* BVerfGE 89, 155 ... 110

Bundesverfassungsgericht, 1 BvR 1036/99, judgment of 9 January 2001 ... 19

Bundesgericht, III ZR 294/03, decision of 28 October 2004 ... 141-142

Greece

Conseil d'Etat, *Katsarou* v. *Greece*, judgment of 25 September 1998 ... 18

United States

US Supreme Court in *Marbury* v. *Madison,* 5 US 137 (1803) ... 111

ICSID

AMCO v. *Indonesia* (Merits) 89 *ILR* 451 ... 56

MIX
Papier aus verantwortungsvollen Quellen
Paper from responsible sources
FSC® C105338

If you have any concerns about our products,
you can contact us on
ProductSafety@springernature.com

In case Publisher is established outside the EU,
the EU authorized representative is:
Springer Nature Customer Service Center GmbH
Europaplatz 3, 69115 Heidelberg, Germany

Printed by Libri Plureos GmbH
in Hamburg, Germany